W9-CTV-136

CHECKMATE!

CHECKMATE!

THE PATTERNS OF THE WINNING MATING ATTACKS AND HOW TO ACHIEVE THEM

George Koltanowski

and

Milton Finkelstein

Doubleday & Company, Inc., Garden City, New York

Library of Congress Cataloging in Publication Data

Koltanowski, George, 1903–
Checkmate!

1. Checkmate (Chess) I. Finkelstein, Milton, joint author. II. Title.
GV1450.3.K6 794.1'24 76-42341
ISBN 0-385-12068-0

Printed in the United States of America
FIRST EDITION

CONTENTS

INTRODUCTION

Our editors insisted that *Checkmate!* did not need an extended introduction, for the mere skimming of its pages would show any player that it opens the door to easy and confident victories in chess situations that occur repeatedly in any player's games. But we have been permitted a few pages to establish why this book was written, how to use it, and to define its limitations.

Masters and players close to master ability will learn little from *Checkmate!*, for they became chess stars by knowing the ideas the book contains. On the other hand, people who have just learned the moves need a book directed to beginners before they can understand the concepts elaborated in these pages. But all other players can benefit immeasurably by understanding the technique of forcing checkmate that forms the core of this new kind of chess book.

In their combined hundred years of chess play and study the authors have examined more than a million recorded games of chess between players at every level of ability. They have paid special attention to those that ended in checkmate. They have seen how certain mating positions occur repeatedly, effected with ease by masters who recognize mating patterns quickly and carry out their attacks almost automatically in familiar situations. In the games of less competent players we have often seen the chance missed, the attack falter, and the deserved win gone astray.

Blindfold play has sharpened the ability of one of the authors to visualize a position many moves away, its final setting thus being just as evident as that before a calculation and a decision that leads to checkmate. The other author, in some thirty years of training young players, has been repeatedly amazed by their ability to learn what can be called standard positions—positions that always succumb to the same idea and its proper sequence of moves. The learning of when and how to checkmate calls for a combination of the ability to visualize and familiarity with standard positions in which checkmate follows from a forced series of moves.

Can you already "see" a position several moves away? If so, you may be able to solve many of the positions in this book without the use of board and chessmen. If not, make it a habit to set up each position, work out its solution, and then build your ability to visualize by setting up the position again and "seeing" its solution from the chessboard and in time from the diagram. A warning is in order. If you simply read this book, looking at diagrams and their solutions, you may become more familiar with standard mating positions but you will do little to increase your playing strength.

Each chapter follows a similar pattern of developing ideas. A standard mating position is introduced and explained. A series of positions is analyzed, each accompanied by an "analysis" paragraph that shows you the method of moving toward the winning moves. Take the time to study each analysis before you seek or attempt any moves. The ideas it contains, related to those in the analysis of other positions in the chapter, have been organized to help you become adept in recognizing mating patterns and then executing the mates. And, conversely, knowing what makes a position ripe for a mating attack will aid you in avoiding those weaknesses that can make you the target of an effort to checkmate.

The book ends with a checkmate quiz; it is suggested that you should not examine this quiz until you have completed the twenty-five chapters that introduce, apply, and combine the mating ideas basic to improving your play. Instead, consider each chapter a separate learning experience that should be mastered before you move on to the next one. Explanations of terms appear where they are needed, dozens of complete games show you how an advantage is turned into a win, and the illustrative positions demonstrate that the same stratagems succeed against masters and amateurs alike. But all this material means little unless you try to learn it in proper sequence.

Checkmate! is also an introduction to some of the great names of chess history and an explanation of the chess world—the realm of the players, beginners to chess masters, who experience joys and agonies that reflect the amazing ability of chess to dominate the hours of play and, for many, entire lifetimes. Our apologies to the many chess friends among the world's great players whose efforts have been omitted because of lack of space, and our special thanks to those whose positions were included. Note that White and Black are generally referred to as "he," a decision reflecting convenience rather than a lack of appreciation of the women who have, as the book demonstrates, so often deservedly risen to the highest ranks within the chess world.

Checkmate! uses standard descriptive notation. The pieces are abbreviated as follows:

K = King　　**N** = Knight
Q = Queen　　**B** = Bishop
R = Rook　　**P** = Pawn

The squares on the chessboard are named according to the rank and file they occupy, the ranks running left to right and the files from one player to the other. The ranks are numbered 1 to 8; the files are given the name of the piece that stands on the first rank at the beginning of the game. The board is divided vertically into two halves—the King's side and the Queen's side. The R, N, and B on the King's

QR1 QR8	QN1 QN8	QB1 QB8	Q1 Q8	K1 K8	KB1 KB8	KN1 KN8	KR1 KR8
QR2 QR7	QN2 QN7	QB2 QB7	Q2 Q7	K2 K7	KB2 KB7	KN2 KN7	KR2 KR7
QR3 QR6	QN3 QN6	QB3 QB6	Q3 Q6	K3 K6	KB3 KB6	KN3 KN6	KR3 KR6
QR4 QR5	QN4 QN5	QB4 QB5	Q4 Q5	K4 K5	KB4 KB5	KN4 KN5	KR4 KR5
QR5 QR4	QN5 QN4	QB5 QB4	Q5 Q4	K5 K4	KB5 KB4	KN5 KN4	KR5 KR4
QR6 QR3	QN6 QN3	QB6 QB3	Q6 Q3	K6 K3	KB6 KB3	KN6 KN3	KR6 KR3
QR7 QR2	QN7 QN2	QB7 QB2	Q7 Q2	K7 K2	KB7 KB2	KN7 KN2	KR7 KR2
QR8 QR1	QN8 QN1	QB8 QB1	Q8 Q1	K8 K1	KB8 KB1	KN8 KN1	KR8 KR1

side are called KR (King's Rook), KN (King's Knight), and KB (King's Bishop). In the same way, the pieces on the Queen's side are called QR, QN, and QB.

Notice that each square has two names, one as read from the White side and the other as read from the Black side. In standard descriptive chess notation each player's moves are considered as made from his side. The squares are therefore named from his side. As the illustration shows, White's K1 is the same as Black's K8 and Black's KB3 is the same as White's KB6.

Moves are read from the side of the board of the player who makes them. First the piece (or Pawn) is named, a dash indicates it is moving, and then the square to which it moves is named. The letter × indicates a capture of whatever Pawn or piece follows the ×. Thus, P—K4 means the KP is moved to the fourth square on its file and B × Q means a Bishop captures a Queen. When two pieces of the same kind can move to the same square, the notation indicates in parentheses the square from which the piece that makes the move has come. Thus, a move like R(K1)—K5 means that the Rook at K1 has moved to K5.

The following abbreviations are used throughout the book:

— mate = checkmate
— ch = check
— dis ch = discovered check
— dbl ch = double check
— ! = a very good move (as in N × P!)
— ? = a poor move (as in K—B1?)

The following values of the pieces are assumed:

1 = value of a Pawn (always called a Pawn and never a piece)
3 = value of a Bishop or a Knight
5 = value of a Rook (although some prefer 4½ or 4¾)
9 = value of a Queen (generally equal to two Rooks or three other pieces)
2 = the difference in value between a Knight or a Bishop and a Rook, usually called "the exchange."

Our special thanks to our chess-playing editors, Harold Kuebler and James Menick, and to Alan Kifferstein, who reviewed and corrected the entire manuscript, for their invaluable suggestions for its improvement and their amazing ability to find that extra line of play that a player might attempt. And our enduring affection to the dozens of players who examined individual chapters or permitted us to demonstrate a sequence of positions during the long months in which *Checkmate!* remained uppermost in our minds.

GEORGE KOLTANOWSKI
MILTON FINKELSTEIN

CHECKMATE!

CHAPTER 1

Checkmate by a Pawn

The chessboard is the playing field of the eternal optimist. In the lifetime of any chess player, with its thousands and sometimes hundreds of thousands of games, hope remains alive in even the poorest positions, so often galvanized and then transformed by the sudden appearance of a winning attack when an opponent errs. It is at such times that the remembered assault in a typical mating attack brings victory. A line is opened; the enemy King position seems to lack defenders; your pieces are in position to attack; you can use your knowledge to produce a combination and often a checkmate.

Any piece but the King can checkmate. It may seem proper for the heavy pieces—Queen and Rooks—to sweep across the board to attack and mate an opponent's King. But it is even more memorable to mate with a Pawn, the least valuable of chessmen when a game begins. The Pawn, attacking only one or two squares at a time, can make its way to the enemy King, attack it, and win the game!

Here's an example of the latent power of the Pawn that you will probably memorize and show to your chess friends for years to come. Then again, it may go down in your mind as THE POSITION THAT SHOULD NOT BE SHOWN. You will see the reason for this after you have played through the amazing series of moves in a composition by a Hungarian player that ends with a Pawn mate. Set up the position on Diagram 1 and play through a beautiful forced checkmate in ten moves!

DIAGRAM 1

White to Play and Mate in 10 Moves

DIAGRAM 2

White Has Mated with His Only Pawn!

1. **R—N7** **Q × R**
2. **B × Pch** **K × B**
3. **Q—N8ch** **Q—N2**

Black returns the Queen to make the mate a little harder to execute. If he plays . . . . K—R4 on his third or fourth move, then White mates at once by Q—N4.

4. **Q × Qch** **K × N**
5. **Q—N4ch** **K—K4**
6. **Q—R5ch** **R—B4**

If 6. . . . . P—B4; 7. Q—R8 mate.

7. **P—B4ch** **B × P**

If 7. . . . . N × P; 8. R—K4ch leads to mate one move earlier after 8. . . . . P × R; 9. P—Q4 mate!

8. **Q × Nch** **B × Q**

If 8. . . . B—K6 instead, then 9. Q × B is mate!

9. **R—K4ch** **P × R**
10. **P—Q4 mate!**

You can best appreciate the beauty of this composition by comparing its original and final positions. Black has been forced to occupy the squares around his King. In the end, this means the King has no escape from the final Pawn check. Surrounded by his own Pawns and pieces, he is conquered by a lowly Pawn supported by White's King.

TERMS TO KNOW

Supported—A term used to describe the protection of a Pawn or piece, so that anything taking that Pawn or piece can be recaptured. Thus, a King cannot capture a supported Pawn.

Why do we call this THE POSITION THAT SHOULD NOT BE SHOWN? Well, doesn't it leave you with the feeling that there is hope in even the most clearly lost position? You can show it if you wish, but do not be surprised if those who have seen it play on against you even when they are as much as a Queen and two Rooks behind. They will refuse to resign, for haven't you just proven that mate is possible even when they have nothing left but a King and a Pawn?

It often is. A Pawn can make the move that mates whenever four conditions exist:

1. The Pawn can reach a square where it checks the enemy King.
2. The Pawn is supported.
3. No enemy piece or Pawn can take the Pawn.
4. The enemy King has no escape squares. That is, the King cannot move out of check.

TERMS TO KNOW

Escape square—A square to which a King can move to get out of check.

You can summarize these conditions in a single sentence. *A supported Pawn checks a King that has no escape squares.* Pawns have mated Kings in openings, middle games, and endgames. Such mates are more frequent in the endgame, for there are then fewer enemy pieces available to protect the squares around a King. The easiest way to understand the typical mate with a Pawn is to examine a simple final position in which a Pawn has mated a King on the edge of the board.

TERMS TO KNOW

Edge of the board—The first and eighth ranks and the KR and QR files.

The open board—All of the chessboard except the edge of the board.

DIAGRAM 3

Black is checkmated. All four of our conditions exist.

1. A White Pawn checks the Black King.
2. The Pawn is supported by the White King.
3. Black has no way to take the Pawn.
4. Black's King has no escape squares.

White's last move was to advance the Pawn from N6 or to

capture a Black Pawn or piece on N7. Black is checkmated because any move by the King would lead to its capture. This final position occurs hundreds of times in every player's chess career. It is common enough so that every player should know it well enough to plan for it.

An Idea from Paul Morphy

Checkmate with a Pawn was a central theme in many of the early chess problems composed in the nineteenth century. Many of them were based on the conclusions of games between chessmasters. Paul Charles Morphy of New Orleans (June 22, 1837–July 10, 1884) was the first American chess genius. He won the first United States championship in New York in 1857 and then spent two years playing in Europe. Morphy defeated all comers, including the then-recognized world champion, Adolf Anderssen of Germany. Unable to arrange a match with the reluctant British champion, Howard Staunton, he returned to the United States and retired from competitive chess. Yet his short career had changed the game for all time. He simplified its play according to careful principles of development and direct attacks built about an advanced understanding of what became standard patterns of achieving checkmate. He was never concerned with teaching his techniques, which others have come to understand by studying his games. But he did compose one chess problem to illustrate one of his favorite stratagems—the advance of a Pawn into the enemy King position and the resulting mate.

DIAGRAM 4
White to Play and Mate in Two Moves

A word about chess problems, several of which will appear in this book to illustrate mating ideas. In each case, White moves first. There is only one move—called the *key move*—that permits mate to follow in the required number of moves. Each possible answer to the key move is called a *variation*. This Morphy problem has only two variations. Let's look at them. Set up the position on your chessboard.

One of the variations leads to mate by a Pawn. Just suppose that the White Pawn were at N7. This would be checkmate—a position similar to the one in Diagram 3. The key move, then, is one that will result in the removal of the Black Pawn now on White's N7. Morphy does this by a sacrifice.

TERMS TO KNOW

Sacrifice—Moving a Pawn or piece to a square where it can be captured, usually to achieve some objective; trading a piece of greater value for one of lesser value.

Forced sacrifice—A sacrifice your opponent must accept.

Clearance sacrifice—A sacrifice that opens a file, rank, diagonal, or a single important square for your use.

1. **R—R6!**

This is the key move. Mate follows on White's second move in each of the two variations.

a. 1. **R—R6** **P × R**
2. **P—N7 mate**

The supported Pawn, protected by White's King, checks a King that has no escape square.

b. 1. **R—R6** **Any Bishop move**
2. **R × P mate**

This time a supported Rook checks a King that has no escape squares.

Examine both variations on your chessboard. Note that Black's only answers to 1. R—R6 were to capture the Rook or to move the Bishop. The final position in Variation A is the typical mate by a Pawn.

Now you should be ready to apply the rule for a Pawn mate to some positions that have occurred countless numbers of times in the play of even the best chess players in the world. Set up each position. Examine the analysis of the position, intended to direct your thinking to the correct moves. Then note your answer before turning to the answer on page 345. Remember—each of these positions is a basic application of the method of mating with a Pawn on the edge of the board.

DIAGRAM 5
White Mates in One Move

ANALYSIS

Do you have the four conditions necessary for mate by a Pawn?

— Can a Pawn check?

— Is the Pawn supported?

— Is Black unable to capture the checking Pawn?

— Does the Black King lack an escape square?

If all your answers are *yes,* then the mating move is obvious!

1. ________ **mate**

DIAGRAM 6

White Mates in Two Moves

ANALYSIS

Your first move must set up the four conditions needed for mate by a Pawn. Don't be frightened by the fact that Black can Queen a Pawn. Your move comes first. Can you prevent Black's King from escaping and also threaten mate by a supported Pawn?

1. ________ ________
2. ________ **mate**

DIAGRAM 7

White Mates in Two Moves

ANALYSIS

There is only one line of play. You can find it if you answer two questions.

— Can you force the Black King to R1?

— Your N at K8 supports any Pawn or piece at KN7. Can a Pawn check—and mate—there?

1. ________ ________
2. ________ **mate**

DIAGRAM 8

White Mates in Two Moves

ANALYSIS

Most of the pieces are still on the board. White could mate by P—K6 if the Black B on B4 were not protecting that square. Your key move must therefore be one that removes that protection! It doesn't matter what material you sacrifice. All you must do is to make Black lose control of K6! Remember that your Bishops then cut off all escape squares for the Black King.

1. ________ ________
2. ________ mate

The four positions you've just examined are common examples of possible mates with a Pawn. You may never be a Paul Morphy, but you can certainly learn to use some of the ideas with which he was so successful. Here is one of his games that features a King being forced into the open board and finally being mated by a Pawn at the edge of the board. Morphy gave his opponent the odds of a Rook. Remove White's Queen Rook before playing through the game.

White	Black
PAUL MORPHY	AMATEUR

New York, 1857

1. **P—K4** **P—K4**
2. **N—KB3** **N—QB3**
3. **B—B4** **B—B4**
4. **P—QN4**

This is the characteristic move of the Evans Gambit—the offer of a Pawn to gain time for rapid development of the pieces.

4. **....** **B × NP**
5. **P—B3** **B—R4**
6. **P—Q4** **P × P**
7. **O—O** **N—B3**

Black would like to castle and remain material ahead. But Morphy makes a move that prevents his opponent's King from leaving the K-file.

8. **B—R3!** **B—N3**
9. **Q—N3** **P—Q4**
10. **P × P(Q5)** **N—QR4**
11. **R—K1ch** **B—K3**

DIAGRAM 9

Morphy now sees an attack beginning with the sacrifice of his Queen and ending with a mate by a Pawn. All of Black's moves are forced once he takes the White Queen.

12. **P × B!** **N × Q**
13. **P × P dbl ch** **K—Q2**
14. **B—K6ch** **K—B3**
15. **N—K5ch** **K—N4**

16. B—B4ch K—R4
17. B—N4ch K—R5
18. P × N mate!

DIAGRAM 10

The final position meets our four conditions for the Pawn mate. Black's King is attacked by a Pawn. The Pawn is supported by a Bishop. Black cannot capture the Pawn with any of his pieces. The Black King has no escape squares. Although Morphy had to see that the final position could be forced, he could not have planned for it unless he understood the conditions necessary for mate by a Pawn.

Sometimes mate by a Pawn occurs early in the game. It becomes a possibility whenever you have a supported Pawn on the fifth or sixth rank near the enemy King. Here is the position after Black's eleventh move in the Rubinstein Variation of the Max Lange attack. White has given up a Pawn for a King-side attack. White pounces at once, for a Pawn mate can be threatened!

DIAGRAM 11

12. N × KBP K × N
13. N—N5ch K—N1

If 13. . . . . K × P; 14. R × Bch wins the Black Queen. 13. . . . . K—N3 is best.

14. P—KN4 Q × NPch?
15. Q × Q B × Q
16. P—B7 mate!

DIAGRAM 12

Checkmate! A supported Pawn attacks a King that has no escape squares!

You can mate with a Pawn in the center of the board too. This usually requires the co-operation of several of your pieces, each of which cuts off one or more of the enemy King's possible escape squares. Here is a position based on a victory in Vienna, 1897, by Carl Schlechter, one of the great players at the turn of the century. Schlechter, playing Black, sees a way to combine two Bishops, two Knights, and two deadly Pawns to force mate.

DIAGRAM 13

Set up the position. It is Black's move. His Queen is attacked, but he sees a mating attack. Suppose he could force White's King into the open board. This could be done if the Black Pawn now at KN5 could check at KB7. Black therefore sacrifices his Queen to get that Pawn check—and the forced checkmate that follows.

1.	....	**P × N!**
2.	**B × Q**	**P—B7ch**
3.	**K—K2**	**B—N5ch**
4.	**K—Q3**	**N—N5ch**
5.	**K × N**	

This is the position Black knew he could force when he sacrificed his Queen. The White King will have no escape squares after:

5.	....	**P—B4 mate!**

Examine the final position. There are several squares near the White King to which it might hope to escape. But two are blocked by its own Pawns on K3 and Q4. Black's Knight cuts off Q3 and Q5. One Black Bishop cuts off K5 and KB4, while the other supports the mating Pawn and also prevents the Black King from escaping to KB3. Thus, a protected Pawn checking a King without escape squares means CHECKMATE!

What can you learn from such a position? You see that the almost automatic response—to move a Queen or another attacked piece—is not always best. When your position permits a Pawn advance against an exposed King, even though the move means you sacrifice a Queen or piece, then look at that advance anyway. If you can force the enemy King into the open board, you may be able to trap it there. To do that you must be able to cut off its escape squares, and then check it with a protected Pawn or a piece. Result—Checkmate!

Diagram 14 illustrates one way to checkmate. White has sacrificed a Knight to bring Black's King to an exposed position. There it stands, lacking escape squares because it is cut off by White's Queen, Rook, and Bishops. White can now checkmate in two moves.

DIAGRAM 14

MAURIAN — AMATEUR

Paris, 1860

Note that a check by a supported Pawn will mean checkmate. Such a check can come only at White's KB6—now protected by a Black Knight. What move removes that protection and results in checkmate?

1. B—B6ch **N × B**

Black has no other move.

2. P × N mate!

The Pawn (protected by the White Rook at KB1) checks the Black King, while White's Queen and Bishop cut off all possible escape squares.

Try the two positions that follow as a check of your understanding. The analysis following each diagram should help you find the continuation that leads to mate.

DIAGRAM 15

White Mates in Two Moves

ANALYSIS

Black could be mated if White's Rook were at KR7, where it could be supported by the Bishop at QN1. Black could also be mated if the Black Bishop were off the board and White's Pawn were at KN7. What move makes both of these variations possible? Call them *a* and *b*.

a. 1. ________ ________
2. ________ **mate**

b. 1. ________ ________
2. ________ **mate**

(Remember: Answers begin on page 345)

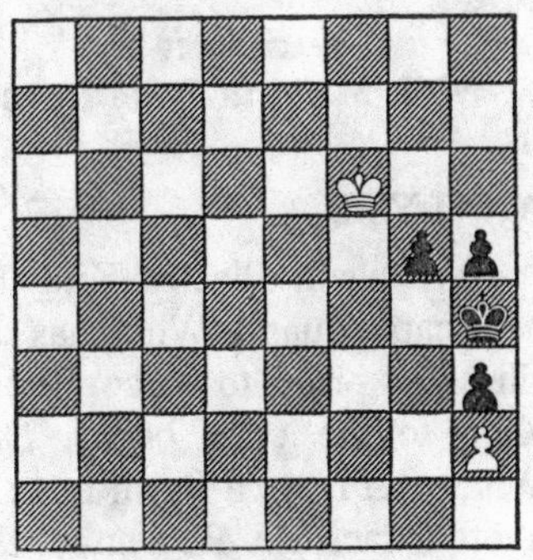

DIAGRAM 16
White Mates in Three Moves

ANALYSIS

Study this position carefully. It is one of the best-known endgame positions in which a Pawn mates a King at the edge of the board. White must begin by cutting off Black's escape squares. Then all Black can do is advance his KNP. Can you see how White then forces the Pawn mate?

1. ________ ________
2. ________ ________
3. ________ **mate!**

(Answer on page 345)

There you have it. We have reviewed the basic ways in which you can mate with a Pawn—on the edge of the board and on the open board. This chapter, and each chapter in this book, ends with a series of quiz positions composed or selected from chessmaster play. They are of increasing difficulty, but can all be solved if you understand the ideas discussed in the chapter. In each case, set up the position. Then read the analysis following the diagram before you decide on the moves that lead to mate in the indicated number of moves. Remember:

1. A supported Pawn can mate if that Pawn cannot be captured, and
2. The attacked King has no escape squares. Answers are on Page 345.

DIAGRAM 17
White Mates in Two Moves

ANALYSIS

Black's King is at the edge of the board. If White can advance a protected Pawn to R7, then Black is mated. If you can find a move that provides that support to the R7 square, a Pawn mate must follow. Note that White's Bishop at K4 cuts off Black King's escape to R1 or N2.

1. ________ ________
2. ________ mate

DIAGRAM 18
White Mates in Two Moves

ANALYSIS

Black's King has no escape squares. White's Rook prevents escape to Black's first rank. The White Bishop at QB5 cuts off any later escape to Black's K2. Thus, a check by a supported Pawn can lead to mate. How does White force this mate?

1. ________ ________
2. ________ mate

DIAGRAM 19
White Mates in Two Moves

ANALYSIS

Here again Black's King has no escape squares. White has sacrificed a piece to force Black's King to the open board. Now White can force a Pawn mate by another sacrifice. Remember that it is the mate that wins, not having a few pieces more or less!

1. ________ ________
2. ________ mate

DIAGRAM 20
Black to Mate in Three Moves

ANALYSIS

Black has forced the White King to the open board. Now a pair of checks can drive that King closer to Black's King—to a square where White will have no escape squares. All Black will then need is a supported Pawn that can check—and mate—the White King!

1. .... ________
2. ________ ________
3. ________ ________ **mate!**

DIAGRAM 21

White Mates in Three Moves

ANALYSIS

This is the end of a game between the Czech masters Karel Hromadka (White) and Karel Opocensky (Black) played in 1931. White begins by sacrificing a Rook to give his other Rook control of Black's third rank. Then he sacrifices his Knight to remove the Pawn at Black's K5. A Pawn mate follows to end the game! Can you see the sequence of moves?

1. ________ ________
2. ________ ________
3. ________ **mate!**

DIAGRAM 22

White Mates in Three Moves

ANALYSIS

This position is the final sequence of moves in a famous endgame study by A. S. Kakovin, published in Russia in 1936. You should find it easy if you understand the solution to the position of Diagram 21. White has forced Black to occupy most of the squares around the Black King. This means no escape squares. If White can now force Black to block his Q4 square too, then a Pawn mate may be possible. Take your time!

1. ________ ________
2. ________ ________
3. ________ **mate!**

REMEMBER!

1. Be alert for positions in which the enemy King lacks escape squares and you can check with a supported Pawn.
2. Be ready to consider sacrifices to block enemy escape squares when such blocking makes a Pawn mate possible.
3. Most Pawn mates occur on the open board when your other pieces have cut off enemy escape squares.

CHAPTER 2

Checkmate by a Bishop

One of the most important lessons to be learned from the play of chessmasters is to make effective use of open lines. Successful players place their pieces on squares where they have maximum mobility—that is, where they can sweep the board. In game after game from master tournaments, and in your own play as well, you will find the Bishop to be an effective surprise weapon. For example, this elementary opening trap has probably defeated you in your beginner days, or won a game against some careless opponent who opened with 1. P—KB4. Play through these moves on your chessboard.

1. **P—KB4** **P—K4**
2. **P × P** **P—Q3**
3. **P × P** **B × P**

If White permits it, perhaps by a move like 4. N—QB3, then Black wins at once by 4. . . . . Q—R5ch; 5. P—KN3, Q × Pch; 6. P × Q, B × P mate. So White usually makes a move that prevents 4. . . . . Q—R5.

4. **N—KB3** **P—KN4**

Now Black threatens 5. . . . . P—N5 and, if the White N moves away, the same mate threatens on White's KN3. So, worried about 5. . . . . P—N5, the inexperienced opponent makes a suicidal move to prevent it.

5. **P—KR3?** **B—N6 mate**

It happens again and again. Too many players see only one threat at a time! (See Diagram 23)

TERMS TO KNOW

Diagonal—A line of consecutive squares of the same color.

Long diagonal—A diagonal that crosses the center of the board (the squares K4, Q4, K5, Q5). Long diagonals begin at a player's R1, R2, or N1 on either the K-side or the Q-side.

Short diagonal—Any diagonal except a long diagonal, such as the line of squares QB1, QN2, QR3, or Q1, K2, KB3, KN4, KR5.

Open diagonal—A diagonal containing no Pawns or pieces between a Queen or Bishop and the square or piece it is attacking.

Interpose—To place a Pawn or piece on a square where it blocks an attack.

DIAGRAM 23

Diagram 23 illustrates a checkmate by a Bishop on a short diagonal. Mate by a Bishop is more common on long diagonals, and for good reason. Once a player has castled, his King is in one corner of the board. Mate by a Bishop may then become possible if the following conditions exist:

1. The King is on an open diagonal on which no protected Pawn or piece can be interposed.
2. The King has no escape squares, being blocked by its own Pawns or pieces or unable to move to nearby squares controlled by enemy Pawns or pieces.
3. The attacking Bishop cannot be captured.

Diagram 24 is the simplest illustration of mate by a Bishop.

DIAGRAM 24

Note how the three conditions for a Bishop mate are met:

1. Black's King is on an open diagonal. Black cannot interpose to block the attack by White's Bishop.
2. Black has no escape squares, his Pawn and Bishop occupying the adjacent squares.
3. Black cannot capture the White Bishop.

Don't expect your opponents to commit chess suicide by placing their King in such positions. But understand that you can often force a King to a square where a Bishop mate is possible.

There are three chief ways to do this:

1. Checks force your opponents to occupy possible escape squares so that your Bishop's check means mate.
2. Sacrifices break open the diagonals near the enemy King, finally opening one that permits a Bishop mate.
3. An attack forces the enemy King to move into the open board while your pieces cut off its escape squares. A Bishop check on either a long or a short diagonal then mates.

Diagram 25 illustrates the use of checks to prepare for mate by a Bishop.

This position can quickly be transformed into one similar to Diagram 24. It is White's move. If he can force the Black Rook to occupy Black's KN1 and also free the Bishop for a check on the long diagonal (White's QR1 to KR8), then mate may be possible.

DIAGRAM 25

1. **R—K8ch** **R—N1**

Black has no other reply. He must interpose this Rook. But now the long diagonal is open for the Bishop.

2. **B—Q4 mate**

White had to answer three questions to be certain of this mate:

— Will the Black King be on an open diagonal without escape squares?
— Will Black be able to interpose on that diagonal?
— Will the White Bishop be immune from capture?

Here are two more positions in which White checkmates with a Bishop after one or more checks have forced Black's pieces to cut off the King's escape squares.

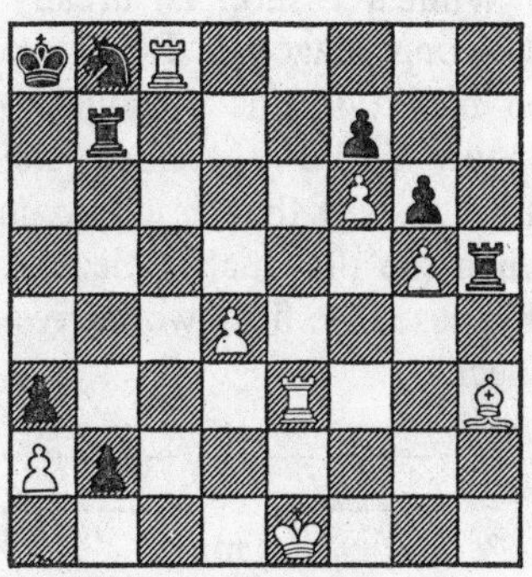

DIAGRAM 26

White Mates in Two Moves

(Answers on page 345)

ANALYSIS

Black threatens to win quickly by Queening his NP. But White can force mate with a Bishop by prying open the long diagonal. What checking move does this?

1. ________ ________
2. ________ **mate**

DIAGRAM 27

White Mates in Three Moves

ANALYSIS

White's Bishop is already on the long diagonal. Black would be mated if this diagonal were open. White therefore makes three moves that result in mate when the diagonal is cleared. In this case, the first two moves are checks.

1. ________ ________
2. ________ ________
3. ________ **mate**

You must often sacrifice material to open an enemy King position so that a Bishop can mate along a diagonal. Diagram 28 shows a direct method of finishing off a won game quickly.

DIAGRAM 28

White is far ahead in material. The Black King has no moves. All White has to do is open the long diagonal, when a Bishop check will be mate. The move that does this at once is 1. P—R6. Black then loses at once. Only his NP can move. It can advance to N3 or N4, or take the White Pawn. Any of these moves has the same result—the opening of the long diagonal to end the game after White's 2. B—K5 mate. The position teaches an important lesson. Be ready to sacrifice material to open a diagonal when the enemy King has no escape squares, no enemy piece can interpose to prevent mate on that diagonal, and your checking Bishop is immune from capture.

Try to find the solutions to these two positions that illustrate sacrifices to break open a diagonal to permit mate by a Bishop.

DIAGRAM 29

White Mates in Two Moves

ANALYSIS

This position is similar to the one in Diagram 27. But this time the clearing of the long diagonal requires a sacrifice. Remember: after the sacrifice Black's King must remain without escape squares. The King must not be able to move to R2, N2, or N1.

1. ________ ________
2. ________ **mate**

DIAGRAM 30

White Mates in Four Moves

ANALYSIS

There are two ways to mate in this position, both based on a Bishop attack on the long diagonal. Note that Black's King has no escape squares, and will be mated if our three conditions for mate by a Bishop can be met. A Queen sacrifice does the job!

1. ________ ________
2. ________ ________
3. ________ ________
4. ________ **mate**

Plus a second way to mate in 3!

Salo Flohr— Who Almost Made It!

It really happens. A young unknown chess player visits a chess tournament where he plays rapid games with the participating masters for small stakes. By the end of the tournament he has made more money than any of the prizewinners. The story was told of a young Czech named Salo Flohr in the late 1920s, after he had emptied the pockets of some of the world's best-known players at a tournament in Berlin. Walter Browne, later champion of the United States, also came to the chess world's attention because of his ability at rapid play.

Salo Flohr's skill at speed chess (five minutes allowed each player) was soon matched by his success in international play. Between 1931 and 1937 he made the best record among the world's grandmasters, playing in ten important tournaments in which he lost a total of only two games! He was scheduled to play and expected to win a match for the world championship then held by Alexander Alekhine. But World War II came before the match could be held, and Alekhine died soon afterward. Flohr, by then a Russian citizen, was unable to maintain his supremacy by the late 1940s. He began to make mistakes, his poorer tournament results soon reflecting a decline in his playing strength. The man everyone expected to make it to the top of the chess ladder had been stopped by events and Father Time—both beyond his control. Diagram 31 shows the kind of slip that came with increasing frequency, and finally led to Flohr's retirement.

DIAGRAM 31

Black Could Have Mated in Three Moves!

Flohr, playing Black, drew this game instead of winning it. He has obtained a position in which he could have mated with a Bishop. First he had to make a move that cut off White's escape squares. Then he had to clear the long diagonal. Perhaps he should not be criticized too harshly for missing the winning line, for it is as subtle as it is brilliant!

1.	**Q—B8ch**
2. B—N1	

Now White's King has no escape square. Can White clear the long diagonal for a Bishop check? A Queen sacrifice would have done the job.

2.	**Q—B6ch!**
3. B × Q	**B × B mate**

Too bad. Flohr almost made it, but here, as in too many of his later games, he weakened after building up a winning position.

Not all mates by a Bishop occur by an attack along an open long diagonal. Sometimes the final attacking move is a capture or a check from close range. The position in Diagram 32, from a game won by the American master Samuel Factor in 1921, has occurred many times in games by other players. It develops when White plays poorly in the King's Gambit, permitting his King to be hemmed in at KN1. Black now wins quickly by sacrificing his Queen, forcing the White King to an exposed square where it is mated by a supported Bishop.

DIAGRAM 32

Black Offers a Queen Sacrifice. When It is Accepted, He Mates in Five Moves!

1.	....	**Q × N**
2.	**P × Q**	**B—B4ch**
3.	**K—R2**	**P—N6ch**
4.	**K—R3**	**B—B1ch**
5.	**Q—N4**	**B × Q mate**

The mate takes 6 moves if White plays 3. Q—Q4, B × Qch; 4. B—K3, B × Bch; 5. K—R2, P—N6ch; 6. K—R3, B—B1 mate. The 5-move mate occurred in the game.

Once you see that a mate by a Bishop is possible after the enemy King has been forced to an unprotected position on the edge of the board or out on the open board, all you must do is to decide on the sequence of moves that will force the King to the square on which it will be mated. Here are two positions you should be able to solve easily if you remember the three keys to a mate by a Bishop—an open diagonal, an enemy King without escape squares, and an attacking Bishop that cannot be captured.

DIAGRAM 33

White Mates in Three Moves

ANALYSIS

This is a typical position, one you will meet in this or a similar form many times in your chess career. The Black King can be forced to the open board where it will be mated by a Bishop. But on what square will you mate it?

1. ________ ________
2. ________ ________
3. ________ **mate**

DIAGRAM 34

G. KOLTANOWSKI — AMATEUR

Blindfold Exhibition—England, 1937

White Mates in Three Moves

ANALYSIS

This type of position also occurs frequently when a Queen has broken into an enemy King position. You should then try rearranging the pieces in your mind. Suppose the Black King were at Black's KB1 while the White Queen cut off its escape to adjacent white squares. Then a Bishop check at R6 would be mate! Two Queen moves can force this.

1. ________ ________
2. ________ ________
3. ________ **mate**

Perhaps you've found these mates with a Bishop easy. Well, sometimes it is very difficult to find a series of moves that will lead to that desired Bishop on a diagonal attacking a King without escape squares. The position on Diagram 35 is one of our favorites. Play through the moves to the mate and gain new respect for the beauty of an active chess imagination. We have here the end of a swashbuckling offhand game in which the players castled on opposite sides of the board and then opened lines for direct attacks on the castled Kings.

DIAGRAM 35

White Can Mate in Five Moves!

Black would win quickly if it were his move. To begin with, he threatens 1. . . . . P—Q8 (= Q)ch, which wins quickly, or 1. . . . . R—N8ch; 2. R × R, R × Rch; 3. Q—B1, R × Q mate or P × Q(= Q) mate. But it is White's turn to move, and he comes through first because his Bishop can occupy the long diagonal at the killing moment. Therefore:

1. R × Pch! R × R

Black would be mated after 1. . . . . K × R; 2. Q—R2ch, Q—R6 (forced); 3. Q × Q mate (for the White Pawn at B5 cuts off the Black King's escape square.

2. **Q—K5ch** **R(R2)—N2**

Here 2. . . . . R(N1)—N2 would permit an immediate mate by any Bishop move, for Black would then have no way to interpose a piece against the attack by the White Rook on QR8.

3. **Q—R2ch** **Q—R6**

And what other move is there to delay the mate? If Black plays 3. . . . . R—R2, then 4. B—K5 is mate at once.

4. **Q × Qch** **R—R2**
5. **B—K5 mate**

DIAGRAM 36

Look back to Diagram 24. In effect, White's play has resulted in the basic mate with a Bishop!

Look back to the position of Diagram 35. What thoughts led White to find the moves that brought him to the mate?

1. He had to recognize the possibility of reaching the basic position of a Bishop mate on the long diagonal.
2. To reach that position, he had to understand that the Black King could be locked in the corner without escape squares —blocked by its own pieces on R2 and N1.
3. The key to the final position was that a White Rook and a White Queen prevented Black's Rooks from interposing to block the mate on the long diagonal.

Once White's thoughts had moved through these points, the moves leading to mate almost called themselves out from the original position!

Do you understand how to mate with a Bishop? Remember that *your Bishop must check on an open diagonal while the enemy King has no escape squares, no protected piece can be interposed to block the check, and your Bishop cannot be captured.* Let's conclude with six positions of varying difficulty that will permit you to demonstrate your mastery of this basic checkmate technique!

DIAGRAM 37

G. KOLTANOWSKI — P. WEBB

Blindfold Exhibition, 1941

White Mates in Two Moves

ANALYSIS

Mate is not forced in this position, but White wins a Queen if his opponent does try to prevent the mate. So, assume that Black tries to keep the material even (as he did in the game), and find the quick mate with a Bishop.

1. ________ ________
2. ________ **mate**

DIAGRAM 38

White Mates in Two Moves

ANALYSIS

Your Bishop is already on the long diagonal. Your other Bishop cuts off Black's only possible escape square. If you can open the long diagonal and then move your King to discover an attack by the Bishop, then Black is mated. Remember, it matters not that you sacrifice material—so long as you then mate!

1. ________ ________
2. ________ **mate**

TERM TO KNOW

***Discovered check (dis ch)*—A check** unmasked when a piece on the rank, file, or diagonal involved is moved, thus opening that line for the check.

DIAGRAM 39

KOSSIKOV — KALINSKI

Soviet Union, 1974

White Mates in Three Moves

ANALYSIS

Black resigned after White's first move in this position. White has just sacrificed two Rooks on the KR file to open a key diagonal. Now he has a simple mate in three that depends on a Bishop. The mate is easy to find once you see which diagonal is critical!

1. ________ ________
2. ________ ________
3. ________ mate

DIAGRAM 40

White Mates in Two Moves

ANALYSIS

This is a common endgame position. Black's King lacks escape squares. If only White could check with his Bishop! Once you see that the Rook at K7 is protected by your Knight, the mate is easy.

1. ________ ________
2. ________ mate

DIAGRAM 41

Black Mates in Three Moves

ANALYSIS

White would be mated if the long diagonal had no White Pawns on it. The task, then, is to remove these Pawns and any piece that tries to interpose on the diagonal. With these hints the forceful mate in three should be obvious.

1. .... ________
2. ________ ________
3. ________ ________ mate

DIAGRAM 42

White Mates in Two Moves

ANALYSIS

White has an easy mate in two, so long as he realizes he must block the Black King's escape squares while attacking on the long diagonal. Fortunately, a Rook move discovers a check by the Queen so that Black lacks time to create an escape square for his King.

1. ________ ________
2. ________ **mate**

NOTE: show the mate after each of Black's possible first moves.

REMEMBER!

1. Look for a Bishop mate when your opponent's King is on an open diagonal and lacks escape squares.
2. Similarly, when a Bishop can check at a square adjacent to the enemy King and thereby mate it, place a piece in position to support the Bishop.
3. Be prepared to sacrifice material to force a diagonal open for your Bishop when its attack on that diagonal leads to mate.

CHAPTER 3

Checkmate by a Knight

"Everything was going well until that Knight check!" How often have you heard that complaint from someone who has just lost an important game? Or, more important, how often have you yourself muttered the same words? Any player, beginner to grandmaster, can be surprised by a Knight move. Other pieces move in straight lines, and it is relatively easy to see from one end to the other of a rank, file, or diagonal. But the Knight can wander across the board defying the straight lines that catch the eye. This permits it to make sudden appearances on squares where it then has a fatal effect on the course of a game.

One of the memorable attacks using the Knight was played by the Italian master Monticelli against the grandmaster Ewfim D. Bogolyubov. Grandmasters, accustomed to winning international tournaments, are players with far better records than the lower rated international masters. Monticelli, an also-ran in the important tournaments, was still one of the best players in Europe. Given the opportunity, he could win as brilliantly as anyone else. Bogulyubov, one of the giants of the game in the 1920s and 1930s, was an unsuccessful challenger for the world's championship in 1934. But in this game Monticelli was in charge, producing a classic example of the hidden power of the Knight. Set up the position before the final attack.

DIAGRAM 43

Black Mates in Four Moves!

Monticelli was Black. All of his pieces (and his KRP) cover squares near the White King. Now he must find the mate. The problem is that White has too many escape squares. The first step must therefore be to limit those escape squares.

1. . . . . **N—K7ch!**

The Knight is sacrificed. White must capture it, for if 2. K—R2, Black plays 2. . . . . Q—N7 mate.

2. **R × N** **R—B8ch!**

The purpose of this second sacrifice is to make room for Black's Queen at R8. If White refuses the sacrifice by 3. K—R2 Black can mate at once by 3. . . . . Q—R8 mate or 3. . . . . R—R8 mate.

3. **K × R** **Q—R8ch**
4. **K—B2**

Now we see the meaning of Black's first move. White's K2 is blocked by his Rook. As things stand, the Black Queen controls the long diagonal and White's first rank. The only escae square still available to the White King is K3. However:

4. . . . . **N—N5 mate**

Because the Knight controls White's K3 while attacking the King.

Mates by a Knight are easiest to find when the enemy King is locked in a corner of the board. The position of Diagram 44 occurs quite often. It is the simplest example of mate with a Knight.

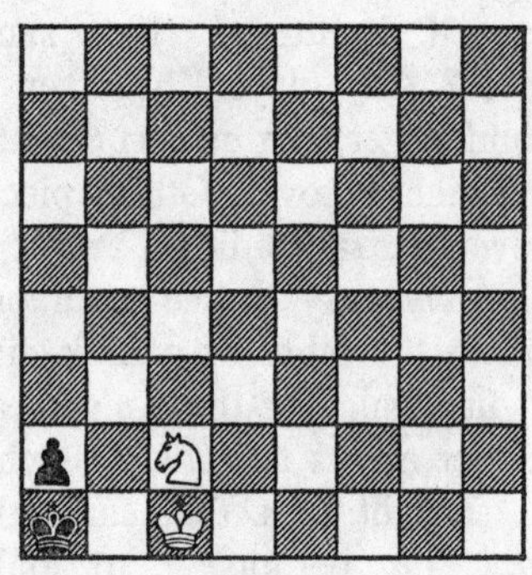

DIAGRAM 44

As in all checkmates, a King lacking an escape square is here attacked (and therefore mated) by a piece that is itself immune from capture. Once an enemy

King can be forced into a corner square in an ending of King and Knight against King and Rook Pawn, the mate can be forced if White can achieve the position of Diagram 44. The position in Diagram 45 occurs frequently, and is only two short moves removed from that of Diagram 44.

DIAGRAM 45

White Mates in Two Moves

The Knight prevents the Black King from moving to Black's R7. The White King prevents an escape to the N-file. White mates in two by forcing the Black Pawn to advance (making R7 unavailable to the Black King), meanwhile vacating the White KB2 square for a Knight check—and mate.

1.	**K—B1**	**P—R7**
2.	**N—B2 mate**	

Inexperienced players sometimes make the mistake of blocking their positions and then permitting a Knight check that mates during the opening. Let's look at two such opening monstrosities to illustrate the danger a Knight invasion can bring. The first is a problem rather than an opening line you are ever likely to play for either side. TASK—Black mates from the opening position in three moves, moving only his Queen's Knight.

1.	**P—QB4**	**N—QB3**
2.	**P—K3**	**N—N5 (or N—K4)**
3.	**N—K2??**	**N—Q6 mate**

DIAGRAM 46

There it is, the task completed. Try it out on your friends. And if they tell you that it is nonsense, for no player would permit such an easy mate in the opening, show them this short game lost in 1950 by an experienced Russian tournament player.

White	Black
PAUL KERES	R. ARLAMOVSKI

CARO-KANN DEFENSE

1.	P—K4	P—QB3
2.	P—Q4	P—Q4
3.	N—QB3	P × P
4.	N × P	N—Q2
5.	Q—K2	N(N1)—B3 ??
6.	N—Q6 mate	

DIAGRAM 47

Any player can be mated by a Knight—and any player can learn to use the Knight to mate. Remember that the ideal position is one in which the enemy King has no escape squares. A check by your Knight can then be mate. The problem is often that an enemy piece controls the square to which you wish to move your Knight. What to do? Look for a sacrifice that forces that piece to move away, while leaving the enemy King still without escape squares. Here is an example of such a mating attack.

DIAGRAM 48

White Mates in Two Moves

ANALYSIS

White can mate if he can play N—B7 without losing the Knight to the Black Queen. A Queen sacrifice leaves Black without escape squares by forcing the Black Queen to give up its control of Black's KB2. Can you see White's winning move?

1. ________ ________
2. ________ **mate**

Sometimes the enemy King is on its second rank with its first rank controlled by one of your Rooks. In such cases, if the King is at its R2 or N2, it is in effect still in the corner of the board, with limited possibilities of escape. Mate with a Knight is still possible, as illustrated by the position of Diagram 49.

DIAGRAM 49

VAN DEN ENDEN — PRASZAK
Lublin, Poland, 1974

White Mates in Two Moves

ANALYSIS

Suppose the White Queen were not on the board. White could then mate by N—R5, for the Black King has no escape squares. The winning move depends on the fact that a White Knight at R5 also controls Black's KB3. Take your time. The startling sacrifice is not obvious!

1. ________ ________
2. ________ **mate**

But enemy Kings often leave the corner of the board. Checkmate with a Knight may still be possible if the King lacks escape squares. This can occur when your opponent's Pawns or pieces block nearby squares, or when your own Pawns or pieces control them. All you then need is a Knight check (and mate) from a square not controlled by your opponent.

More commonly, you must create such a blocked enemy King position by forcing your opponent's pieces to squares where they block the King's escape from the later Knight check. Begin by examining this complex position in which two sacrifices leave a King trapped and ripe for mate by a Knight.

DIAGRAM 50

DRUGANOV — PANTALEIEV
Correspondence game, 1956

Black Mates in Three Moves

You can best understand this mate by following the thoughts that must have led Black to success.

1. All of my pieces are active. I would like to mate by N—N6. How?
2. I must clear the diagonals for my two Bishops so that they control the escape squares Q7 and QB7. This means I must

move away my Knight and get White to move away his Bishop.

3. That will leave White's Q1 available for the King's escape. How can I force White to occupy that square with a piece?
4. In doing all this, I must remember that my Queen has to leave its present square to make room for my Knight now at R8.
5. All is clear. First I force the White Rook to Q1. A Queen sacrifice does that. Then I check with my Knight at K7 to force White to capture with his Bishop. All lines are then under control for the Knight mate. That does it!

1.	**Q—Q8ch!**	**R × Q**
2.	**N—K7ch**	**B × N**
3.	**N—N6 mate**	

The analysis of the next two positions should help you to discover similar mates based on the blocking of escape squares. Once such blocking has been achieved, the King is subject to check—and mate—by a Knight.

DIAGRAM 51

GRIGORIEF — HABITCH
Schaffhousen, 1931

Black Mates in Two Moves

ANALYSIS

This ending has been reached after several sacrifices by Black have forced the White King to its present position—where its only escape square is at its R5. A Knight check (at Black's B5) will also control White's escape square—and be mate! What move, by introducing a new mate threat, gives Black time to play N—B5 mate?

1\. . . . . ______

2\. ______ ______ **mate**

DIAGRAM 52

White Mates in Three Moves

ANALYSIS

On what square can the Black King be mated? Suppose it were at its K2 and a Black Bishop were at its KB3 to block the King's escape. Then White could mate with N—B5. How can this situation be forced? Remember that sacrifices can be used to force an opponent to occupy a square!

1. **P × Pch!** ________
2. ________ ________
3. ________ **mate**

Rudolf Spielmann— The Brilliant Win Comes First!

It must be frustrating to be talented and only partly successful. Rudolph Spielmann (1883–1942) was such a person. One of the chess world's child prodigies, he became famous early in his career for his brilliant attacks and endless search for combinations. Of course, attacks and combinations are not always possible, and Spielmann's hunt for more than existed in many a chess position brought him losses as well as victories. He was often a prizewinner but only occasionally finished first during a generation of tournaments. His book, *The Art of Sacrifice in Chess,* was printed in a dozen languages and became a world-wide best seller. Its analysis of his best combinations inspired a generation of young players, including the American masters who became world famous in the 1930s when their team won the Chess Olympiad four times.

The Spielmann combinations flashed around the chess world. One of the most amazing came in his game against R. Walter at Teplitz, 1928. Spielmann, playing White, has bored in with Queen and Knight, reaching this position with the Black King on B4.

DIAGRAM 53

What next? The White Bishop prevents Black's King from escaping to Q3. Every other square near the King is occupied by one of its own pieces or controlled by a White Pawn. Black will be mated if White can find a Knight check while Black's King is still trapped. Study the position for a few minutes before you look at the answer at the top of the next page. If you see it quickly, then be proud! There may be a touch of Spielmann in you! Problem—what to do about Black's B?

Opportunities for Queen sacrifices to prepare for a mate by a Knight appear frequently. Consider a player's usual method of attacking the opponent's castled King position. He tries to bring his Queen and perhaps a Knight and another piece to bear on the Pawns in front of that King. When there are few enemy pieces able to defend against the onslaught, sacrifices become possible to force the enemy King to a square where it can be mated. The next two positions illustrate Queen sacrifices permitting mate by a Knight.

DIAGRAM 54

A. THOMPSON — G. MACKENZIE

New York, 1866

Black Mates in Four Moves

ANALYSIS

Captain Mackenzie was one of the best players in the United States in the Age of Morphy. His opponent has misplayed a King's Gambit and thinks his King is now safe at QB3. But Black plays 1. . . . . Q × QPch. If White declines the sacrifice and plays 2. K—Q2, he is mated by 2. . . . . Q—K6ch; 3. K—B3, B—N2ch; 4. K—B4, B—R3 mate. White accepts the Queen sacrifice and is mated at his K4. What are the moves?

1.	....	**Q × Pch**
2.	**K × Q**	______
3.	______	______
4.	______	______
		mate—by a Knight!

DIAGRAM 55
KARALAIC — NICOLIC
Pristina, 1973
White Mates in Two Moves

ANALYSIS

This mate by a Knight occurred when Black accepted White's offer of a Queen sacrifice. Had he refused it, he would have been left with a lost ending. So assume that there is a square at which you can offer your Queen, and then assume further that Black does take it. Mate by a Knight then follows because Black has no escape squares. What Queen move won this game?

1. ________ ________
2. ________ **mate**

So much for mate by a Knight. It can occur in the ending when the enemy King is pinned against the edge of the board or trapped in the corner. It is easiest when the King is hemmed in by its own pieces. It can also occur on the open board when the King lacks escape squares. And, for those who dare to force matters, one or more sacrifices can force the King to a square where a Knight can mate. Try the six positions that follow to check your understanding of these techniques of mate with a Knight.

Solution to Spielmann-Walter (Diagram 53)

1. Q × Nch! B × Q (forced)
2. N × P mate

DIAGRAM 56
White Mates in Five Moves

ANALYSIS

Don't be frightened by the fact that this is a mate in five. Your task is simple. While keeping the Black King pinned down at its R8, force Black to advance Pawns. Finally, when Black is forced to play P—R7, you will have a position similar to the ones in Diagrams 44 and 45. Look back at them before you attempt this one.

1. ________ ________
2. ________ ________
3. ________ ________
4. ________ ________
5. ________ **mate**

DIAGRAM 57

Black Mates in Three Moves

(From a position in one of the first chess books, by Greco in 1516!)

ANALYSIS

This is an example of forcing the enemy King into the corner, where it is hemmed in by its own pieces and subject to mate by a Knight. How can you force the White King to KR1? Once there, how can you prevent it from returning to KN1? Why not consider a Queen sacrifice? Many games are won each year by the technique illustrated by this attack!

1. .... ________
2. ________ ________
3. ________ ________ **mate**

DIAGRAM 58

VIRTANEN — BJORQUIST

Correspondence game, 1974

White Mates in Four Moves

ANALYSIS

This is another attack that occurs frequently. The key to the win is that the Black King can be forced to its N1 while a protected White Pawn is at White's KN7. Then, with the Black King lacking escape squares, a Knight check is mate. The mate depends on two sacrifices—a Rook followed by a Queen. The first clears a line; the second makes use of it. On what square does the Knight mate?

1. ________ ________
2. ________ ________
3. ________ ________
4. ________ **mate**

DIAGRAM 59

White Mates in Three Moves

ANALYSIS

Consider this position an introduction to the double check—an attacking technique important later in this book. The win here depends on a check by the White Queen and Knight—simultaneously. That means you must open the long diagonal on which the Queen, Knight, and Black King stand. You can do this if you force the Black Rook to R2 instead of its present N2. You will then have a double check that mates a King trapped in the corner without escape squares.

1. ______ ______
2. ______ ______
3. ______ **double check and mate!**

DIAGRAM 60

White Mates in Two Moves

ANALYSIS

This composed position illustrates a mate by a Knight on the open board. Note that any move by your Knight unmasks a check by your Bishop that forces the Black Knight back to its K3—where it has no escape squares. That means a check by a Knight is mate—if it doesn't check from a square that must remain open to control an escape square. Confusing? Just avoid getting back to the position from which you began!

1. ______ ______
2. ______ **mate**

DIAGRAM 61

DANIEL HARRWITZ —
ADOLF ANDERSSEN
Match, Breslau, 1848

White Mates in Three Moves

ANALYSIS

Harrwitz was a chess professional of the mid-nineteenth century, serving in that capacity in London and later in Paris. The clubs that hired him knew his play was often brilliant—a showpiece for their activities. In this game he used an attack beginning with a double check to force a mate with a Knight. His famous opponent had just played P × P, discovering a check on the White King. But White mates by driving the Black King to the open board.

1. ______ **dbl ch** ______
2. ______ ______
3. ______ **mate**

REMEMBER!

1. As in other mates, one by a Knight is possible only when the enemy King lacks escape squares.
2. When the enemy King lacks escape squares and your Knight can check, seek sacrifices to remove enemy defenders of the square on which the mate can occur.
3. Similarly, other attacking moves by your pieces can force enemy pieces to occupy squares adjacent to the enemy King, when a Knight check mates a King that no longer has escape squares.

CHAPTER 4

Checkmate by a Rook

"Let me show you how I beat ——" How many times have you heard that phrase, the introduction to what may be an exciting game or another illustration of someone's blunder? But then, how can you refuse to look at a game that may contain a position or an idea that is well worth remembering? The chess imagination is at times miraculous, exploding what seem to be quiet positions to produce the most brilliant of checkmates. One of the most complex finishes in recent years involved a mate with a Rook. And yet, it was completely logical. A player saw a way to force his opponent's King to a square where it had no escape from a Rook check!

The game was played in a 1973 Russian tournament. The Russian master Zaichev was mowing down the opposition until he was paired against a relative unknown named Alexandrov. They reached this position.

DIAGRAM 62

Zaichev, playing Black, threatens mate in one by . . . . Q—R7, for the Black Bishop cuts off the White King's escape. But it is White's move, and Alexandrov saw a win that must be seen to be believed! Suppose he could force Black's King to its QR1, open the QR file, prevent its escape via QN1, and then check—and mate—with a Rook on the QR file! Alexandrov sees that he can do all this if he sacrifices freely and plays his moves in the proper sequences. He mates in eleven moves—with Black's responses forced all along the way. Play through the moves first without studying the notes. Then go through them again with the notes.

1. Q × Nch!

The Queen sacrifice is the key to all that follows. It opens lines on which the remaining White pieces can co-ordinate their activity to force the mate.

1.		**K × Q**
2. **N—N5 dbl ch**		**K—N1**

Black's King has no other move.

3. R—Q8ch!

The mating attack fails without this move. White must force the Black Rook to leave the K-file so that there will be no defense to White's B—B4ch, the move that forces Black's King into the corner. If White had played 3. B—B4ch, Black could have defended with 3. .... R—K4.

3.	**R × R**
4. **B—B4ch**	**N—K4**

Black sacrifices his Knight to delay the mate. He could later have delayed it another move by sacrificing his Rook on Q3.

5. **B × Nch**	**K—R1**

Now White plays to open the QR file. His method is as sharp as it is instructive.

6. **N—B7ch**	**K—N1**
7. **N × B dbl ch**	**K—R1**
8. **N—B7ch**	**K—N1**
9. **N—Q5ch**	**K—R1**
10. **N—N6ch!**	**P × N**

White has created his desired position. Black's King is at QR1. A Bishop prevents its escape to QN1. The QR file is open. Mate follows.

11. R—R1 mate

DIAGRAM 63

There it is—an attack to remember. Once Alexandrov had visualized the final position, his moves came like clockwork. After all, he knew the four conditions necessary for mate by a Rook:

1. The enemy King lacks escape squares.
2. A Rook can attack it on a rank or file.
3. The Rook is immune from capture.
4. The Rook check cannot be blocked by the interposing of a protected piece or Pawn.

TERMS TO KNOW

Open file—A file containing no Pawns.

Open rank—A rank on which there are no Pawns or pieces between a Rook (or Queen) and whatever it is attacking.

Kings in close opposition—When a King can cut off a rank or file to an opposing King, as each King does in Diagram 64.

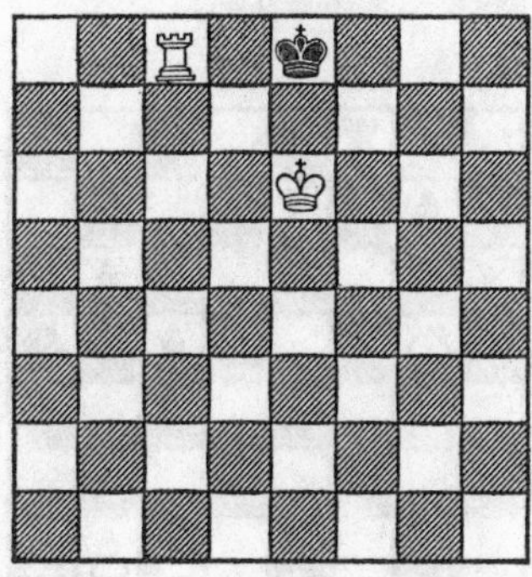

DIAGRAM 64

The position of Diagram 64 is the kind of mate that often ends a game in which King and Rook oppose a lone King. The Rook attacks the Black King, which has no escape squares on its first rank and cannot move to the second rank because the White King is in close opposition. This is mate with a Rook on a rank. It is one of the three ways in which you can checkmate with a Rook:

—on a rank
—on a file
—from an adjacent square.

Let's go back a bit to see what White move could have forced Black into close opposition to make the checkmate possible.

DIAGRAM 65

The White Rook is on KN4. It could be on any square from which it can move to the open QB file without itself being captured. In the position of Diagram 65, White now plays 1. R—QB4. The Rook must move to the QB file to cut off the escape of Black's King. Now the King can make only one move, 1. . . . . K—K1, when White can mate as in Diagram 64 with 2. R—B8 mate.

This is called a mate on the eighth rank (or back rank). Most such mates occur when the enemy King has no escape squares on its first rank and cannot move to the second rank because its own Pawns or enemy pieces prevent such moves. In the ending, such a blocking of escape squares is often accomplished by a King in close opposition. Once you note that you have an open file for your Rook, and that the opposing King is on your eighth rank without escape squares, your problem is to get a Rook to that rank. Diagram 66 shows a common win based on mate by a Rook.

DIAGRAM 66

White mates in two moves. The material is even, but not the positions of the two sides. Black's King has no escape squares and can be attacked by a White Rook. White plays 1. R—Q8ch, R × R; 2. R × R mate.

This, of course, is an ideal position and a mate easily learned and used. But most mates on the eighth rank require the aid of one or more other pieces to cut off escape squares. The trick is to be able to visualize the final position. For example, in Diagram 67 White can mate in four moves in an attack that must use all four White pieces. The Black King must be forced to its QR1, where the White Knight cuts off its escape via QR2. A Rook check on the eighth rank would then be mate if the two Black Rooks can be removed. Given the first two moves of the winning procedure, can you see its conclusion? Be ready to sacrifice!

DIAGRAM 67

White Mates in Four Moves

ANALYSIS

Remember that you will mate with a Rook on the eighth rank while the Black King is at its QR1.

1.	**B × Pch**	**R × B**
2.	**R × Rch**	**R—B1**
3.	________	________
4.	________	**mate**

Sometimes a single advanced Pawn cuts off two escape squares while a third is blocked by the opponent's own Pawn or piece. Diagram 68 illustrates such a blocked back rank. Here a sacrifice forces the Black King to its K1 square, when a White Rook can mate on the eighth rank. It's fortunate that White has this win, for Black also threatens to win with a Rook check on the back rank!

DIAGRAM 68

White Mates in Three Moves

ANALYSIS

The key to this mate is that the White Pawn at K6 controls Q7 and KB7. Thus, once the Black King is at its K1, it will have no escape squares on its second rank. How can you force the King to that square?

1.	________	________
2.	________	________
3.	________	**mate**

We have examined examples of mate by a Rook on the file and on the rank. Less common, but just as important for your technique, is the mate by a protected Rook from a square adjacent to the enemy King. Diagram 69 is a good illustration.

DIAGRAM 69

White Mates in Three Moves

ANALYSIS

The Black King's scope is limited by White's advanced Pawns

and by the Black Rooks. White wins by driving Black's King to a square where it cannot escape from a Rook check on an adjacent square. White begins by forcing the King to its second rank.

1. ________ ________
2. ________ ________
3. ________ mate

All mates with a Rook are variations of these three basic attacks—on the rank, on the file, and from an adjacent square. Let's examine one more of each type.

DIAGRAM 70
White Mates in Two Moves

ANALYSIS

This is another mate on an adjacent square. Black's King's escape routes are blocked by its Bishop and White's King, Bishop, and advanced Pawn. All White needs is a pair of Rook moves to mate.

1. ________ ________
2. ________ mate

DIAGRAM 71
White Mates in Four Moves

ANALYSIS

This position is based on a threat in a game between M. Vidmar and R. Teichmann in the Carlsbad, 1907, tournament. If it were White's move, he could mate brilliantly in four moves—ending with a Rook check and mate on the eighth rank. To aid you in finding the difficult sequence of moves in this combination, the final position is given in Diagram 72.

How does White force mate? Look at the final position. White's Queen and one Rook have been

DIAGRAM 72
Final Position

sacrificed, while Black's KRP is gone. What moves led from Diagram 71 to Diagram 72?

1. ________ ________
2. ________ ________
3. ________ ________
4. ________ **mate**

DIAGRAM 73
Black Mates in Three Moves

ANALYSIS

Examine this position closely. The White King is locked in the corner. If the White Pawn at KR2 were gone, a Black Rook check on the file would be mate, for White would have no escape squares. Even if the White King were at R2, a Rook check would be mate because White could not move to KN3.

1. .... ________
2. ________ ________
3. ________ ________ **mate**

That's all there is to it. Mating with a Rook requires the ability to recognize positions in which a King without escape squares can be checked on the rank, the file, or an adjacent square. Sometimes such mates are obvious and merely require the forcing of a check. More often the enemy King must be forced to the square where that check is fatal, or its pieces removed from squares where they can interpose or capture the checking Rook. The eight positions that follow provide practice in simple mates and in positions where forcing moves and sacrifices are necessary to make the mate occur.

DIAGRAM 74
W. STEINITZ — AMATEUR
London, 1890
White Mates in Three Moves

ANALYSIS

Wilhelm Steinitz, one of the great world champions and perhaps the first scientific chess master, sought patterns leading to winning chess formations and demonstrated them again and again. Here the pattern is clear. White could mate with a Rook if the Black Rook at KB7 were replaced by a White Knight on the same square. How does Steinitz force that change in the position—and then mate with his Rook?

1. ________ ________
2. ________ ________
3. ________ mate

DIAGRAM 75
White Mates in Two Moves

ANALYSIS

One of the advantages of having a protected Pawn at KN7 in this position is that it will in turn protect a Rook at R8—if White can get his Rook to that square! White has sacrificed everything but his Rook to reach this position. Now he mates in two moves no matter what Black does.

1. ________ Any move
2. ________ mate

DIAGRAM 76
White Mates in Two Moves

ANALYSIS

This is another mate on the eighth rank. In an otherwise even position, Black has just blundered by playing his Rook to K1. White quickly forces the Black King away and then mates. No wonder a basic goal of successful chess players is to make certain that a King on the first rank has an escape square!

1. ________ ________
2. ________ mate

DIAGRAM 77
White Mates in Three Moves

ANALYSIS

This position is typical of many in which mate on a file can be forced. Black threatens to win at once by . . . . R(2) × P mate, but it is White's move. He sees that he can make Black move his King to the QR file, open that file, and then mate along it!

1. ________ ________
2. ________ ________
3. ________ mate

Akiba Rubinstein—Tragic Victim of His Times

War and the waves of hatred that swept the world during his lifetime destroyed the great potential of one of the most talented and imaginative chess players of our century. His name was Akiba Rubinstein, and his story is a commentary on the failings of our times. The youngest of twelve children in a poor Jewish family, he had begun training to be a rabbi when introduced to chess. His progress was so rapid that he decided to become a chess professional instead. Rubinstein became one of many ghetto Jews who escaped the restrictions then placed on those of his religion by entering an honored profession whose members were exempt from most discriminatory regulations.

His rapid progress from 1906 on seemed certain to make him world champion. A match with world champion Emanuel Lasker was set for 1914, but World War I delayed it. Rubinstein was in Berlin during the war years, where he went bankrupt and then developed a persecution mania that broke his powers of concentration and destroyed his chess ability. He made several more efforts to play, but finally retired from the game in 1932. The coming of the Nazis made him a target of real persecution, and he collapsed. His final years were spent in a sanitarium, where he died in 1961. Yet in his lifetime he had produced dozens of new chess ideas and had proven that the six hours daily he spent in the study of chess theory could make a grandmaster a model of precise play.

One of Rubinstein's most memorable wins involved a mate with a Rook as the final point of an astounding combination.

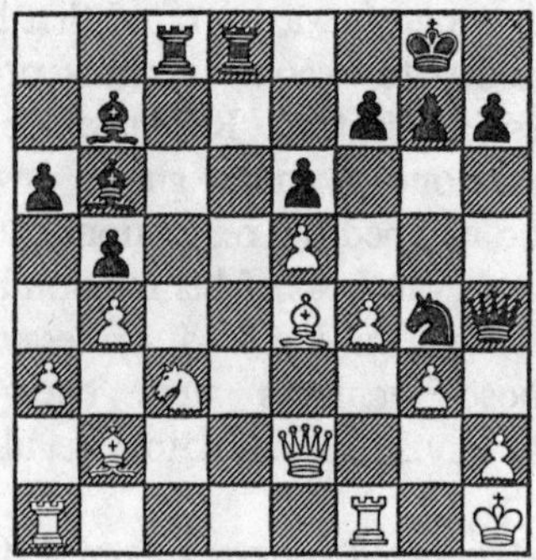

DIAGRAM 78

ROTLEVI — RUBINSTEIN
Lodz, 1907

Black to Play and Win

ANALYSIS

White has just played 1. P—KN3 to attack Black's Queen. Rubinstein continued with the brilliant Queen sacrifice, 1. . . . . **R × N!** When Rotlevi took the Queen by **2. P × Q,** the attack continued with **2. . . . . R—Q7!** Suddenly Black's mate threats could not be met.

a. 3. **B × B** **R × Q**
4. **B × R** **R × P mate**

b. 3. **Q × N** **B × Bch**
4. **R—B3** **R × R**
5. **Q—N2** **R—KB8ch**
6. **R × R** **B × Q mate**

Rotlevi therefore played 3. Q × R, and after Rubinstein's 3. . . . . B × Bch; 4. Q—N2. How did Rubinstein now force resignation? Play through the moves from Diagram 78 and then add Black's winning move.

1.	**R × N**
2. **P × Q**	**R—Q7**
3. **Q × R**	**B × Bch**
4. **Q—N2**	________
5. **Resigns** (Why?)	

DIAGRAM 79

Black Mates in Five Moves Beginning with 1. . . . Q × Nch; 2. P × Q

ANALYSIS

This mate on the eighth rank is made possible by the exposed position of White's King and the fact that Black's Bishops can drive that King to its KN1. There, lacking escape squares, it cannot avoid mate by the Rook. Black therefore begins with 1. . . . . Q × Nch; this opens the KR6 square for the first Bishop check. What forcing moves then result in mate?

1.	....	**Q × Nch**
2.	**P × Q**	______
3.	______	______
4.	______	______
5.	______	______ **mate**

tack at all costs, reached this position in which, despite White's attack on a Rook and a Bishop, Black forces mate in 5—by a Rook on the eighth rank! Black's first move threatens 2. . . . . Q × P mate, so White stops this threat by 2. Q × B. How does Black then offer his Queen to force the mate? The key to his win is the pressure of his Bishop on the long diagonal!

1.	....	**Q—R5!**
2.	**Q × B**	______
3.	______	______
4.	______	______
5.	______	______ **mate**

DIAGRAM 80

LARSEN — LJUBOJEVIC
Milan, 1975

Black Mates in Five Moves

DIAGRAM 81

CHEMOUILLET — KIESERITZKY
Paris, 1840

Black Mates in Three Moves

ANALYSIS

Two of the most imaginative players in the history of chess, both aggressive and ready to at-

ANALYSIS

Nineteenth-century masters also understood the mate with a Rook. This one takes place on

the open board. White has just played N × B. If Black recaptures the Knight, White will play P—Q4 and create an escape square for his King at K3. Instead, Black sees a way to mate with a Rook. White could have delayed the mate by interposing his Knight along the way, but didn't. So, your task is to find the two Queen moves by Black and the final mate, with White making only the King moves he played in the game. Black's goal is to cut off escape squares on the KN file to prepare for a Rook mate on the rank.

1.	**Q—____**	
2. **K—____**	**Q—____**	
3. **K—____**	**R—____**	**mate**

REMEMBER!

1. Mates by a Rook are most common when an enemy King is on an open file and lacks escape squares, or in a similar condition on its first rank with escape squares blocked by its own Pawns.
2. Most mates by a Rook occur when the Rook acts in combination with another piece that supports it on the mating square or cuts off enemy escape squares.
3. Once the enemy King has been forced to a position where mate by a Rook becomes a possibility, examine sacrifices that force open the line on which the mate will occur.

CHAPTER 5

Checkmate by a Queen

The Queen's lethal potential derives from its great mobility. It moves quickly across the board, its sweep of ranks, files, and diagonals giving it control of more squares than any other piece. This great scope makes a Queen's invasion of an enemy position the frequent prelude to mates. No player is immune from sudden mating attacks based on the Queen's power—and no player can be successful without understanding how and when a Queen can be used to force a mate.

Alexander Alekhine, regarded by many chess authorities as the best chess player of all time, had to learn chess through bitter experience. Yet he rarely repeated his mistakes, developing an attacking technique that made him world champion in 1927. But in 1911, a rising star of nineteen, Alekhine misplayed an opening against the Swiss master Johner—and then played on to the end in a lost position. Finally, Johner announced a mate in four that illustrates the power of a supported Queen against an exposed King that soon lacks escape squares.

DIAGRAM 82

ALEKHINE — JOHNER

Carlsbad, 1911

Black Mates in Four Moves

This mate illustrates how attacking moves by a Queen on the rank, file, and diagonal can be combined to achieve victory.

1. . . . . **Q—B7ch**

Johner begins with an attack on the diagonal. His Queen is supported by the Bishop on K6.

2. **K—Q1** **Q—B8ch**

Now the Queen attacks on the rank—like a Rook. White's only move is to interpose his own Queen, which cuts off his King's possible return to K1.

3. **Q—K1** **Q—Q6ch**

That does it. With this check on the file, the White King has no move. The only reply is to interpose and lose his Queen.

4. **Q—Q2** **Q × Q mate**

(See Diagram 83)

This mate illustrates the most common mate by a Queen. It is supported and attacks a King without escape squares on an adjacent square. Note that the Queen's ability to move like a Rook or a Bishop gives it control of all five squares adjacent to the King.

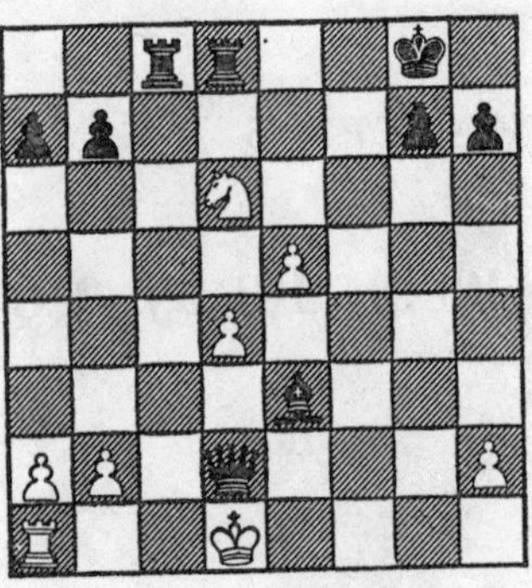

DIAGRAM 83
**Final Position—
The Black Queen Mates
from an Adjacent Square**

Understanding mate by a Queen follows understanding of its ability to do anything a Rook or a Bishop can do. Diagram 84 illustrates a mate by a Queen on a diagonal (like a Bishop), while Diagram 85 shows one in which the Queen mates like a Rook.

DIAGRAM 84
Mate by a Queen on a Diagonal

DIAGRAM 85

Mate by a Queen on a Rank

Mates by a Queen are more common than any others. They are often made possible by sacrifices that open lines to permit the entry of a supported Queen. Diagram 86 occurred in a 1971 Russian tournament in which a Queen mates because his opponent lacks escape squares. Here again the Queen's power to check on the rank, file, and diagonal is

DIAGRAM 86

White Mates in Four Moves

illustrated in an attack that was preceded by the sacrifice of a Rook and Bishop to remove the Pawns near the Black King.

1. Q—R5ch K—B3

If Black had played 1. . . . . K—N2, then White would have mated quickly by 2. Q—B7ch, K—R1; 3. Q—R7 mate (by a supported Queen on a square adjacent to an enemy King).

2. Q—B7ch K × N
3. Q—B5ch K—R5
4. Q—R5 mate

There it is—mate by a supported Queen that has first attacked like a Bishop, then checked on a file and a rank like a Rook, and finally mated on an adjacent square.

Mate with a Queen, then, depends on three factors:

1. The enemy King must be driven to a square (or be on a square) where it lacks escape squares.
2. This lack of escape squares is easier to force because the Queen can threaten moves like a Rook or a Bishop at more squares than any other attacking piece.
3. In addition to possible mates like a Rook or a Bishop, the Queen's ability to invade a position along any open line gives it the power to move

quickly to squares adjacent to the enemy King.

The Queen's great scope and the speed with which it can move from one part of the board to another makes it dangerous to adopt any opening in which too many Pawns near the King are moved. The worst opening moves possible can lead to such sequences as the two chess jokes called the Fool's Mates.

1. **P—KB3?** **P—K4**
2. **P—KN4??** **Q—R5 mate**

Or, with Black playing the same moves,

1. **P—K4** **P—KB3?**
2. **P—Q4** **P—KN4??**
3. **Q—R5 mate**

Of course, you do not expect your opponents to make such absolute blunders. If they do so more than once, find other opponents. Yet they may make another kind of error, failing to see a mate threat in the opening based on the power of the Queen. This short game has been played dozens of times in the experience of every master who gives simultaneous chess exhibitions.

1. **P—K4** **P—K4**
2. **N—KB3** **P—Q3**
3. **B—B4** **N—QB3**
4. **P—B3** **B—N5**
5. **Q—N3** **B × N??**

DIAGRAM 87

White Mates in Two Moves

The mate is possible because of the power of a supported Queen to attack on both the file and the diagonal.

6. **B × Pch** **K—K2**
7. **Q—K6 mate**

How do you recognize when a mate by a Queen is possible?

1. You must be able to force the enemy King to a square where check by the Queen will be mate. This may mean checks to make the King move to that square.
2. You must look for a check that will force an interposition that then allows you to use your Queen to check on a rank, file, or diagonal to force mate.
3. You should try to advance a Pawn or get one or more other pieces that can support your Queen at a square adja-

cent to the enemy King when that King lacks escape squares.

Diagram 88 illustrates a mate in which a Queen forces an interposition and then mates by switching its attack from a rank to a diagonal. Diagram 89 illustrates a mate on an adjacent square made possible by the great mobility of the Queen and its ability to switch its attack from a rank to a file.

DIAGRAM 88

White Mates in Two Moves

ANALYSIS

Given time to create an escape square by . . . . R—R1 or . . . . P—N3, Black could easily draw and might even win. But White has a dangerous Queen check that forces Black to interpose on his Q1 and thus eliminate his King's only escape square. How does White then use the Queen's power to move along the diagonal to mate?

1. ________ ________
2. ________ **mate**

DIAGRAM 89

White Mates in Four Moves

ANALYSIS

Most of the Pawns are gone, and open lines invite an attack. The Black King is trapped in the corner, and will be mated at White's KN7 if a way can be found to use the White Queen on the long diagonal. Suppose the Black Rook were off the QR file. Then a White King move would unleash the mating power of his Queen. White's first move is therefore 1. R—Q8ch!, which forces Black's Rook to capture! Can you see the continuation after that?

1. **R—Q8ch!** ________
2. ________ ________
3. ________ ________
4. ________ **mate**

TERMS TO KNOW

Battery—Two or more pieces bearing down on the same square so that one supports another when it moves to that square. When there are three or more pieces in a battery, sacrifices can be used to remove the target square's defenders.

Target square—The square you must control to carry out a mating attack—often the square on which one of your pieces will deliver mate.

The most common mating battery in the endgame (and sometimes in the middle game) is a Queen on an open file or diagonal plus an advanced Pawn close to a King on the edge of the board.

DIAGRAM 90

White Mates in Two Moves

ANALYSIS

White mates with the Queen if he can control the Black King's possible escape squares from an adjacent square. In this position his goal is KN7. How can he force Black to a square where mate at KN7 follows?

1. ________ ________
2. ________ **mate**

DIAGRAM 91

White Mates in Two Moves

ANALYSIS

White's Rook cuts off the Black King's escape to the K-file. Once again mate can be forced at KN7, after the invasion of the King position by a checking Queen.

1. ________ ________
2. ________ **mate**

Another important battery is the combination of a Rook and a Queen on an open file when the enemy King is on the first rank and lacks escape squares. Mate can then be possible, the Queen acting like a Rook—moving on file and rank.

DIAGRAM 92
White Mates in Two Moves

ANALYSIS

Mate would occur in the same way if the White Queen were a Rook. Once you see that the Black King lacks escape squares, you realize all you need is a checking piece immune from capture on your eighth rank. How do you achieve that goal?

1. ________ ________
2. ________ **mate**

It is important to realize that a Queen can quickly shift its attack from one side of the board to another. Diagram 93 illustrates the use of a battery as sacrifices open lines leading to a mate by a supported Queen.

DIAGRAM 93
White Mates in Six Moves

ANALYSIS

Here we have a battery (2 Rooks and a Bishop) bearing down on the target square QB8. The square is attacked three times and defended three times. White will win if he can get a fourth piece into the battery—his Queen. A sacrifice opens the road to the long diagonal—KR2 to QN8.

1. **R × Nch!** **N × R**
2. **Q—R2ch**

Black's Queen must remain on the first rank to prevent mate on the target square. Thus, if 2. . . . . Q—K4; 3. R × N mate.

2. **. . . .** **R—K4**

Now White cannot play 3. Q × Rch (with the idea of 4. R × N mate) because Black's reply 3. . . . . Q × Q would be check!

3. **R × Nch** **Q × R**
4. **Q × Rch** **Q—B2**

Now White mates by checking on the rank and capturing on the target square.

5. **Q—K8ch** **Q—B1**
6. **Q × Q mate**

One of the most common mating batteries is a Queen and a Bishop on the same diagonal aimed at a target square. If that target square is defended, your goal becomes the removal of the defender. Diagram 94 illustrates the removal of a defender to force a mate.

DIAGRAM 94
White Mates in Two Moves

ANALYSIS

Imagine that the Knights were not on the board. White would then mate at once by Q × P, his Queen supported by his Bishop. Your goal, then, is to remove the Knights—a simple task in this position.

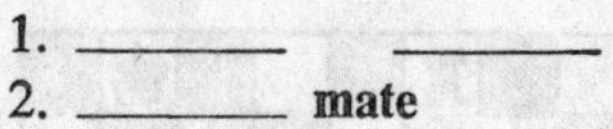

1. ________ ________
2. ________ **mate**

The combination of Queen, King, and Pawn, as in the final position of Diagram 95, can cut off all of a King's escape squares. Memorize the final position's array of pieces on the QB file, for such a mate is often possible in endings where you have just Queened a Pawn.

DIAGRAM 95
White Mates in Two Moves

ANALYSIS

Your goal is to attain a position in which the opponent's King has no escape squares. There is no time to waste here, for Black is threatening to take White's Bishop. But that Bishop makes the first move, and mate follows.

1. **B × Bch!** **K × B**

Black has no other move.

2. **Q—B8 mate**

Some positions are curiosities—important not because they can occur frequently but because they explain some unusual method of using pieces. Diagram 96 shows such a position. Black's King is trapped in a corner square, but defended by its Queen and Rook. But White can mate with a Queen because his pieces co-ordinate their attack.

DIAGRAM 96

White Mates in Four Moves

ANALYSIS

The mate takes place on the KR file. To achieve it, White's Queen must quickly move across the board.

1. **R—R7ch** **Q × R**
2. **Q × Rch** **Q—N1**

Now Black's Queen is pinned to the first rank. When White advances his Pawn to check the Black King, that King must move to the square on which it will be mated.

3. **P—N7ch** **K—R2**
4. **Q—R5 mate**

Play through this position again to appreciate White's method of bringing his Queen to KR5!

The possibility of mate by a Queen often permits sacrifices of material. In a match game between Richard Reti and Max Euwe, Reti permitted Euwe to invade his first rank and win two Rooks. Meanwhile, Reti had built a mating battery that he used to force Euwe's King to a square where mate by a Queen followed.

DIAGRAM 97

White Mates in Two Moves

ANALYSIS

On what square will the Black King have no escape? The White Queen cuts off the K-file. A check by the Bishop can force the King to QB1. If it then has no escape except on a diagonal, then a Queen check on that diagonal means mate!

1. ________ ________
2. ________ **mate**

Once a Queen has invaded a King position, mate may follow on a rank, file, or diagonal if the King has no escape squares. Diagram 98 illustrates a common method of cutting off such escape squares. Black has a deadly check with his Queen at R8, but it does not mate so long as White's King can escape to his K2.

DIAGRAM 98

GAMARRA — AJIAN

Mar del Plata, 1974

Black Mates in Two Moves

ANALYSIS

When a King is on its first rank and can escape to a single square on its second rank, then a check on the diagonal can force that escape route to be blocked. When an opponent has blocked the escape with one of his own pieces, mate can follow. How does Black use this idea to win in this position?

1. . . . . ________
2. ________ ________ **mate**

One of the weakest pawn formations is that of Black in Diagram 99. By playing . . . . P—N3 while he has a Pawn at K3, Black has opened his position to the invasion of enemy pieces. With a White Pawn at KB6, mate can follow if a Queen can be brought to KN7.

DIAGRAM 99

White Mates in Two Moves

ANALYSIS

Material is even, but not the positions. Black's deadly weakness is the hole at his KR3. Remember that a supported Queen on a square adjacent to a King can mate!

1. ________ **Any move**
2. ________ **mate**

Alexander Deschapelles— One of the Founders of Modern Chess

A man who was for a while the best chess player in the world gave up the game when he began to lose frequently to his own best pupil. The man was Alexander Louis Honoré Lebreton Deschapelles (1780–1847), a child of the French Revolution and a participant in the struggles for human equality that followed it. The son of a Marshal of France, young Alexander served in the French army, losing his right arm fighting against the Prussians. He then turned to games, becoming France's leading chess expert and Europe's most successful whist player. Deschapelles played for money, and made a good living from both games!

Playing chess at a time when few players understood the value of systematic development, Deschappelles profited from his gambler's instinct when his opponents tried to attack at all costs. At his best, with superior natural ability and an early understanding of the kinds of attack that could lead to checkmate, Deschapelles could give odds to the best of his opponents. John Cochrane, one of the best English masters, once received odds of KBP and two moves from the French expert. Thus, Black began without that Pawn and White made two moves before Black could begin. Cochrane, certain this advantage would help him win quickly, neglected his development and concentrated on pushing K-side Pawns. Deschapelles was to move in a position that cried out for mate by a Queen—which Deschapelles found!

DIAGRAM 100
COCHRANE — DESCHAPELLES
St. Cloud, France

Deschapelles has regained his Pawn and developed his pieces, meanwhile forcing the White King to its KR2. He now permits

Cochrane to win a Pawn and mates quickly.

1. .... **Q—K2**
2. **R × P**

Otherwise, Cochrane must have reasoned, the Black QNP would advance and threaten to become a Queen.

2. .... **Q—R5!**

An opponent who snatches at a Pawn will probably snatch a piece as well!

3. **R × B** **Q—B7ch!**

Deschappelles had seen a mate based on forcing White to block his escape square at KN2. The final position became a model for every chess player since Deschappelles! See Diagram 86—a position reached 150 years after this game was played!

4. **B—N2** **R × Pch!**
5. **K × R** **Q—R5 mate**

Mate by a supported Queen when the enemy King lacks escape squares!

The six positions that follow permit you to apply your understanding of the chief ways to force mate with a Queen. As you study them, remember that the Queen usually needs the aid of other pieces—to support it when it mates on an adjacent square or to cut off escape squares when it mates on a rank, file, or diagonal. Of course, when a battery bears down on a target square and the opponent lacks the material to maintain that square's defense, direct and forceful attacking moves or exchanges often bring an easy mate.

DIAGRAM 101

ARTHUR DAKE — M. DI PAULA
Baltimore, 1935

Black Mates in Two Moves

ANALYSIS

Who says an international master doesn't make mistakes? In this game from a simultaneous exhibition, Dake snatched at Black's KNP, permitting a mate in two that he could have avoided by Q—Q1. The key to the mate is the cutting off of escape squares by Black's Knight after the first move.

1. .... ______
2. ______ ______ mate

DIAGRAM 102

W. LOVEGROVE — A. J. FINK
San Francisco, 1916

Black Mates in Five Moves

ANALYSIS

This position illustrates a mate by a Queen supported by a Rook on the seventh rank. Once Black has played his first move, he threatens havoc because of a discovered check by his Bishop. Black sees that any hope of defense depends on removing that Bishop. But in taking it, he will open the long diagonal for a deadly Queen check that is followed by a mate.

1. .... **R × B!**
2. **R × P** **R × N dis ch**
3. **R × B** ______
4. ______ ______
5. ______ ______ **mate**

DIAGRAM 103

D. BRONSTEIN — V. GOLDENOV
Kiev, 1944

White Mates in Three Moves

ANALYSIS

David Bronstein, a chess prodigy in the 1940s and still one of the world's most imaginative chessmasters in the late 1970s, demonstrated the use of two batteries in this game. His Rooks aim at QB8, while his Queen and Bishop threaten mate by a supported Queen at K7 or Q8. Black's defense depends on his supported Queen holding the Q1 square. But if that Queen were no longer supported, or moved away from Q1, then White would mate. What moves force one of these two disasters? Give the lines of play after Black's possible replies to White's first move.

1. ______ ______
2. ______ ______
3. ______ **mate**

DIAGRAM 104
I. GUNSBERG — A. SCHALLOP
London, 1866
Black Mates in Three Moves

DIAGRAM 105
White Mates in Six Moves

ANALYSIS

Black has outplayed his opponent and now has an easy win—a mate by a Queen in three moves, made possible by White's lack of escape squares and the advanced Pawn on Black's KN7. He sees that his Queen can mate as a Rook would in a similar position if it were on the KR file. A sacrifice forces the desired position.

1. .... ______
2. ______ ______
3. ______ ______ mate

ANALYSIS

Don't be frightened by the need to see six moves ahead. This is an example of a battery working around a corner. The target square is QR7, for a Queen on that square would mean checkmate. But the Queen cannot get to that square unless the White Bishop and both Rooks are out of the way. That being the goal, sacrifices are in order, and they begin with 1. B—Q6ch, to continue with the gift of both Rooks. Remember that every move must be a check—for Black will otherwise attack the White King and mate it instead!

1. **B—Q6ch** ______
2. ______ ______
3. ______ ______
4. ______ ______
5. ______ ______
6. ______ **mate**

DIAGRAM 106
White Mates in Three Moves

1. ________ ________
2. ________ ________
3. ________ **mate**

ANALYSIS

This is another use of a battery to force mate, with QN7 the target square at the end. The attack is similar to that of Diagram 102, whose solution you should review before trying to find this mate in three. Just remember that a Queen combines the moves of a Rook and a Bishop!

REMEMBER!

To mate with a Queen, you must be able to recognize or create a position in which:

— an enemy King without escape squares is trapped on a rank, file, or diagonal your Queen can reach; or

— a supporting Pawn or piece covers a square to which your Queen can move to mate on a square adjacent to a King without escape squares; or

— a battery bearing on a target point near the enemy king permits sacrifices to remove defenders or to force the King into one of the two kinds of position described above.

CHAPTER 6

The Epaulettes Mate

Epaulettes are the decorated boards placed on the shoulders of a dress uniform. The term has been used to describe the kind of checkmate illustrated in the four diagrams that follow.

DIAGRAM 107

DIAGRAM 107—The White King's escape squares on the rank are occupied (and therefore blocked) by its Rooks. This is an epaulettes mate on the edge of the board.

DIAGRAM 108

DIAGRAM 108—Here two Pawns or a Rook and a Pawn form the epaulettes on the open board while escape to the next rank is cut off by a Rook (or Queen in some positions). In effect this epaulettes mate is the same as one on the edge of the board.

DIAGRAM 109

DIAGRAM 109—Two angular squares are occupied by anything but a Knight while the King is attacked by a supported Queen on an adjacent square.

DIAGRAM 110

DIAGRAM 110—A King lacks escape squares because of an epaulettes formation and is mated by attack by any piece. Thus this would be mate if the White Knight were replaced by a Pawn at QR4, a Knight at QR3, QB3, or Q6, a Rook at QB5 or Q5, or even a Queen at QR4, QB5, or Q5. There would also be a mate if a White Queen or Bishop could capture Black's Bishop.

The epaulettes mate is harder to visualize than the more direct mates we have examined in previous chapters. Most mates depend on the action and placement of your own pieces. The epaulettes mate depends as much on the poor placement of your opponent's pieces. The Russian player Usachev, playing Black in the position of Diagram 111, recognized a possible epaulettes mate. Suppose the White King could be forced to its K2 square. Then suppose further that its Q2 were cut off. Any check would then be mate. The play was simple and direct.

DIAGRAM 111

1. . . . . B—B6ch

If White now plays 2. N × B, Q—K6 is mate. And on 2. K—B1 Black wins a Rook by 2. . . . . B × R. So White seeks safety at K2.

2. K—K2 Q—K6ch!

The Queen is sacrificed to free the Q5 square for the mate that will follow.

3. N × Q N—Q5 mate

This is an epaulettes mate with pieces on the angular squares Q1, Q3, and KB1.

What must you see before you can plan for an epaulettes mate?

1. The enemy King's escape routes are blocked or can be forced to be blocked by an epaulettes formation.
2. The mating piece can be brought (and supported if necessary) to the square on which it delivers the mate.
3. A battery bearing on that target square can be used to remove defenders or pieces that would otherwise interpose. This means a readiness to sacrifice to achieve the epaulettes mate position.

DIAGRAM 112
White Mates in Two Moves

ANALYSIS

The squares near Black's King are open to invasion. White's Rook battery on the KB file permits him to force an epaulettes position with a sacrifice that also opens a diagonal for his Queen. Look at Diagram 107 if you do not see the solution at once.

1. ________ ________
2. ________ **mate**

DIAGRAM 113
White Mates in Two Moves

ANALYSIS

This time the epaulettes position involves two angular squares. The material is even, but White has a killing check that is followed by an epaulettes mate. Look at Diagram 109 if you do not see the solution at once.

1. ________ ________
2. ________ **mate**

Epaulettes mates usually occur in the middle game or ending, but can appear in opening attacks usually beginning with a Bishop sacrifice at KB7 followed by moves that force the enemy King to the open board. A line in Philidor's Defense that illustrates such a mate should be in every player's repertoire.

1. **P—K4**	**P—K4**
2. **N—KB3**	**P—Q3**
3. **B—B4**	**B—K2**
4. **P—Q4**	**P × P**
5. **N × P**	**N—Q2?**

This error permits quick execution. Black's best move is 5. . . . . N—KB3 so that he can castle quickly and bring his King to safety.

DIAGRAM 114

6. **B × Pch!**	**K × B**
7. **N—K6!**	

Strangely, Black now loses his Queen or is mated. The win of the Queen follows 7. . . . . Q—K1; 8. N × BP, Q—Q1; 9. Q—Q5ch, K—B1; 10. N—K6ch.

If Black tries to save the Queen he must permit an epaulettes mate.

7.	**K × N**
8. **Q—Q5ch**	**K—B3**
9. **Q—KB5 mate**	

Such mates can and do occur. Sometimes your opponent needs a shove to make one possible. For example:

DIAGRAM 115

WASJUKOV — SEITZEV
Berlin, 1969

White Mates in Two Moves

ANALYSIS

White would have an epaulettes mate if he could play Q × KP. But the Black KP has a defender. If that defender can be forced to advance to B3, the epaulettes mate would become possible. Fortunately, Black's King has no escape squares, and a check on the diagonal would force the BP to advance to interpose.

1. ________ ________
2. ________ **mate**

Paul Morphy understood the epaulettes mate and made good use of it. Diagram 116 shows a position he reached as White in a game against an amateur in 1857. His attack is similar to the one shown in Diagram 112—and further illustrates the value of a Rook battery on an open file.

ANALYSIS

Black has just played . . . . P × P(N3). Morphy recognizes an epaulettes position with a King on the edge of the board flanked by two Rooks. His problem is to force that position. His solution is to give up his Rooks!

1. ________ ________
2. ________ ________
3. ________ **mate**

Given the epaulettes position, mate can result from a Pawn move as easily as from a Queen's attack. The Dutch master Prins has had an uneven career, but in his game against Canada's best player, at the Carlsbad tournament in 1948, Prins provided the chess world with one of its most memorable mating attacks.

DIAGRAM 116
White Mates in Three Moves

DIAGRAM 117
White Mates in Three Moves

ANALYSIS

Prins has given up a piece to force the Black King to an exposed position on the open board. Now his thoughts must have followed this sequence:

— An epaulette position might be possible if the Black Pawn at his Q4 were at his QB5.

— Once that happens, the White Rook at Q2 cuts off escape to the Q–file. The Black King would then in effect be on the edge of the board.

— If the Black King could then be forced to his QN4 while the White Queen holds the long diagonal from his QR7, mate can follow.

1. **R—B4ch!** **P × R**

Black could have played 1. . . . . K—Q3; 2. Q × Bch, K—K2; 3. Q × QP, when White's extra Pawns ensure the win. Instead he takes the Rook.

2. **Q × RPch** **K—N4**
3. **P—R4 mate**

This position merits study. The epaulettes position had to be created and, once forced, could be utilized because Black's Rooks and Queen were on the other side of the board. Result—a Pawn mates because the epaulettes position of Black's Pawn and Bishop makes escape impossible.

Ossip S. Bernstein— Mr. Surprise of the Chess World!

How well can you play if chess is not your main interest, if you do not play for years at a time, and when you do play it is for fun and not for glory? If you have the natural talents possessed by one of the best occasional players in chess history, then you can do very well indeed! Ossip Samoilovitch Bernstein (1882–1962), doctor of law, Russian expatriate, and long one of the best players in France, won few tournaments. He let years pass without entering competition, but never lost his skill. In fact, one of his best results was his first place in Montevideo, 1961, when he was seventy-nine! His great understanding of tactics made him Mr. Surprise every time he did enter a tournament. For fifty years grandmasters had to tell one another the latest tale of how Dr. Bernstein had shocked them with some amazing attack—often ending in checkmate.

Bernstein's special style was disconcerting. He tried to gain small advantages in the opening —a lead in development or doubled Pawns near the enemy King. He then used such advantages to keep his opponent on the defensive while he prepared a final attack that often included a sacrifice that could not be refused. He offered gifts in the opening that disconcerted his opponents, often leading them to make second-best moves once they had seen the trap behind the offer of a Pawn or piece. For example, in a game against Adolph Albin in Vienna, 1904, Bernstein had offered his QR in a position that would have led to this mating attack—a semi-epaulettes finish.

DIAGRAM 118

Position that might have occurred in Albin—Bernstein, Vienna, 1904, if Albin had played to win the Black QR offered by Bernstein

ANALYSIS

It is Black's move in this position (threatened but one that did not occur). He would now win by some such line as:

1.	....	**Q × NP**
2.	**R—KB1**	**B—KN5**
3.	**N—R4**	**B × Pch**
4.	**R × B**	**Q—N8ch**
5.	**R—B1**	

Now White's King is in a semi-epaulettes position in which Black can mate in two moves.

5.	....	**Q—K6ch**
6.	**Q—K2**	**Q × Q mate**

Albin saw this attack would defeat him if he took the Black QR, and played a series of exchanges and Pawn moves that weakened his position instead. The position of Diagram 119 was finally reached, with Black to move. He delivered an epaulettes mate five moves later! Surprise!

DIAGRAM 119

1.	....	**R—K3!**

White cannot capture this Rook without losing his Queen.

2.	**Q—Q7**	**R—Q3**
3.	**Q—R4**	

And now for the direct attack on White's King position.

3.	Q—K7

Black threatens Q × BP mate or B × BP mate. White must defend the KBP.

4. **R—KB1**	**Q × N!**
5. **P × Q**	**R—N3 mate**

Epaulettes! White could have dragged the game along by not taking the Black Queen—but would then have been a piece behind in a lost position.

DIAGRAM 120

Epaulettes mates often result from control of your seventh rank when your opponent's King is on his first rank. In such situations you must first be able to force the epaulettes position—by sacrifices if necessary. You then need only a check to mate.

DIAGRAM 121

DE LABOURDONNAIS — AMATEUR
Paris, 1833

White Mates in Four Moves

ANALYSIS

De Labourdonnais replaced Deschapelles as France's leading player in the 1830s. Like his former teacher, he played for stakes and had to keep his audiences happy with sacrificial mating attacks. This was one of his best crowd-pleasing efforts as he set up an epaulettes mate by two sacrifices.

1. **N—K6ch**	**K—K1**
2. **Q—Q8ch!**	**B × Q**
3. **R-B8ch!**	**R × R**

There it is. The epaulettes have been formed while White controls his seventh rank. Black's King has no escape—if White can check with another piece.

4. **N—N7 mate**

The six positions that follow illustrate epaulettes mates. They often demand a willingness to sacrifice material. But once you can visualize an epaulettes position, all that remains is to calculate whether or not you can deliver that final check as illustrated in the first four diagrams of this chapter.

DIAGRAM 122

A. NIMZOVICH — AMATEUR
Berlin, 1920

White Mates in Three Moves

ANALYSIS

Aron Nimzovich, considered an eccentric by his contemporary chess masters, was an innovator whose theoretical contributions have become basic to success in master play today. One of his contributions was to improve understanding of the use of open lines. In this game, with the Black King already in an epaulettes position, Nimzovich showed that open lines can also work around a corner. He would have an epaulettes mate if his Rook were at QB7. How does he get it there in three moves?

1. ________ ________
2. ________ ________
3. ________ **mate**

DIAGRAM 123

G. BERTOLA — K. MEIER
Switzerland, 1975

White Mates in Three Moves

ANALYSIS

It is obvious that the Black King is in an epaulettes position. White would mate at once by 1. Q—B6 if Black could not interpose his Bishop. But wouldn't there be a mate if the Bishop were removed? What is needed is an attack by another piece that can be sacrificed to prepare for the epaulettes mate.

1. ________ ________
2. ________ ________
3. ________ **mate**

DIAGRAM 124

KORCHNOI — PETERSON
Soviet Union, 1965

White Mates in Three Moves

ANALYSIS

Viktor Korchnoi, regularly listed among the ten best players in the world, owes much of his success to a deep knowledge of opening play that often permits sudden attacks against less well prepared opponents. This is evident from his games even though he denies being a student of the openings. In this game he had sacrificed a piece to open up Black's K-side. Now he sees a Queen sacrifice that leads to an epaulettes mate similar to that reached in Diagram 121.

1. ________ ________
2. ________ ________
3. ________ **mate**

DIAGRAM 125

TAL — TRINGOV
Interzonal Tournament, 1964

White Mates in Two Moves

ANALYSIS

Mikhail Tal, perhaps the most unpredictable and imaginative of all Russian grandmasters, was the youngest world's champion in modern chess history. He was in top form in 1964. In this game he sacrificed two pieces in the opening to force an uncastled King into an epaulettes position (Bishop and Knight blocking escape). Now he can close the trap by forcing Black's King to its QB2.

1. ________ ________
2. ________ **mate**

DIAGRAM 126

White Mates in Four Moves

ANALYSIS

Black's Rooks form a natural epaulettes position if the Black King can be forced to its KN2 and the White Queen can then attack it at White's KN5. But this calls for checking moves along the way, for Black would otherwise break free by any of a dozen possible freeing, exchanging, or attacking moves.

1. ________ ________
2. ________ ________
3. ________ ________
4. ________ **mate**

DIAGRAM 127

Black Mates in Three Moves

ANALYSIS

White's King is in the epaulettes position—a Rook at each side and no escape squares. All Black needs is a clearing of the QB file. Black counts—two pieces in a battery attack White's QB2 and two pieces defend the square. But one of these is the White King, which will then be in another epaulettes position. Is there a check—and therefore mate—possible on Black's third move?

1. .... ________
2. ________ ________
3. ________ ________ **mate**

REMEMBER!

1. Learn to recognize the epaulettes mate positions!
2. Be ready to sacrifice to complete an epaulettes mate posi-

tion if you then see how to deliver the final check—and mate.

3. Most epaulettes mates occur when your attack forces your opponent to occupy squares near his King. Therefore, if you can see an attacking move that leads to such defensive play by your opponent, look further for a possible epaulettes mate.

CHAPTER 7

Mate with a Rook and a Bishop

Keres—The Unpredictable Tactician

Picture yourself playing an opponent you know to be one of the most dangerous attacking players in the world, his mind ever searching for that distant mating attack. His face betrays no emotion; his moves are at times mysterious, their meaning evident only when you see how his planning has forced the game into some unclear but uncomfortable direction. You seek replies for potential onslaughts—but they come anyway, because your opponent has masked his real attack behind the ones you thought you saw. In the end you may find yourself mated by the grandmaster whose chess career included more mates than were achieved by most of his contemporaries. This was Paul Keres, whose brilliant record of tournament success spanned more than forty years from his appearance on the chess scene in the early 1930s to his death in 1975.

Keres won many games through his understanding of the value of open lines—ranks, files, and diagonals along which his pieces could apply pressure and execute final attacks. Living in a small town in Estonia when in his teens, he got his early chess competition from playing by mail—the special field called correspondence chess, in which a player has two or three days to reply to the move his opponent has sent. Keres developed a powerful attacking technique in his years of correspondence play, for an opponent with plenty of time must be faced with the hidden threat as well as the obvious one. In 1933 Keres won a game against an opponent named Wilkins by a surprising final attack ending with mate by a Rook and a Bishop.

DIAGRAM 128
KERES — WILKINS

White's control of open lines has left the Black King without escape squares. He sees a potential mate by R—Q8, if he can first remove the defense of Black's Q1 by a Knight and a Rook. Once he saw this possibility, he was able to ignore the fact that Black was attacking his Bishop on N5. The problem is to open the target square Q8, and a pair of sacrifices does that to produce a mate in three moves.

1. **N × Pch!**	**R × N**
2. **Q × Nch**	**P × Q**
3. **R—Q8 mate**	

The first two moves could have been played in reverse order. The final position illustrates one of the key mating positions possible with the combined use of a Rook and a Bishop.

The next five diagrams illustrate basic mates possible with a Rook and a Bishop. Note the two conditions that exist in all of them:

1. One of the two pieces cuts off escape squares while the other checks and mates.
2. The enemy King is blocked by its own pieces or yours at squares around the point where a rank or file and a diagonal meet.

DIAGRAM 129

ANALYSIS

The Bishop mates while the Rook cuts off escape squares. This is often called the Morphy Mate, from his use of it during his short chess career.

DIAGRAM 130

ANALYSIS

The Rook mates while the Bishop cuts off escape squares. This is often called the Pillsbury Mate from its use by Harry Nelson Pillsbury, the best American player of the 1890s.

DIAGRAM 131

ANALYSIS

This variation of the Pillsbury Mate is common because it is often possible for a Rook to check on the eighth rank. Note that the Bishop can be on several of the squares on the long diagonal, while the Rook can be on several squares on the eighth rank.

DIAGRAM 132

ANALYSIS

Mate with a Rook and a Bishop can also occur on the open board. This position has frequently appeared in chess problems (composed positions in which White must mate in a given number of moves). The Rook cuts off four possible escape squares and is protected from a distance by a Bishop which also checks and mates.

DIAGRAM 133

ANALYSIS

This position is similar to that of Diagram 132, both depending on a self-blocking by an epaulettes type of formation. Here the Rook mates while protecting the Bishop which in turn is cutting off two escape squares.

The possibility of mate by a Rook and a Bishop explains why players try so hard to open lines leading to the enemy King position. Mate can follow when the player recognizes and uses three conditions:

1. Either the Rook or the Bishop is able to check while the other controls possible escape squares.
2. The enemy King's possible escape squares are limited to the rank or file controlled by the Rook and the diagonal or diagonals controlled by the Bishop.
3. If an enemy piece defends the square on which you want to give the check that mates, search for a sacrifice that removes that defender—as Keres did in the position that began this chapter.

The positions examined in the rest of this chapter illustrate the variety of ways in which the basic mates with a Rook and a Bishop can be achieved. As you examine them, keep in mind that it is the point of intersection of a diagonal and a rank or file that is always critical.

DIAGRAM 134
White Mates in Two Moves

ANALYSIS

This is a common mating position. The White Rook controls the open KR file. If the White Bishop can cut off Black's escape to his KB1 and prevent a return to his KN2, then mate will result.

White first checks and then discovers a second check which is mate.

1. ________ ________
2. ________ **mate**

DIAGRAM 136

White Mates in Three Moves

DIAGRAM 135

White Mates in Three Moves

ANALYSIS

The key to mate with the Rook and Bishop is to force a position in which the two pieces work together along two intersecting open lines. Sometimes you must sacrifice to open those lines. This position would be mate if the Black KNP were absent. White's goal is therefore to remove that Pawn and force the Black King back to its KN1. Look at Diagram 130 before you try to find the winning moves.

1. ________ ________
2. ________ ________
3. ________ **mate**

ANALYSIS

As in Diagram 135, a battery is bearing down on the enemy King position. A sacrifice again forces a variation of the Pillsbury Mate (see Diagram 130). To find the obvious sequence of moves you must first visualize that typical mate with a Rook and a Bishop!

1. ________ ________
2. ________ ________
3. ________ **mate**

DIAGRAM 137

White Mates in Two Moves

ANALYSIS

Look at Diagram 129 before you seek the mate in this position. This time the Bishop mates while the Rook cuts off escape squares—as in a Morphy Mate. Your problem is to force the Black King to a square where such a mate is possible.

1. ________ ________
2. ________ **mate**

DIAGRAM 138

White Mates in Two Moves

ANALYSIS

This is the end of an offhand game by Morphy played against two French noblemen, both amateurs, during what must have been an uninspired performance at the Paris Opera. But Morphy, playing White, was inspired, producing one of those games chess writers describe as "immortal." Look back at Diagram 131 before you look for the simple sacrifice that opens a line for a mate by a Rook and a Bishop.

1. ________ ________
2. ________ **mate**

DIAGRAM 139

White Mates in Three Moves

ANALYSIS

Once learned, this example of mate by a Rook and a Bishop will not be forgotten. To find the win, you must first visualize a Bishop at White's QB7 where it controls White's QN6 and QN8. Then visualize an open QR file on which a Rook mates a King that lacks escape squares.

1. ________ ________
2. ________ ________
3. ________ mate

DIAGRAM 140

S. WINAWER — AMATEUR
Poland, 1890

White Mates in Four Moves

ANALYSIS

Sometimes a mate by a Rook and a Bishop can appear when your opponent has misplayed the opening. White had sacrificed a piece to open Black's King-side. He then saw he could force a variation of the Pillsbury Mate (see Diagrams 131 and 132). A Bishop check forces the Black King to the first rank to avoid an immediate mate. Then a Queen sacrifice permits mate by a Rook and a Bishop.

1. ________ ________
2. ________ ________
3. ________ ________
4. ________ mate

DIAGRAM 141

PILLSBURY — LEE
London, 1899

White Mated in Five Moves

ANALYSIS

The Pillsbury Mate can be possible whenever your Bishop controls escape squares and your Rook can check on an open rank or file. This is one of the best examples provided by Pillsbury in a career that saw many games in which he sacrificed to obtain open lines.

Examine the position. If the Black Queen were not on the KN file, White could play R—N1ch and achieve a Pillsbury Mate.

1. **Q—B3!** **Q × Q**

Black could have avoided the mate by giving up his Queen or retreating it to KN3. But White would then have won a Rook or more after 2. B × R with the additional threat of 3. Q × R.

2. **R—N1ch**	**K—R1**
3. **B—N7ch**	**K—N1**
4. **B × P dis ch**	**Q—N5, N6 or N7**
5. **R × Q mate**	

DIAGRAM 142
White Mates in Four Moves

ANALYSIS

Both sides threaten mate with Rook and Bishop. Were it Black's move, he would play 1. . . . . B—B7 dis ch and, after White interposed his Knight at R7 or R5, mate would follow with 2. . . . . R × N. But it is White's move, and he has a brilliant win in which Black is mated either at the edge of the board or on the open board. White begins with the only move that can open the QR file. Can you find the win, including the mates after Black's three possible third moves?

1. ________ ________
2. ________ ________
3. ________ ________
4. ________ **mate**

DIAGRAM 143
White Mates in Two Moves

ANALYSIS

Mate with a Rook and a Bishop on the open board requires a relatively blocked position. In this one all White has to do is force the Black King to a square where it is mated by a Bishop while a Rook prevents its escape.

1. ________ ________
2. ________ **mate**

The four positions that follow summarize basic mating ideas using a Rook and a Bishop. Consider that each position has a focal point—the squares around the intersection of a rank or file and a diagonal. If you decide mate is possible on a target square, check first to make certain that you can remove any defender of that square—by a sacrifice if necessary.

DIAGRAM 144

White Mates in Three Moves

ANALYSIS

This position quickly turns into a Pillsbury Mate—the Rook mating while the Bishop controls an escape square. The final position is common, depending on the movement of the White Bishop from a short diagonal to a long diagonal.

1. ________ ________
2. ________ ________
3. ________ mate

DIAGRAM 145

White Mates in Two Moves

ANALYSIS

Look at the position. Suppose Black's KNP were absent. What mate in one would follow? Once you see this, all you must do is find a move that forces that NP to move. It must be a forceful move, for Black is threatening mate by 1. . . . . Q—N8!

1. ________ ________
2. ________ mate

DIAGRAM 146

White Mates in Five Moves

ANALYSIS

This is another typical winning attack with Rook and Bishop. It depends on a seesaw maneuver in which the Rook clears away a Pawn that might otherwise advance to block the long diagonal. Once that has been done, a Morphy Mate follows, the Bishop mating while the Rook controls escape squares. Positions like this one led to the chess adage—*Beware of the open file you create when you snatch a Knight Pawn!*

1. ________ ________
2. ________ ________
3. ________ ________
4. ________ ________
5. ________ **mate**

DIAGRAM 147

Black Mates in Three Moves

ANALYSIS

This too is a typical position, similar in its final mate to that of Diagram 139. Black has a battery on his open Rook file that can be used to clear the file for a mating move. Just imagine the position with the White KRP gone!

1. .... ________
2. ________ ________
3. ________ ________ **mate**

REMEMBER!

1. A Rook and a Bishop can mate when both bear down on the enemy King position along open lines and one can check while the other blocks the King's escape.
2. Such a mate follows one of the patterns presented in this chapter. Once you are familiar with these patterns, you will be able to recognize the opportunities to use them.
3. A pattern may exist but be blocked by a defender. You should then consider a sacrifice that removes that defender.

CHAPTER 8

Mate with a Rook and a Knight

Mate with a Rook and a Knight is often called the Arab Mate, for Middle Eastern chess writings of the Middle Ages paid special attention to the moves of the Knight and its ability to mate alone or with the aid of another piece. The Rook and the Knight were the only pieces whose moves remained unchanged when the rules of chess were modernized in the fifteenth century. For that reason, Arab writings on the game remain valid today—at least as they concern the Arab Mate.

The first four diagrams, with only the pieces needed for the mates remaining on the boards, illustrate the four basic positions in which a Rook and a Knight can mate.

DIAGRAM 148

ANALYSIS

This is the basic position of the Arab Mate. The Rook mates while supported by the Knight. At the same time, the Knight holds the possible escape square at Black's KN1.

DIAGRAM 149

ANALYSIS

This time the King is away from a corner square. Again the Rook mates because the Knight is covering the possible escape squares on the R-file. The Black King (or any other piece) provides support to the Rook.

DIAGRAM 150

ANALYSIS

This is similar to the epaulettes mate, for Black's King is hemmed in by its own pieces. The White Rook prevents escape to the N-file, while the Knight mates. Note that the Knight could also mate from QB5.

DIAGRAM 151

ANALYSIS

This time the mate occurs on the open board. Such a mate by a Rook and a Knight can take place only when the eight squares normally available to a King are controlled. The Rook covers four of them; the Pawn covers KB4 and Q4; the Knight supports the Rook and covers KB5; the King (or a Bishop on the same square) controls Q5 and Q4.

There it is. The Arabs worked it out, and their findings remain true today. They demonstrated the three conditions that can lead to a mate by a Rook and a Knight.

1. Either the Rook or the Knight can check (and mate), usually while it is supported by the other piece. The enemy King must lack escape squares. See Diagrams 148 and 151.
2. The key to most mates with a Rook and a Knight is the control of one or two squares adjacent to the King by the Knight. One such square can be the one on which the Rook is mating. See Diagrams 148 and 151 again.
3. In most cases, mate requires the assistance of one or more Pawns or pieces (and sometimes the King) to control possible escape squares near the enemy King, or to support the mating piece. See Diagrams 149 and 151. Alternately, a King's own pieces may block its escape. See Diagram 150.

To learn how to mate with a Rook and a Knight, you must first recognize the basic positions in which it is possible. That means you must be able to visualize how a move or two can force one of the mates shown in Diagrams 148–151. The following diagrams will help you understand how Arab Mates can be forced.

DIAGRAM 152

White Mates in Two Moves

ANALYSIS

The material is even, but the White Knight at QB6 plus an open file for the White Rook invites the Arab Mate shown in Diagram 148. Once the Rook reaches a square where it cuts off Black's second rank, the mate must follow.

1. ________ ________
2. ________ mate

DIAGRAM 153

White Mates in Three Moves

This position was reached in a game between Golmayo (White) and Mattison in a tournament played at the Hague in 1928. Attack and counterattack had left the pieces scattered around the board, each player having a Rook on his eighth rank. But White's Knight at K4 makes his position superior, for he can use it to force an Arab Mate. A Rook check drives the Black King to its first rank and the Knight then enters at B6 to force the King to R1. Then we have the mating position of Diagram 148.

1. **R—B7ch** **K—N1**

If 1. . . . . K—K1; 2. N—B6 mate (for the Bishop at his QN4 gives White control of his KB8).

2. **N—B6ch** **K—R1**
3. **R × P mate**

DIAGRAM 154

KOLTANOWSKI — HALSEY

Blindfold Exhibition, Omaha, 1958

White Mates in Two Moves

ANALYSIS

Sometimes a sacrifice is necessary to force the Arab Mate. In this game White had to visualize the position if the Black Rook at N2 were at R2 (instead of the Black Pawn now on that square). Then mate would be possible because the White Rook would be supported at its N8 by the Knight. A Queen sacrifice does the trick!

1. ________ ________
2. ________ **mate**

DIAGRAM 155

ROSSOLIMO — REISSMAN

Puerto Rico, 1967

Some positions require extended analysis, especially when they call for understanding of exceptional grandmaster play. The best players seem to sense the existence af basic checkmates, for they see the entire board and all possible co-ordination of the pieces. In this game Rossolimo had sacrificed a Pawn to bring his Knights forward, and has just played N—B6ch, to which Black has answered . . . . K—R1. Suddenly the Black King is ripe for an Arab Mate, if only White can find a way to check with a Rook on the Rook file. The only way for such a check to occur is by opening the KR file. Observe Rossolimo's method—an amazing feat that becomes simple and almost obvious once you remember that no piece is sacred so long as sacrificing it leads to checkmate!

1. Q—N6!

The Queen is placed on a square where two Pawns can capture it, and where it also threatens 2. Q × RP mate. Consider what happens if Black takes the Knight:

1. . . . . P × N; 2. Q × P(B6)ch, K—N1; 3. R—N3ch, N—N4; 4. R × N mate (Or 2. . . . . N—N2; 3. R—KN3, R—KN1; 4. N × Pch wins Black's Queen)

And suppose he takes the Queen:

1. . . . . RP × Q; 2. R—R3 mate
or
1. . . . . BP × Q; N × Pch, P × N; 3. R—R3 mate

Black therefore tries another move to prevent White from playing Q × P mate.

1.	**Q—B7**
2. R—R3	

Now White threatens 3. R × P mate. If 2. . . . . P—R3; 3. R × Pch, P × R; 4. Q × Pch, Q—R2; 5. Q × Q mate and the result is similar to the Arab Mate.

2.	**Q × Q**
3. N × Qch	**BP × N**
4. R × P mate	

The Arab Mate after all!

DIAGRAM 156

Black Mates in Three Moves

ANALYSIS

White threatens immediate mate by R—B8. But it is Black's move, and he sees that an Arab Mate is possible:

—Play the Knight to KB6
—clear the seventh rank
—mate on KR7

It isn't complicated at all if you see how to force the White King to its R1 and then force the NP to move!

1. . . . . _______
2. _______ _______
3. _______ _______ **mate**

Anastasia's Mate

This form of the mate with Rook and Knight obtained its name from a novel by Wilhelm Heinse, *Anastasia und das Schachspiel (Anastasia and the Game of Chess)*, published in 1803. Chess was a popular theme in early modern literature, and Heinse's book included reference to this position in which a Rook and a Knight mate.

DIAGRAM 157
Anastasia's Mate

Note that the Rook mates while the Knight controls the two squares to which the Black King might otherwise move. At the same time, a Black Pawn occupies the square next to the King on which it could normally escape the check. This mating position was not new, but writers on chess picked up the name as they described final attacks that threatened or included some variation of this mate. Diagram 158 shows the standard attack, one played again and again by experienced players as the Anastasia Mate became part of the master's repertoire.

DIAGRAM 158
White Mates in Three Moves

ANALYSIS

The goal is to force the position of Diagram 157. Three conditions must be met:

1. The Knight should be at K7 to control N6 and N8.
2. The Black King should be at

its R1 or R2 with the R-file open.
3. A Rook must be able to check and mate on that open file.

Therefore:

1. **N—K7ch** **K—R1**
2. **Q × Pch** **K × Q**
3. **R—R3 mate**

The Most Feared Chess Master of His Time

Every player likes one type of position better than others. He plays best when he can get that comfortable feeling that comes from being on familiar ground. But each player also has his weaknesses. He may make mistakes when defending; he may not know the ending as well as the opening or the middle game; he may dislike open or closed positions. Dr. Emanuel Lasker of Germany became the most successful chess master of his time (he was world champion from 1894 to 1921) by playing to force his opponents into the types of positions they had found most difficult in their past games. This meant constant study of the games of other leading players and the careful change of strategy from game to game to bewilder his opponents. No player was so successful in this psychological approach to the game until Robert J. Fischer shocked the chess world and became word champion by complicating his games in ways his opponents found too much to handle. No wonder men like Lasker and Fischer were feared; each game became a test of one's ability to survive the unfamiliar or to defend against the unexpected!

Lasker was a confident man, as interested in philosophy as in chess. He felt his chief accomplishment was his writing and lecturing—much of it on matters other than chess. But at a lecture in 1937 at Columbia University his audience insisted on asking the aging master questions about chess. What odds might the deity give a player of his ability once he had arrived at the section of heaven certainly reserved for chess masters? His reply was greeted by a burst of applause: "No more than a Bishop."

Lasker understood every kind of checkmate, and often used threats of mate as part of his psychological arsenal. After all, it takes time and energy to find the best defense to a mate threat, and this worried his opponents. In 1895 Lasker introduced a line in the Ruy Lopez Opening that can lead to the Anastasia Mate. For years afterwards other masters worried that some quick win might result from an unusual move by the then world champion.

RUY LOPEZ

1.	**P—K4**	**P—K4**
2.	**N—KB3**	**N—QB3**
3.	**B—N5**	**N—B3**
4.	**O—O**	**N × P**
5.	**R—K1**	**N—Q3**
6.	**N—B3**	**N × B**
7.	**N × P**	**N × N(K4)**

DIAGRAM 159

Players who prefer the Black side of the Ruy Lopez usually expect to have time to develop their pieces and to organize a defense against any White plan of attack. But in Lasker's new variation Black has been wandering about with his Knights and is now subjected to a crushing onslaught that wins a piece or mates.

8. **R × Nch** **B—K2**
9. **N—Q5** **O—O**

There is no way Black can prevent White from capturing the Bishop at Black's K2.

10. **N × Bch** **K—R1**
11. **Q—R5**

Suddenly White has the basic attack position that can lead to the Anastasia Mate (see Diagram 158). In addition, he threatens to win a piece by 12. N × B, for the Knight can then escape if Black moves his attacked Knight to safety.

11. .... **N—Q5**

DIAGRAM 160

White Mates in Two Moves

ANALYSIS

If you do not see the final two moves of Lasker's analysis, look back to Diagram 157 and 158. The mating idea should be part of your chess arsenal from now on!

12. ________ ________
13. ________ **mate**

The Anastasia Mate on the thirteenth move of a game! No

wonder playing Lasker left chess masters so shaken!

What are the characteristics of a position in which you can mate with a Rook and a Knight?

1. In the Arab Mate the Knight usually supports the Rook and can also control another square adjacent to the enemy King.
2. In the Anastasia Mate, the Knight prevents escape on two diagonal squares while the Rook mates on the rank or file. At the same time, the enemy King is blocked by one of its own Pawns.
3. Always consider sacrifices that force the enemy King to the square where mate with a Rook and Knight can occur, or to open a rank or file for the final Rook check and mate.

The seven diagrams that follow will enable you to apply these ideas in a variety of positions in which mate with a Rook and a Knight can be forced.

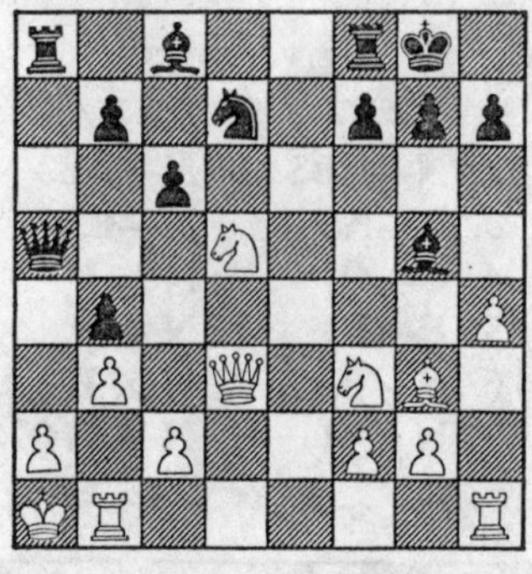

DIAGRAM 161

White Mates in Three Moves

ANALYSIS

This position demands a sacrifice. Note that Black threatens mate by 1. . . . . Q × P. How can White avoid the mate? He doesn't have to seek a defense, for he can play the standard attacking moves of the Anastasia Mate! The order of the moves may be a little different, but the final position isn't.

1. ________ ________
2. ________ ________
3. ________ **mate**

DIAGRAM 162

VIDMAR — EUWE
Carlsbad, 1929

White Mates in Two Moves

ANALYSIS

Always examine your own immediate threats as well as those of your opponent. White is clearly in danger of being mated by a move like Black's 1. . . . . Q—R7 mate. But he also sees that he could mate if he could force the Black King to move to its KB1. The Knight would then control the Black escape squares at K7 and KN7. The problem: what move can force the Black King to move to a square where it will be mated?

1. ________ ________
2. ________ mate

DIAGRAM 163

Black Mates in Two Moves

ANALYSIS

Black must find a decisive continuation, for White will otherwise win quickly by advancing and Queening the Pawn at his Q7. Fortunately, Black can mate in two with a Rook and a Knight—an opportunity made possible by the position of the White Rook on KN4, where it blocks possible flight by the White King. A sacrifice does the trick—and Diagram 151 will remind you of the goal if you do not see the final position at once.

1. .... ________
2. ________ ________ mate

DIAGRAM 164

Black Mates in Two Moves

ANALYSIS

Although White's King is on the open board, it cannot move freely. This means it will be mated if Black can find a check to which there is no defense. The Rook battery points the way.

1. .... ________
2. ________ ________ mate

DIAGRAM 165

White Mates in Two Moves

ANALYSIS

This is similar to Diagram 164, for again a well-timed check leads to mate by a Rook and a Knight. Suppose the Black Pawn at Black's Q3 were at its B4 instead. How could White then mate in one move? All you have to do is find the move that forces that Pawn to move!

1. ________ ________
2. ________ mate

DIAGRAM 166

Black Mates in Three Moves

ANALYSIS

The Black Knight at his N5 controls White's possible escape squares at his KR2 or KB2. A combination suggests itself if the White Rook can be forced to leave the KB file and thus be unable to interpose at KB1. What move does this? And what sacrifice then follows?

1. .... ______
2. ______ ______
3. ______ ______ mate

DIAGRAM 167

White Mates in Three Moves

ANALYSIS

The Black King is penned in by its own pieces. Its only move if attacked on the Q-file is to return to K1. How can White force it to do that? Since Black threatens to create an escape square by a Bishop move, White must begin with a check! If only the Rook at N3 could move to Q3 with check!

1. ______ ______
2. ______ ______
3. ______ mate

REMEMBER!

1. Recognize the basic mating positions of the Arab Mate and the Anastasia Mate—the two most common ways to mate with a Rook and a Knight.
2. Most mates with a Rook and a Knight require a sacrifice to open a line or to clear a square for a check and mate. Be ready to make such a sacrifice if you see you can then force one of the four positions at the beginning of this chapter.

CHAPTER 9

Mate with a Knight and a Bishop

The Chess Olympiads, held every two years, are the most popular of all chess competitions. Each country sends its team, usually containing the nation's best players. The teams are divided into four or five groups for a preliminary series of matches, with the highest ranking teams in each group advancing to a championship final round robin. Alternately, a Swiss System is used, in which teams play opponents who have achieved the same or similar scores in their previous play. In any event, the Olympiads are the great opportunity for relatively unknown players to play the world's leading grandmasters. Sometimes an unknown is a world star in the making whose victories add a new name to the roster of the world's best. But more often the grandmasters and well-known international masters win steadily, for they know more about the techniques and ideas that lead to victory. In the 1970 event, held at Skopje, Yugoslavia, the Polish master Bednarski had White against an unknown named Novissere. Bednarski advanced pieces while Novissere pushed his center Pawns. Finally a position was reached in which Bednarski could use his understanding of how to mate with a Knight and a Bishop to force a quick win.

DIAGRAM 168

Black has just captured White's Knight at B3. The normal reply to any capture is to recapture. But Bednarski played a surprise move instead.

1. Q—R6!

This Queen sacrifice is made possible by the immediate mate that would follow on 1. . . . . B × Q; 2. N—K7 mate. The White Bishop then controls Black's N2 and R1, and the Black King has no escape squares. This is one of the basic mating positions with Bishop and Knight.

1.	**B × B**
2. P × B	

The mate with Knight and Bishop is gone, but White now threatens 3. Q—N7 mate.

2.	**Q × BP**
3. N × Qch	**K—R1**
4. Q × RP mate	

Mate with a Bishop and Knight when the enemy King is at R1 or N1 with its escape squares blocked by its own Pawns or pieces or controlled by your pieces is often called the Bird Mate, after an English master of the mid-1800s who used it effectively. The following three diagrams illustrate the three common forms of the mate.

DIAGRAM 169

ANALYSIS

Black's King is at N1 with its R1 square occupied by its own Rook. The White Bishop at R6 cuts off escape to Black's B1 or N2. Thus, the check by the White Knight is mate. Note that the Knight could also mate from Q7—a position similar to that threatened by Bednarski in the game just examined.

DIAGRAM 170

ANALYSIS

Mate is also possible with King, Knight, and Bishop against

a lone King. The Bishop mates while the King and Knight cut off escape squares. Set up this position and then move your pieces to the other formations that result in similar mates:

BLACK KING ALWAYS AT R1.

a. White K at R6; B at N7; N at B6 or Q7

b. White K at R6; B at QB7; N at QN6

c. White K at QB8; N at QN5; B mating anywhere on the long diagonal

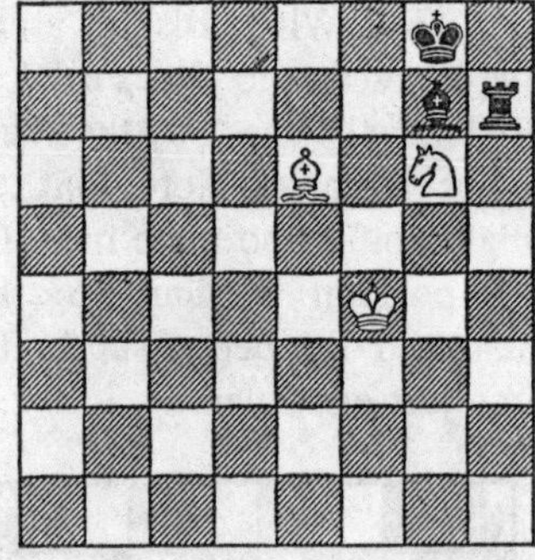

DIAGRAM 171

ANALYSIS

Mate with a Knight and a Bishop is also possible when the enemy King is on its first rank and its escape is blocked by its own Pawns or pieces. White's last two moves in this position were a Knight check when Black's King was at its KR1 and then a Bishop check (= mate) at K6. Note that the Knight prevents escape to Black's B1 or R1.

What are the characteristics of positions in which a Knight and a Bishop mate?

1. The enemy King is usually on the edge of the board; more usually in a corner of the board.
2. Its escape squares are blocked by its own pieces or Pawns.
3. The most common position includes your own Bishop controlling a diagonal left open by the advance or removal of the enemy Pawn at N2. This creates a hole at the opponent's R3 or B3. See Diagram 169.
4. Either your Knight or your Bishop then cuts off possible escape squares while the other piece checks and mates.

DIAGRAM 172

White Mates in Two Moves

ANALYSIS

Your goal is to know and recognize the positions that permit mate with a Knight and a Bishop.

This is one of them (see Diagram 169). The Black King lacks escape squares, and will be mated if a Knight can check it. You have two possible checks, but the Black Queen will capture any Knight that moves to White's Q7. Count. What do you do?

1. ________ ________
2. ________ mate

DIAGRAM 173

Black Mates in Two Moves

ANALYSIS

The White King cannot move. White needs two moves to create an escape square at his KB1. But Black can check and mate with a Knight before that escape square can be opened. How does he do this?

1. .... ________
2. ________ ________ mate

DIAGRAM 174

Black Mates in Three Moves

ANALYSIS

This position illustrates a sacrifice that opens lines for mate by a Knight and a Bishop. Black gives up his Queen to force White's King to N2. Then a Bishop check cuts off escape to permit mate by a Knight. In one form or another, this attack has occurred in dozens of tournament games.

1. .... ________
2. ________ ________
3. ________ ________ mate

DIAGRAM 175

Black Mates in Five Moves

ANALYSIS

Don't be surprised by the five-move requirement of this position. It is really the same attack you saw in Diagram 174. But this time you must first remove the two Black Rooks from the long diagonal. Fortunately, this can be done without giving White an escape square!

1. .... _______
2. _______ _______
3. _______ _______
4. _______ _______
5. _______ _______ **mate**

DIAGRAM 176

White Mates in Four Moves

ANALYSIS

Here is a position in which Black gave up two of his pieces to force a set of passed Pawns that cannot be prevented from making a new Queen. But in the process the Black King is trapped and will be mated if White can achieve the kind of position discussed under Diagram 170. How does the White King support the piece that finally mates?

1. _______ _______
2. _______ _______
3. _______ _______
4. _______ **mate**

DIAGRAM 177

White Mates in Four Moves

ANALYSIS

It matters little that your opponent can Queen a Pawn—so long as you can still force mate. Here again the enemy King is trapped. It will be mated if it can be checked by the White Bishop. Can you see the circuitous route that culminates in mate?

1. ________ ________
2. ________ ________
3. ________ ________
4. ________ **mate**

DIAGRAM 178

White Mates in Three Moves

ANALYSIS

Look at Diagram 171 before you seek the winning moves in this position. Suppose White's Knight could check without being captured. That would force the Black King to its N1, where a Bishop check would be mate. A sacrifice opens the N6 square for the Knight!

1. ________ ________
2. ________ ________
3. ________ **mate**

There it is. You can mate with a Knight and a Bishop when one of the pieces cuts off escape squares while the other attacks the King. Sometimes the Knight and Bishop can do this alone, especially when the enemy King is blocked by its own pieces. At other times the Knight and Bishop need the assistance of your King or a piece or Pawn to dominate escape squares or to support the mating piece. Try to visualize the possible mate first. If it seems possible but is blocked by some enemy piece or the need to open a line, consider the possibility of a sacrifice to remove that piece or open that line.

The positions that follow further illustrate ways of mating with a Knight and a Bishop. Sacrifices are important in most of them.

DIAGRAM 179

ASTHER — BIRD
London, 1853

Black Mates in Three Moves

ANALYSIS

This is an early example of the Bird Mate. Bird was talented but won few tournaments. He was given to wild attacks that at times neglected development. But in this game he had outplayed his opponent, giving up a Rook to develop his pieces. With four pieces bearing down on the King position, Bird saw a way to mate with Knight and Bishop—thereby giving chess literature the Bird Mate!

1. .... **N—K7ch**

This finish is characterized by effective pins—situations where a piece cannot move because its move would expose a King to capture. Here the White Rook is pinned by a Bishop and the White Bishop by a Rook. In the final position it will be a Queen that pins the Pawn that might otherwise capture the mating piece.

2. **K—R1** **R × Bch**
3. **R × R** **N—N6 mate**

A Toast to Gosta Stolz!

Gosta Stolz, Sweden's star in nine Olympiad competitions between 1937 and 1954, possessed a sense of humor and capacity for fun that made him popular at every tournament. On one occasion he proved his apparent immunity to alcohol. He and two other players wandered into an inn during some off hours of a tournament at Hastings, England. The Swedish grandmaster finished off four pots of jam and then offered to buy drinks for his friends. The jam must have made him thirsty, for he had a black beer, an Irish whiskey, a Guinness, a cognac, a scotch, a liqueur, and (the other two by then having dozed off) no one knows how much more. He shepherded them back to the tournament and proceeded to win his game. Since his opponent was half asleep, it's best to omit his name. Stolz often won without the aid of stimulants, for he tended to confuse his opponents by sharp tactical threats. Diagram 180 shows a position he discussed in the analysis of one of his wins. Realizing it might occur and working out a defense to it had probably had a sobering effect on that opponent!

DIAGRAM 180

White Mates in Three Moves

ANALYSIS

Black, far ahead in material, threatens a quick win by 1. . . . . R × Q or 1. . . . . Q × Bch. Yet White can mate if he can force the Black King to its R1. A double check (the King must move on a double check) follows a Queen sacrifice. The question is—on what square does the Knight give its part of the double check?

1. ________ ________
2. ________ ________
3. ________ **mate**

DIAGRAM 181

LECHTYNSKY — PACHMAN

Czechoslovakia, 1968

White Mates in Two Moves

ANALYSIS

This position is similar to that of Diagram 180. White has just sacrificed his Queen at KR7. Now a double check can force the Black King back to R1, where it will have no escape squares and can be mated by a Knight check.

1. ________ ________
2. ________ **mate**

DIAGRAM 182
SCHMID — CASTALDI
Bern, 1957
White Mates in Two Moves

ANALYSIS

Again a Queen sacrifice forces a mate. All White has to do is gain control of the long diagonal, on which a check can mate a Black King that has no escape squares. If Black refuses the sacrifice, mate follows anyway with Bishop and Knight or with Queen (acting like a Bishop) and Knight.

1. ________ ________
2. ________ **mate**

DIAGRAM 183
ROBATSCH — JANSA
Sochi, 1974
White Mates in Five Moves

ANALYSIS

It seems incredible that mate by Knight and Bishop can result from this position—yet it happened! Black has just snatched White's QBP, expecting 1. B × B, Q × B; 2. R—B1, Q—B3; when he is safe and a Pawn ahead. But he failed to see that his King and Bishop are on the same diagonal!

1. **Q—Q2!**

Surprise Number One! The Black Bishop cannot take the Queen, for it is pinned by White's Bishop. And if Black plays 1. . . . . B × B, then White wins Black's Queen!

1.	**. . . .**	**Q × QP**
2.	**B × Bch**	**P—K4**
3.	**N × P!**	

Surprise Number Two! The White Bishop at KN2 is attacking Black's Queen.

3. .... Q × Q

Surprise Number Three! Can you see the Bird Mate in two moves?

4. ________ ________
5. ________ **mate**

DIAGRAM 184

Black Mates in Three Moves

ANALYSIS

Note the characteristics that point to a possible mate by a Knight and a Bishop. Black's Bishop on the long diagonal would cut off White's escape if the diagonal were open. The Black Knight could then deliver the mate at R6. But how can Black open the diagonal? The sacrifice should be obvious!

1. .... ________
2. ________ ________
3. ________ ________ **mate**

DIAGRAM 185

White Mates in Two Moves

ANALYSIS

White could mate if the Black Pawn were not at N2. Black would then succumb to N—R6 mate. In such a situation a sacrifice is in order, especially if it involves a move that also threatens mate. White made a Queen move in this position that caused immediate resignation. How does he force mate in two?

1. ________ ________
2. ________ **mate**

REMEMBER!

1. There are three typical positions in which you can mate with a Bishop and a Knight. In each of them one of your pieces cuts off escape squares while the other checks and mates.

2. The most common mates with Bishop and Knight occur when your opponent's King is at its N1, cannot escape to B1, and finds its R1 and N2 squares controlled by your Bishop. A check by your Knight then forces mate.

3. Sacrifices are often needed to open a King position to permit mate by a Knight and a Bishop. Consider a sacrifice whenever you recognize the possibility of creating one of the three basic mating positions.

CHAPTER 10

Mate with Two Knights

Meet Sam Lloyd

Perhaps the most ingenious maker of puzzles and brain teasers ever published in the United States, Sam Lloyd was also the premier American chess problemist of the second half of the nineteenth century. His forte was the creation of positions where victory seemed impossible—until some sequence of apparently suicidal moves reconstructed the situation to permit mate. Lloyd played tournament chess infrequently and had mixed results, perhaps because of his tendency to complicate positions in a search for brilliant finishes. Yet there were times when his special penchant for the unusual paid off. In the Paris Chess Congress of 1867, Lloyd had White against a well-known master named Rosenthal. They reached a position in which the American produced an unusual mate with two Knights.

DIAGRAM 186

White has concentrated his pieces on the Queen side while Black has gained control of the King side. Given time, Black will advance his KRP and win. But Lloyd is ready to unleash a winning attack on the Black King. If only he could force that King to its R1 square the combination of Rook and two Knights might force a mate. The only move that can achieve the forcing of . . . . K—R1 is a Knight check at White's Q7. But the Black Queen covers White's Q7. So Lloyd offers his Queen to clear the road for his Knight.

1. Q × B! **Q × Q**

Otherwise White has won a Bishop.

2. N—Q7ch **K—R1**
3. N—B6 dis ch **N—R3**

Black had no other move. His King could not return to N1. Now White can mate, his two Knights working in harmony. One will check and mate while the other cuts off escape squares.

4. N—N6 mate

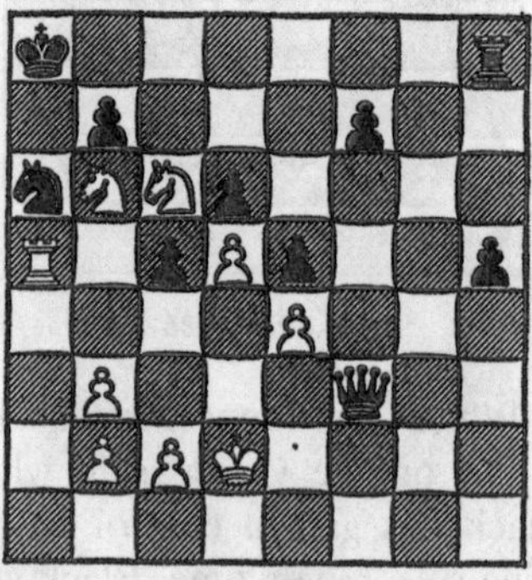

DIAGRAM 187

The final position illustrates the characteristics of a mate with two Knights.

1. The enemy King lacks escape squares.
2. Two squares near the King are usually held by one of the Knights while the other Knight checks and mates.
3. Often, a sacrifice is needed to remove a defender of the square on which the mate occurs.
4. Alternately, a sacrifice can force your opponent to block an escape square when he must capture the sacrificed piece.

But some examples are needed to clarify these ideas.

DIAGRAM 188

ANALYSIS

White is mated. Note how all possible escape squares are under Black's control. The Black King controls White's KB1 and KB2. The crisscross effect of the Black Knights prohibits White's escape to K2, Q1, or Q2. Thus, one

Knight prevents escape while the other Knight checks (= mates) and also controls one possible escape square.

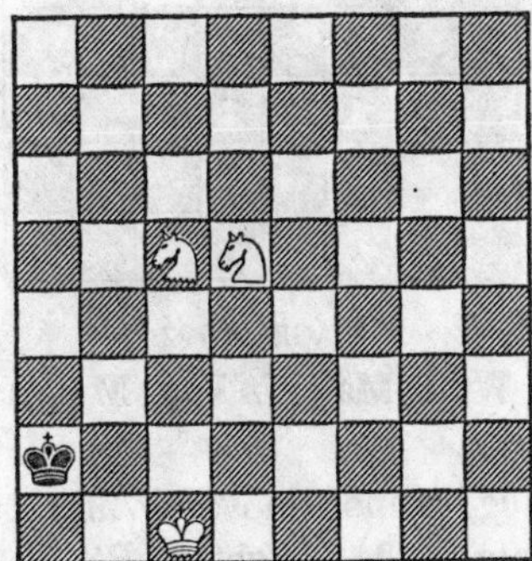

DIAGRAM 189

Black Permits White to Mate in Two Moves

ANALYSIS

Note the word "permits." White would mate by 1. N—B3ch, K—R8?; 2. N—N3 mate. But Black can avoid the mate by playing 1. . . . . K—R6. There is no way in which King and two Knights can mate a lone King unless that King deliberately moves into a corner square. Thus, the defense against such a mate when you have a lone King is to avoid the corner squares!

ANALYSIS (Diagram 190)

This position leads to the mate shown in Diagram 188. Note that Black's King has no moves. That means the Black Knight will have to move in reply to White's first move. Suppose the Black Knight weren't on its Q2. On what squares should your Knights then be placed to force mate? The only hint you need is that the White Knight at QB6 remains where it is.

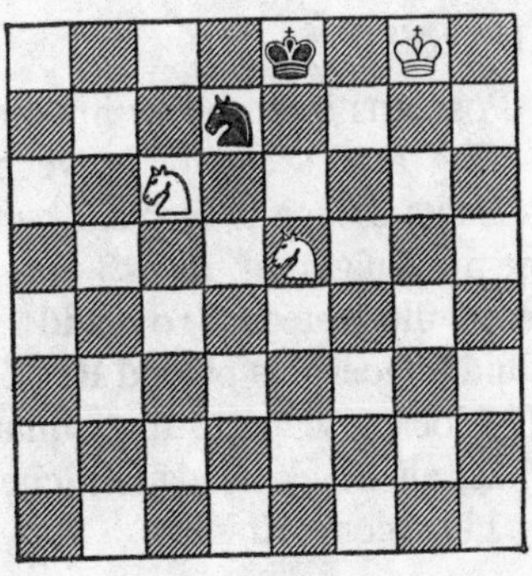

DIAGRAM 190

White Mates in Two Moves

1. ________ ________
2. ________ **mate**

DIAGRAM 191

Black Mates in Two Moves

ANALYSIS

Positions often occur in which a King at R1 cannot move because its escape is blocked by an enemy Knight at its R3—as is here illustrated. To add to White's woes, his pinned Rook at N2 blocks escape to that square. Thus, all Black needs is a check by his second Knight!

1. .... ______
2. ______ ______ mate

TERMS TO KNOW

Waiting move—A move that does not alter your position at a time when all of your opponent's pieces must remain where they are to meet your threats. Examples of waiting moves are a King move to a square where it still does whatever it could have done on its previous square; a Rook move along its rank or file; a Bishop move along its diagonal.

Zugzwang—A term from the German, best translated as "a disagreeable need to move." Zugzwang occurs when all your pieces are needed on the squares they occupy. The movement of any one of them will result in your losing material or being mated.

Diagram 192 is an instructive introduction to both the waiting move and zugzwang. Black's

DIAGRAM 192

White Mates in Four Moves

King cannot move. White can mate if the Knight at R8 could reach a square where it can check without being captured. It could take 9 moves to reach QN1, assuming the Knight would not be captured en route by Black's Bishop. Examine this Knight tour on the board after setting up the position. N—B7; N—Q6; N—K8; N—N7; N—R5; N—N3; N—B1; N—Q2; N—N1 mate. Another route is N—N6; N—B4; N—R5; N—N3; N—B1; N—Q2; N—N1. But why bother with such a laborious effort when there is an easier win through a check (and mate) at either QB4 or QN5?

1.	**N—B7**	**P—K4**
2.	**N—Q6**	**B—R3**

Black could have reversed the order of his first two moves. Now

White can force Black into zugzwang.

3. **K—N1!**

This is an example of a waiting move. The King's task was to prevent a Black escape to N2. The square can be controlled from N1 as well as from B2. The position has been altered by the waiting move but has not really been changed.

3. . . . . **Any Bishop Move**

For Black is in ZUGZWANG! He must move. Only his Bishop can move. He loses on any move he makes with it.

—if 3. . . . . **B—N4; 4. N × B mate**
— if 3. . . . . **B—N2 or B—B1; 4.** N × **P mate**

Endgame positions in which an opponent's King has no escape squares are common, and mates with two Knights can then occur when the opponent cannot defend the square on which one Knight mates while the other cuts off escape squares. But in many more cases the mate requires a sacrifice that removes a defender (as in the Sam Lloyd game that opened this chapter) or forces the opponent to occupy the only available escape square with one of his own pieces.

DIAGRAM 193

Black Mates in Two Moves

ANALYSIS

The Russians call the mate with two Knights the Tchigorin Mate, honoring their strongest nineteenth-century grandmaster, Mikhail Ivanovich Tchigorin. Tchigorin stressed original attacking ideas as opposed to adherence to so-called scientific principles. He edited an early Russian chess magazine in which he presented composed positions similar to this one to clarify ways of using sacrifices. Black sacrifices his Queen to force White to occupy the escape square at his KN2, after which Black's two Knights mate.

1. . . . . ______
2. ______ ______ **mate**

DIAGRAM 194

POWELL — BLACKBURNE
Norwich, 1871

Black Mates in Three Moves

ANALYSIS

Positions like the ones composed by Tchigorin really occur! In this game the English master known as "The Black Death" because he won so often with the Black pieces (and because of his name— Black + Burn) demonstrated that the Bishop sacrifice he had made to open up the White King position was sound. He can now give up his Queen after forcing the White King to the square where it will be mated by the two Black Knights!

1. .... ______
2. ______ ______
3. ______ ______ mate

Sometimes mate with two Knights can occur on the open board, and even in the opening. But the losing player must make a few mistakes along the way—such as the ones made by Black in this tournament game early in this century.

	White	Black
	SEGUIN	HAYNES
	London, 1905	
1.	**P—K4**	**P—K4**
2.	**N—KB3**	**P—Q3**

Philidor's Defense, rarely played today because it gives Black a cramped position. But in this game Black tries to turn it into a gambit in hopes of an early counterattack on the K-side.

3.	**B—B4**	**P—KB4?**

Black hopes White will play 4. P × P, when 4. . . . . B × P gives Black some counterplay. But White continues to develop.

4.	**P—Q4**	**N—KB3**
5.	**N—B3**	**P × QP**
6.	**Q × P**	**B—Q2?**

Another weak move. 6. . . . . N—B3 was better, gaining time by driving the White Queen away from its strong center square.

7.	**N—KN5**	**N—B3**
8.	**B—B7ch**	**K—K2**
9.	**Q × Nch!**	

This spectacular Queen sacrifice is justified by Black's blocked position. If Black now plays 9. . . . . P × Q; 10. N—Q5 mate!

9. .... K × Q

And now, with the White Bishops controlling possible escape squares, the Knights go to work to force mate in three moves.

DIAGRAM 195

White Mates in Three Moves

ANALYSIS

The final position, and the game as a whole, is of the type players love to show to their friends. Black's King can move only to K4. Once there it can be forced to its K5, where it will be mated by the combined action of the White Knights and the restraining influence of the White Bishops. It's the Knights who do all the work as they complete the mating attack that began with the Queen sacrifice!

1. ________ ________
2. ________ ________
3. ________ **mate**

Keeping Out of the Club

Suppose you had the opportunity to join a club whose membership was restricted to international masters and grandmasters. Wouldn't you be anxious to be in such a select group? Vera Menchik, the world's best woman player in the 1920s and 1930s, unwittingly organized such a club, and was herself the only player in the tournament world who could never become a member. Miss Menchik was from time to time invited to compete in a major tournament. She didn't win any of them, and often finished in the cellar. But at each event she managed to win or draw against a few of her male opponents—some of them the best-known names in the chess world. After a few such tournaments, when one of her opponents had joined the list of masters she had beaten, he was greeted with the joke: "I hear you've joined the Menchik Club!" The joke spread, and the grandmasters became determined to avoid membership "this year or any year."

Miss Menchik was invited to play in the strongest tournament of 1929, played at Carlsbad. She added four new members to the club, and was prevented from making it double that number by her tendency to blunder in time trouble. Akiba Rubinstein, then at his peak, played her in one of the final rounds. He was determined to decline membership, and played sharply to reach a position where Miss Menchik permitted him to mate her with two Knights.

DIAGRAM 196

Black Mates in Two Moves

ANALYSIS

Rubinstein, a Pawn ahead, had penetrated the White position with his Knights. Now he played **1. . . . . Q—K5ch.** Miss Menchik might have played on for a few moves with 2. N—B3, Q × Nch; 3. K—R2, Q × Pch; 4. K—R1, Q × P mate. But, tired after a long game and seeing she was lost, she played:

2. **K—R2**

This, of course, permitted an immediate mate by:

2. . . . . ________ **mate**

To mate with two Knights you must be able to visualize the final position. The enemy King must lack escape squares, one Knight cutting them off while the other checks and mates (sometimes cutting off another escape square at the same time). Sacrifices are often needed to remove a defender or to force an enemy piece to occupy an escape square. Most of the positions that follow illustrate such sacrifices, and also show how a square can be vacated for a Knight when the piece on that square can attack the King.

DIAGRAM 197

White Mates in Three Moves

ANALYSIS

The Black King would be mated if White could play N—B2 without fearing its capture. The battery of White Rooks can force Black's Rook into inactivity because of a pair of pins. Note that the White Bishop prevents . . . . P—N6. If a White Rook could only check on the third rank . . . !

1. ________ ________
2. ________ ________
3. ________ mate

DIAGRAM 198

MACZYNSKI — PRATTEN
Portsmouth, 1948

Black Mates in Four Moves

ANALYSIS

Here again the attack begins with a Queen sacrifice, needed to permit the first of three Knight moves that lead to mate. The key to the mate is the assistance of the Black Bishop at its KB6, where it prevents the escape of the White King to its K2 or KN2.

1. .... ________
2. ________ ________
3. ________ ________
4. ________ ________ mate

DIAGRAM 199

White Mates in Three Moves

ANALYSIS

Again a Queen sacrifice, this time to vacate a square needed for the final Knight check and mate. Black's King, blocked by its own pieces, has just moved from K1 to Q1. Suppose the White Queen were not on the board, and that the Black position were unchanged. How would you then place your Knights to force mate?

1. ________ ________
2. ________ ________
3. ________ mate

DIAGRAM 200

WAILA — KIVI
Finland, 1949

White Mates in Three Moves

ANALYSIS

After a Bishop sacrifice at KB7, White's Queen and Knight forced the Black King to its KR4, where its only remaining escape square is its KR5. No wonder the position is ripe for a mate by two Knights that begins with a Queen sacrifice to free White's KB3 square while removing the Black Bishop. The mate depends on the White Bishop's control of its diagonal.

1. ________ ________
2. ________ ________
3. ________ **mate**

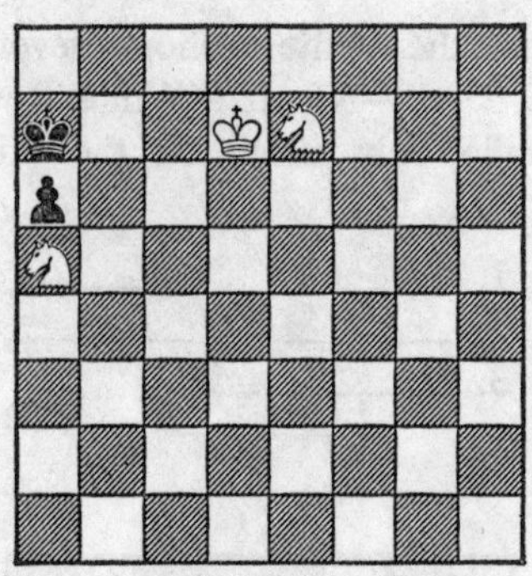

DIAGRAM 201

White Mates in Four Moves

ANALYSIS

Remember that the mate by two Knights is easiest to achieve when the enemy King is on its corner square. How can White force the Black King to its R1? Once this occurs, you have time to move your Knights to their mating position. First cut off possible moves by the Black King and then bring the other Knight to the mating square. All Black will be able to do is to advance his Pawn while awaiting the mate!

1. ________ ________
2. ________ ________
3. ________ ________
4. ________ **mate**

DIAGRAM 202

R. BYRNE — L. SZABO

Spain, 1975

White Resigned after Three Moves. Why?

It is important to sense when an opponent's King can be mated. Black's pieces have left the White King without escape squares. Thus, a check can be mate. Observe how that check is forced!

1. . . . . N—B5

The Knight threatens mate at Black's QN7. But the real value of the move is that it controls White's K3 and releases the other Black Knight for the final mating move.

2. R—N1 P—K4

This time the threat is 3. . . . . P—K5 mate.

3. P × P P—B4

Now White's King cannot escape to its Q4. White resigned because he could not prevent the mate by (either) N × P. All he can do is delay it by 4. R—N7ch, K—K3; 5. R—K7ch, K × R; 6. ANY MOVE, either N × P mate.

What made this mate possible? To begin with, the Black Rook held the seventh rank to prevent escape by the White King to its Q2 or K2. Had White tried to block that Rook by B—K2, it would have meant nothing because the Black Knight still held White's Q2 square. But the key to the mate is the ability of two Knights to control escape squares (White's Q2 and K3) while steps are taken to open another square for the final mate.

DIAGRAM 203

HORVATH — EPERJESI

Hungary, 1971

White Mates in Four Moves

ANALYSIS

Our examination of mate by two Knights closes with an illustration of the use of a battery to remove a defender while leaving a possible escape square occupied by an enemy piece. White begins with a planned sacrifice of Queen and Rook to clear the KN file and force Black's Knight to move. Then the two Knights force mate!

1.	**Q × Pch!**	**R × Q**
2.	**R × Rch**	**N × R**

And the mate is there!

3. ________ ________
4. ________ **mate**

REMEMBER!

1. Mate with two Knights can occur when one Knight can cut off escape squares while the other Knight attacks the enemy King.
2. If your opponent has one escape square your Knights cannot control, consider the possibility of a sacrifice that forces an enemy piece to occupy that square.
3. Remember that King and two Knights cannot mate a lone King. Thus, do not capture your opponent's last Pawn if you see a way to immobilize his King on a corner square and mate with your Knights before that Pawn Queens in time to prevent the mate.

CHAPTER 11

Mate with Two Bishops

Inexperienced players often make the error of trying to win a game quickly by a series of sacrifices whose only goal is to expose the enemy King. They then find themselves unable to complete the attack because they no longer have enough material to mount sufficient pressure against the opponent's defense. Sometimes an opponent meeting such an attack wastes time, fails to defend, or makes the mistake of placing his King on an exposed square where mate is easily forced. A hundred years ago players considered attack imperative from the first move on. Many of them, including some masters, played an opening called the Jerome Gambit. It is so unsound that it has disappeared from chess theory and practice—even though some beginners still attempt it. It made its last important appearance in 1880, when the British master Blackburne demonstrated how to crush the gambit with a counterattack that also illustrated a mate with two Bishops.

White	**Black**
GREEN	BLACKBURNE

London, 1880

1. P—K4	**P—K4**
2. N—KB3	**N—QB3**
3. B—B4	**B—B4**
4. B × Pch?	

White is ready to sacrifice two pieces to attack the Black King with his Queen. White's fourth, fifth, and sixth moves are the characteristic "attack" of the Jerome Gambit.

4.	**K × B**
5. N × Pch	**N × N**
6. Q—R5ch	**P—KN3!**

Before this game Black had usually played 6. . . . . K—K3 to hold the two-piece advantage.

White then has a few attacking moves left that can win against any but the best play by Black. But Blackburne had calculated a win by returning a piece and then permitting White to capture a Rook.

7. **Q × N** **P—Q3**
8. **Q × R** **Q—R5**
9. **0—0**

DIAGRAM 204

What has White achieved by his attack? He has a Rook and two Pawns for his Bishop, but is now subjected to an attack that succeeds because Black can immobilize and later attack the White Queen.

9. .... **N—B3**
10. **P—B3** **N—N5**

Suddenly Black threatens mate by Q × P!

11. **P—KR3** **B × Pch**
12. **K—R1**

If 12. R × B, Q × Rch; 13. K—R1, Q—B8 mate.

12. .... **B—KB4!**

The Bishop move uncovers an attack on the White Queen. Its only move is:

13. **Q × R**

And now Black mates in two moves—with his Bishops!

DIAGRAM 205

13. .... **Q × Pch!**
14. **P × Q** **B × P mate**

Blackburne's play in this game was a final nail in the coffin that holds the dead Jerome Gambit. His victory depended on his understanding of the power of two Bishops to mate when they control a pair of adjacent diagonals. The final position, in which another piece aids the Bishops by controlling one square adjacent to the enemy King, is called the Blackburne Mate. The position of the Bishops at the end of this game illustrate one of the two ways a pair of Bishops can mate.

DIAGRAM 206

ANALYSIS

The basic characteristics of any mate are evident again. The Black King has no escape squares. The White King controls Black's R2 and N2. One Bishop prevents escape to Black's N1 while the other Bishop checks and mates. Such a mate by two Bishops requires open diagonals. White's previous play had to include efforts to open the long diagonals.

DIAGRAM 207

ANALYSIS

This time the King's adjacent squares are blocked by its own pieces, and the White Bishops attack from two directions. One Bishop prevents escape to Black's KN2 or KB1 while the other Bishop checks, prevents escape to Black's KB2, and therefore mates. The typical positions of Diagrams 206 and 207 are the most common ways of mating with two Bishops.

There are therefore two goals that, once achieved, can lead to a mate with two Bishops.

1. With the enemy King lacking escape squares except those that can be controlled by your Bishops, find ways to open the diagonals leading to the King position.
2. Get one Bishop to a square where it cuts off possible escape squares on one diagonal and the other Bishop to a diagonal where it checks and mates.

DIAGRAM 208

BOLBOCHAN — PACHMAN

Moscow, 1956

White Mates in Two Moves

ANALYSIS

Mates with two Bishops require open diagonals. In this game Black had played P—K3 and P—KN3, creating holes in his position. Once White had played B—KR6 to gain control of Black's KN2 and KB1, he was able to plan the Queen sacrifice that now forces a mate similar to that shown in Diagram 207. How does this sacrifice lead to mate?

1. ________ ________
2. ________ **mate**

DIAGRAM 209

ANDERSSEN — SCHALLOP

Berlin, 1864

White Mated in Two Moves

ANALYSIS

After sacrificing two Pawns, White controls the center of the board, where his Bishops are poised for attack. Black's King has no escape squares and a supported check at White's KB7 would be mate. Anderssen therefore played **1. Q × Pch!** and Black was lost. He could have given up material by some such line as 1. . . . . N—K4; 2. Q × Nch, B—K3; 3. B × B, P × B; 4. Q × Pch, Q—K2; 5. Q × Q mate. Instead, he permitted his opponent to have his brilliant finish and played **1. . . . . N × Q,** on which White mated at once.

2. ________ **mate**

DIAGRAM 210

G. KOLTANOWSKI —
SIR HUGH WALPOLE
Keswick, England, 1936

White Mates in Two Moves

ANALYSIS

The Blackburne Mate, with a Knight controlling a possible escape square, often results from a Queen sacrifice that brings the enemy King into the open. A Bishop then checks and mates when the second Bishop controls a key diagonal—as the White Bishop on QB2 does in this position. Assume Black accepts the sacrifice.

1. ________ ________
2. ________ **mate**

DIAGRAM 211

Black Mates in Four Moves

ANALYSIS

Mate by two Bishops sometimes depends on forcing a King to a corner square. Then, if the long diagonals are open, mate follows. In this position White's King cannot leave its first rank. The sweep of Black's Bishop pair forces that King to its R1 where it is mated.

1. .... ________
2. ________ ________
3. ________ ________
4. ________ ________ **mate**

The threat of mate by two Bishops once the long diagonals are opened often justifies a sacrifice if two conditions exist. The sacrifice includes a mate threat (or the gain of material) if it is not accepted. And if it is accepted (as it must be to avoid the new threat), the opening of diagonals permits a Blackburne Mate or some other mate by the two

Bishops. Diagram 212 illustrates a common form of the Blackburne Mate following a Queen sacrifice that must be accepted because it threatens a new mate itself.

DIAGRAM 212

BIRD — BROWN
London, 1872

White Mates in Two Moves

ANALYSIS

Four White pieces bear down on Black's King position, made vulnerable by the holes at KB3 and KR3. White sees that mate is possible after 1. Q × P, for there are then two threats:

a. If Black plays 1. . . . . P × Q; 2. B—R7 mate (Blackburne Mate).

b. If Black does not take the Queen, it will mate on R7 (supported by the Knight) or on R8 (supported by a Bishop). Thus, if 1. . . . . B × N (to prevent 2 Q—R7 mate); 2. Q—R8 mate. And if 1. . . . . ANY MOVE TO BLOCK THE DIAGONAL OF THE WHITE BISHOP AT QN2; 2. Q—R7 mate.

In the actual game, Black played 1. . . . . P × Q and White mated by 2. B—R7 mate. Black could have delayed the mate by one move with 1. . . . . N—R3; 2. Q × N and then mate on the next move.

DIAGRAM 213

Black Mates in Three Moves

ANALYSIS

Mate with two Bishops requires open diagonals. In this position Black's Bishops dominate the board but do not yet attack the White King. But the Blackburne Mate would be possible if the Pawn at White's KN2 were gone. It must be removed at once, for White threatens moves like B × Pch and then P—B5 dis ch with a dangerous attack. Black therefore selects his most forcing move—a Queen sacrifice that is followed by a Blackburne Mate.

1. .... ______
2. ______ ______
3. ______ ______ **mate**

Mate with two Bishops requires control of escape squares along adjacent or intersecting diagonals. The positions that follow illustrate some of the steps that can lead to such control. Sometimes you can mate with two Bishops by simply taking advantage of the opportunity to occupy open diagonals. At other times you must consider sacrifices to open a King position (and the diagonals leading to it) or must make sacrifices that give you time to bring a Bishop to a more effective square.

DIAGRAM 214

White Mates in Six Moves

ANALYSIS

This is a simple proof that you understand the power of two Bishops on adjacent diagonals. One Bishop will hold the Black King in the corner while the other will sweep away the Pawns on the way to mate.

1. ______ ______
2. ______ ______
3. ______ ______
4. ______ ______
5. ______ ______
6. ______ **mate**

DIAGRAM 215

White Mates in Two Moves

ANALYSIS

Edgar Colle was one of that group of masters in the 1920s and 1930s who added new ideas to chess in their search for fresh approaches to such goals as the control of the center. The Colle System, an opening, was named after him. In it, as in his analysis of master games, he tried to show that new twists can enrich old ideas. This position is based on his brilliant win in Berlin, 1926, over Ernst Grünfeld, another chess innovator (originator of the Grünfeld Defense). Colle's analysis suggested a line of play in which he would have sacrificed his Queen to gain time to get his Knight to KB5, from which point it threatened to force a Blackburne Mate or a mate with two Knights. What move for White forces one of these two wins?

1. ________ ________
2. ________ **mate**

DIAGRAM 216

ANGER — DR. TARRASCH

Nuremberg, 1891

Black Mates in Three Moves

ANALYSIS

Black has a choice of winning moves in this position, among them 1. . . . . B × P and 1. . . . . N—N6ch. But he chooses a Queen sacrifice that leads to a mate by his Bishops. The Queen sacrifice is needed to open a long diagonal, after which the Blackburne Mate becomes obvious.

1. . . . . ______
2. ______ ______
3. ______ ______ **mate**

DIAGRAM 217

FLOHR — PITSCHAK

Berlin, 1930

Black Mates in Five Moves

ANALYSIS

Black is ready for a Blackburne Mate, but must first clear a path for his second Bishop. He does this by offering his Queen to threaten two mates— . . . . Q—R7 if the Queen is not captured and . . . . B—R7 if it is taken. All White can do is to look for a check and then try interpositions on the long diagonal. These moves delay but do not prevent the mate.

1. .... Q × P!
2. B × Pch K—B1
3. N(1)—B3

For 3. P × Q permits 3. . . . . B—R7 mate. How does Black win now?

3. .... ______
4. ______ ______
5. ______ ______ mate

DIAGRAM 218

Black Mates in Three Moves

ANALYSIS

Two sacrifices, one to free a blocked Bishop and the other opening a short diagonal for its mating move, force mate in three moves. Look at Diagram 207 before you decide how this position can be transformed into a basic mate by two Bishops. The Bishop at Black's KB1 is the key!

1. .... ______
2. ______ ______
3. ______ ______ mate

Is There a Chess Nobility?

It seems strange that a game that had its origins and much of its early history in the courts of India, the Middle East, and Europe should never have produced a monarch or a nobleman who became a leading player. Never, that is, until our own century. Today Alberic O'Kelly de Galway of Belgium is the only member of any country's nobility who is also a grandmaster at chess. He may have inherited his title, but his rise to international status at chess was won the hard way, by study, continuous play, and a full portion of crushing defeats along the way. O'Kelly became a leading chess author and journalist who specialized in the analysis of difficult and instructive positions from master play. He probably remembers the lesson he learned himself as a youth when he played a match against the Belgian master Devos and found himself the victim of a brilliant attack that culminated in mate by two Bishops.

DIAGRAM 219

O'KELLY — DEVOS

Brussels, 1937

Black Mates in Seven Moves

ANALYSIS

Combinations seven moves deep present no problem to a master when there is only one variation. Every White move in this position is forced. Black observes that his Bishops can attack the White King once it has been forced into the open. A Queen sacrifice begins a journey by the White King that finally sends it back home to be mated!

1.	**Q × Pch!**
2. **K × Q**	**N—N5ch**
3. **K—B3**	

This is forced, for if 3. K—N1, B—K6 mates.

3.	**P—K5ch**
4. **K × P**	

For if 4. P × P, N(2)—K4 mate!

Now the mate should be clear. Black can use his Knights to force the White King back to N1 where it is mated by the Bishops.

4.	_______
5. _______	_______
6. _______	_______
7. _______	_______ **mate**

DIAGRAM 220

White Mates in Two Moves

ANALYSIS

This final position demonstrates a mate by two Bishops when a Rook supports the square on which the second Bishop mates. At first glance the White position seems weak. Black threatens to exchange Rooks and then to win by advancing his RP. He also threatens to win a piece by 1. . . . . P—B5. But White can ignore these threats, for his Bishops can mate by attacking first on the longest and then on the shortest diagonal!

1. _______	_______
2. _______ **mate**	

REMEMBER!

1. The Bishops need open diagonals to cut off escape squares and to deliver the final check that mates the enemy King.
2. Sacrifices are often needed to clear a path for a Bishop or to open the diagonal on which it will mate.
3. The mate can occur when you control two adjacent diagonals that bear on the enemy King position from different directions.

CHAPTER 12

Mate with Two Rooks

Why the Russians Win Chess Tournaments

Russian chess masters have dominated the game since 1945. Only Robert J. Fischer of the United States has been able to defeat them with any regularity. The Russian teams have won every Chess Olympiad they entered—sometimes without losing a single game in the long competition! In 1970 a match was held between a Russian team and the twelve best non-Russian players. The Russians won by a point—a victory somewhat clouded by two blunders made by a Hungarian grandmaster in winning positions. But the chess superiority of the Russians remains clear. It is the result of long years of development at national expense.

Rising players in the Soviet Union are coached by masters and grandmasters whose jobs and incomes are a reward for their chess prowess. A Russian winning an international tournament is treated like a hero—a national asset. His comfort is assured—so long as he continues to contribute to his country's reputation as the chess center of the world. The chess masters are expected to study and write about the game, and must keep up with both current theory and the achievements of past and present chess stars. Ewfim Geller, one of their leading players, won the international tournament at Las Palmas, Canary Islands, in 1976. He showed his knowledge of the games of Paul Keres when he quickly won in a position similar to one reached by Keres almost thirty years earlier!

DIAGRAM 221

GELLER — DEBARNOT
Las Palmas, 1976

White Mates in Three Moves

ANALYSIS

Black's King is exposed, for the White Rooks bear down on it while Black's Queen is far away. Geller's first move caused resignation, for the win is then obvious. It was less obvious that the first move would win so quickly!

1. **Q × Nch!**

If the Black King flees to R1, then the battery of Queen and Rook mate by 2. Q—B8ch, R × Q; 3. R—B8 mate. But how does White win on **1. . . . . R × Q?**

2. ________ ________
3. ________ **mate**

The win becomes less surprising when you realize that a similar position was reached in a game won by Paul Keres from Alexander Alekhine in 1937. Alekhine, world champion for all but two years between 1927 and his death in 1946, had also moved his Queen to QN5, where it could play no part in the defense of his King position.

DIAGRAM 222

KERES — ALEKHINE
Margate, 1937

White Mates in Three Moves

ANALYSIS

The win came with sudden and surprising effectiveness. Keres played 1. Q × Bch! and Alekhine resigned. He must lose a Rook and a Bishop or be mated. Suppose he takes the White Queen:

1. **Q × Bch!** **R × Q**
2. ________ ________
3. ________ **mate**

The wins by Keres and Geller illustrate one of the ways to mate with two Rooks. One Rook mates while supported by the other on a rank or a file. Diagram 223 shows the road to mate when a King can be cut off from its escape to the next rank by one Rook while the second Rook checks and mates.

DIAGRAM 223

ANALYSIS

White is mated. One Black Rook prevents escape to White's second rank while the other Rook checks from a distance on White's first rank and mates. This mate occurs frequently, sometimes because an opponent has been careless and more often when a series of captures has cleared the seventh rank of Pawns.

DIAGRAM 224

(Based on a position first analyzed by P. Damiano in 1512)

ANALYSIS

White mates in two moves. He has the ideal position—two Rooks that can occupy adjacent files. The problem is that the KR file is not open. But a Queen sacrifice can open it and force the mate. Remember: one Rook prevents escape while the other checks and mates on the adjacent file.

1. ________ ________
2. ________ **mate**

DIAGRAM 225

Black Mates in Three Moves

ANALYSIS

The White King is trapped. It cannot leave the KR and KN files. If Black's King were not in the way the Black Rooks could mate through their control of two adjacent files. Black's task is to find a route to a square where his King no longer impedes the combined action of his Rooks.

1. .... ______
2. ______ ______
3. ______ ______ **mate**

The most common mate by two Rooks occurs when they are both on the seventh rank and the enemy King is on its first rank. Diagrams 226 and 227 illustrate the types of positions that can then lead to mate.

DIAGRAM 226

White Mates in Two Moves

ANALYSIS

The White Rook on the seventh rank prevents escape to Black's second rank. If White can get his other Rook to the seventh rank, then either Rook can mate by checking on the eighth rank.

1. ______ ______
2. ______ **mate**

DIAGRAM 227

Black Mates in Three Moves

ANALYSIS

Two Rooks mate when one cuts off escape squares while the other checks. In this position both Black Rooks are on the same rank, where they support one another. Picture the position with the Black Rooks on the squares now occupied by White's KN and KR Pawns.

1. .... ______
2. ______ ______
3. ______ ______ mate

DIAGRAM 228

White Mates in Four Moves

ANALYSIS

Black threatens mate in one at his KN7 (. . . . Q—N7 mate), and White must make checking moves to prevent Black's victory. This means a first move that forces a Black King move in reply. If the Black King were only at its KR2! Then the White Rooks could mate in a manner similar to that of Diagram 227. What move forces the Black King to its R2?

1. ______ ______
2. ______ ______
3. ______ ______
4. ______ mate

DIAGRAM 229

ARONIN — TCHECHOWER

Moscow, 1948

White Plays 1. Q × Pch

ANALYSIS

Sometimes the support of another piece makes the mate by two Rooks easier. The White Knight in this position will support a Rook check at KN7 and permit mate by another Rook at KB8. But first something must be done to get rid of one of Black's Rooks. White played **1. Q × Pch** and Black resigned. He could have dragged the game on a few moves by:

1. **Q × Pch** **K—R1**
2. **Q—K5ch** **B—B3**
3. **N × B** **R × N**
4. **Q × R(6)ch** **K—N1**
5. **Q—N7 mate**
   (or: 4. Q × R(8)ch, R—B1; 5. Q(or R) × R mate

But what happens on 1. . . . . R × Q?

1. **Q × Pch** **R × Q**
2. ________ ________
3. ________ **mate**

DIAGRAM 230

Black Mates in Three Moves

ANALYSIS

It is also possible for two Rooks to mate when they are not doubled (supporting one another on the same rank or file). White has three Pawns for a Knight and has reached a position where he threatens to Queen a Pawn. But Black can sacrifice his Knight and then check first on a rank and then on a file to mate!

1. . . . . ________
2. ________ ________
3. ________ ________ **mate**

We have examined the basic guidelines to mates by two Rooks. What should you do or look for when your Rooks can penetrate the enemy position?

1. When the enemy King is on the edge of the board first occupy the seventh rank with a Rook. Then try to get your second Rook to the seventh rank too so that the combined action of the Rooks can threaten mate.
2. An enemy King at its R1 or elsewhere on the edge of the board can be cut off by a Rook placed on the adjacent rank or file. Then try to check—and mate—with the second Rook.
3. Be ready to sacrifice whenever the result is the removal of a defender or the opening of a line for one or both Rooks; but be certain the mate is possible before you give up any of your pieces!

Mates with two Rooks occur frequently because these pieces are rarely exchanged in the opening. They therefore remain as weapons to be used in the middle game and endgame. The positions that follow, most from middle games, illustrate techniques of forcing mate with two Rooks.

DIAGRAM 231

The Rooks Force Mate!

ANALYSIS

This is a perfect illustration of the power of two Rooks combining their efforts on the seventh and eighth ranks. The Black King is limited to its first and second ranks. Mate may be possible if the White Rooks can invade and work together.

1. Q × Pch!

If 1. . . . . P × Q; 2. R(R8) × Rch, K—B2 or Q2; 3. R(N1)—N7 mate—and if 1. . . . . K—Q1; 2. R × R mate. Black must interpose his Queen.

1. . . . . Q—B2
2. R × P!

Now there are two mate threats at once, and one must succeed.

a. If 2. . . . . Q × Q; 3. R(R8) × R mate
b. If 2. . . . . K—Q1; 3. Q × Qch, K—K1; 4. A choice of mates by Q—K7 or either R × R

DIAGRAM 232

White Mates in Five Moves

ANALYSIS

A King limited to two open files can be mated by two Rooks in the type of position illustrated by Diagram 225. Look at that one before you begin your analysis of this one. White begins with:

1. N—B6ch! P × N

The Knight must be captured, for on 1. . . . . K—R1; 2. Q × P mate

2. Q × Pch! K × Q

The goal has been achieved. The Rooks mate by occupying the open files, and the final check and mate occur because the White Pawns cut off possible escape squares.

3. ________ ________
4. ________ ________
5. ________ **mate**

DIAGRAM 233

Black Mates in Three Moves

ANALYSIS

White's Queen is out of play, yet given time his Pawn on B6 will advance to Queen. But the Black Rooks can seize control of the seventh rank and mate must then follow.

1. .... ________
2. ________ ________
3. ________ ________**mate**

DIAGRAM 234

BAUMSTARK — KOZLOVSKA
Soviet Union, 1971

White Mates in Two Moves

ANALYSIS

This mate depends on the support provided by the White Pawn on B6. All White must do is to force the opening of the seventh rank, when the Black King will have no escape squares. A Queen sacrifice does the trick!

1. ________ ________
2. ________ **mate**

DIAGRAM 235

White Mates in Two Moves

ANALYSIS

Doubled Rooks, one supporting a check by the other, can mate if the enemy King is on a rank without escape squares. Here White has only to visualize the position with the Black Rook at its QB1 off the board, and the sacrifice and mate to follow become obvious.

1. ________ ________
2. ________ **mate**

DIAGRAM 236

Black Mates in Three Moves

ANALYSIS

Mate with two Rooks is easy to see when both Rooks can bear on the same square adjacent to an enemy King that lacks escape squares. That condition can be forced in this position after a Queen sacrifice. The key square is White's KB1! Dozens of tournament games have been won with the attack illustrated by this position.

1. .... ________
2. ________ ________
3. ________ ________ **mate**

Selecting the World Champion

The World Chess Federation (*Fédération Internationale des Échecs or FIDE*) has controlled all world titles since 1948. Until then a world champion could make his own decisions about the defense of his title. Sometimes years passed without a world title match. Sometimes the champions selected weak opponents (as they do in boxing) so that they could keep their titles. Today an organized competition carefully chooses the best player among dozens of zonal champions representing every part of the world. Two interzonal tournaments select six players who join the two highest ranking players of the previous elimination series to determine the new challenger for the world title.

As might be expected, Russian grandmasters have tended to dominate the challenger matches. In 1974 five of the eight were Russians, and one of them, Anatoly Karpov, became the 1975 challenger. When the world champion, Bobby Fischer of the United States, refused to accept the playing rules set by FIDE, Karpov was declared the new world champion.

Lev Polugaevski, one of the Russians in the 1974 and 1977 matches, plays regularly and is renowned for his crushing attacks and forced mates. But he too can be vulnerable, and a lesser player with a good knowledge of checkmate techniques can beat him. This was well illustrated at a German tournament where a player who could never win a match against Polugaevski forced a brilliant mate with two Rooks!

DIAGRAM 237

POLUGAEVSKI — EISING
Solingen, 1974

Black Mates in Four Moves

ANALYSIS

Eising has obtained open files for his Rooks. The mate depends on joining the Rooks on the eighth rank. This cannot be done unless the White Pawn on KN2 is removed, and Eising began with a Queen sacrifice that eliminated that Pawn and led to his grandmaster opponent's immediate resignation! Find the mate after:

1.	**Q × Pch!**
2. **R × Q**	_______
3. _______	_______
4. _______	_______ **mate**

DIAGRAM 238

HARTSTON — WHITELEY
England, 1974

White Mates in Three Moves

ANALYSIS

The British chess world has been in renaissance since the 1960s, and has produced several outstanding players. In this game one of them used his understanding of mate with two Rooks to justify a brilliant Queen sacrifice. Suppose the Black Queen were no longer able to protect his K2 and Q2 squares. White would then have the mate with two Rooks illustrated in Diagram 227.

1. ________ ________
2. ________ ________
3. ________ **mate**

REMEMBER!

1. The most common mates with two Rooks occur when the Rooks dominate the seventh rank and the enemy King lacks escape squares or defense by its pieces. Try to get your Rooks to the seventh rank!
2. Mates with two Rooks also occur when one Rook can cut off escape squares on a rank or file and the other Rook checks and mates. Such mates are common when one Rook is on the seventh rank and the other on the eighth, or when the enemy King is confined to two open files that the Rooks can command.
3. Once the Rooks are poised for one of the basic mates, a sacrifice may be possible to remove a defender or to open a rank or file to permit the Rooks to mate.

CHAPTER 13

Boden's Mate

How Strategy Makes Tactics Possible

The checkmates presented in the previous chapters can be characterized as tactics. That is, they are sequences of moves in typical positions that lead to some desired goal—in our case, to mate. Chess planning and play have been divided into the two areas commonly called strategy and tactics. Strategy refers to long-range planning built about such principles as the development of your pieces, the control of the center, the domination of open lines, and the placement of your pieces on squares where defense is assured and attacks can be launched. In all the mates we have examined a player's pieces were already in position to execute a final attack. But they didn't just happen to be there. The attack had to be planned; a desired position had to be achieved; the pieces had to be placed on squares that then made the mate possible. It is important to understand the kinds of threats that can win games—one purpose of reading this book. But it is equally important to know that it must be your strategy to get your pieces to squares where such threats can become checkmates. You cannot succeed as a tactician unless you are first a strategist.

The mating idea called the Boden Mate (named after a German player of the 1860s) provides an example of how to reap the benefits of long-range strategy. Bishops are most useful on open diagonals. In the Boden Mate they usually bear on the

Queen side after the opponent has castled there. One Bishop checks and mates while the other controls escape squares. The strategy is to place your pieces so that such a mate may be possible. The tactics required may include the sacrifice of a piece to open the diagonal on which a Bishop mates.

DIAGRAM 240

White Mates in Two Moves

DIAGRAM 239

ANALYSIS

This is the basic position of the Boden Mate. The White Bishops control the three squares adjacent to the Black King. They bear on it from different directions, their cross fire eliminating any escape. In the Boden Mate positions the opponent's Pawns or pieces usually occupy two or more squares adjacent to the King—like the Rook and Knight in this position.

ANALYSIS

Correct strategy has prepared for the mate. White's Queen is on an open file and bearing down on Black's King. The White Bishops are on open diagonals, one of them already cutting off Black's escape to his N1 or B2. But a tactical finish is needed. The Black King is still protected by a Pawn and a Bishop. White would mate if he could check with his Bishop at QR6. He must open a diagonal, and can do it with a sacrifice which is also a check.

1. ________ ________
2. ________ **mate**

DIAGRAM 241

Black Mates in Two Moves

ANALYSIS

The control of open lines is an essential part of successful chess strategy. Black's Bishops are poised for the same kind of mate achieved in Diagram 240. Again a King is blocked by its own pieces and all that is needed is the opening of a diagonal for a final check and mate. It matters little that you lose a Queen if its sacrifice is followed by mate!

1. .... _______
2. _______ _______ **mate**

Terrible Teichmann

Richard Teichmann, recognizable at any tournament by the eye patch he wore over his missing eye, was one of the most talented and feared chess masters of the early years of this century. He studied little, depending chiefly on his great tactical ability. This meant he was often unprepared to meet new opening ideas; losses on such occasions prevented him from winning many tournaments. But he still frightened every opponent, beating the best from time to time and almost always crushing weaker players. He was ready to play anywhere, his lazy approach to chess counterbalanced by the fact that he was always in form because he played so often. A formidable strategist, he developed his pieces as quickly as possible, tried to achieve open games (many open files and diagonals), and looked for tactical ideas that could lead to mate. The type of attack leading to the Boden Mate was always in his arsenal, for he knew well how to create and use open diagonals. One of his games, played in 1914, led to a Boden Mate in only thirteen moves. It was quickly printed all over the world, with confusion as to his opponent's name and even whether it was a tournament game or one in which he gave an offhand opponent the odds of a Rook. In any event, it was played, and it does illustrate how correct strategy calls for the placement of your pieces on squares where they can be used to hit at the enemy position.

White	**Black**
TEICHMANN	DAGOVER

Berlin, 1914

1. **P—K4** **P—Q4**
2. **P × P** **Q × P**
3. **N—QB3** **Q—Q1**

This line in the Center Counter Defense is not recommended. Better is 3. . . . . Q—QR4.

4. **N—B3** **B—N5**
5. **B—B4**

The terrible Teichmann wastes no time. He has more pieces in play and immediately threatens 6. N—K5 and, on 6. . . . . B × Q; 7. B × P mate.

5. **. . . .** **P—K3**
6. **P—KR3** **B × N**
7. **Q × B** **P—QB3**

Played to prevent 8. Q × NP or, on 7. . . . . N—QB3; 8. B—QN5.

8. **P—Q3** **Q—B3**

Black hopes to exchange Queens and thus avoid some of the threats posed by White's superior development.

9. **Q—N3** **N—KR3?**

Violating a general strategic rule—to develop your pieces so that they can help you control the center of the board. It is such minor strategic errors that make brilliant short games possible. Now Teichmann leaps in to the kill.

10. **B—KN5** **Q—N3**
11. **N—N5**

The threat is 12. N—B7ch with the win of a Rook. Black is reluctant to play 11. . . . . N—R3, when both of his Knights will be misplaced. Besides, he doesn't see the mate to come, and doesn't realize what has happened until after he takes the Knight.

11. **. . . .** **P × N?**

DIAGRAM 242

White Mates in Two Moves

ANALYSIS

A Boden Mate awaits. It is not yet possible because on 12. B × Pch Black can interpose his Knight. But suppose the Knight were not there to be interposed? The winning move becomes obvious. Remove the Knight and mate must follow on the next move!

1. ________ ________
2. ________ **mate**

Hundreds of tournament games have ended in a Boden Mate. Players whose strategy has been sound and whose opponents have failed to develop properly or keep escape routes open for their Kings become the unhappy victims of first a sacrifice and then a mate enforced by the criss-cross sweep of two Bishops.

1. Look for an enemy King position with limited escape squares, two of them on a diagonal already controlled by one of your Bishops.
2. Seek a sacrifice that opens a diagonal to permit the second Bishop to check and mate.
3. Before attempting the sacrifice, make certain your two Bishops will control every square to which the enemy King might move.

The positions that follow bear striking resemblances. In each the Boden Mate must first be visualized. Then one or more moves open the line for the Bishop that finally mates. It is amusing that some of the greatest players in chess history have been victims of this mate. Perhaps it proves that no player is immune from punishment when he fails to follow sound strategical principles!

DIAGRAM 243
LASKER — ENGLUND
Scheveningen, 1913
White Mates in Two Moves

ANALYSIS

A world renowned engineer and a part-time grandmaster, Dr. Edward Lasker maintained his playing strength for more than fifty years. His books on chess strategy taught two generations of players. Even at ninety his sudden attacks were winning games. This position, one of his early triumphs, becomes a Boden Mate because the White Rook prevents escape to the Queen file.

1. ________ ________
2. ________ **mate**

DIAGRAM 244

BROWN — ESSERY
England, 1913

White Mates in Two Moves

ANALYSIS

This position is so similar to that of Diagram 243 that the solution should come in seconds. Again the Bishops are ready to mate, if only the diagonal from QR6 to the Black King can be opened. A Boden Mate position is always an invitation to sacrifice! And Black made it all possible by playing . . . . Q × QP, winning a Pawn but taking his Queen away from its defensive post near his King.

1. ________ ________
2. ________ **mate**

DIAGRAM 245

MIESES — ELLINGER
Berlin, 1920

White Mates in Two Moves

ANALYSIS

Jacques Mieses, who claimed at eighty that he had passed the danger zone (between seventy and eighty) at which most older people die, and might therefore live to play chess forever, was a speculative player who rarely won tournaments. But he did produce a large share of mates, including this one. The technique should by now be familiar.

1. ________ ________
2. ________ **mate**

DIAGRAM 246

White Mates in Three Moves

ANALYSIS

Sometimes the recognition of a mating pattern saves a difficult game. Black's advanced Pawns seem ready to break White's position open. But White's Bishops are poised for a Boden Mate, if only the diagonal QR6—QB8 can be opened. Two sacrifices are necessary, for the Black Knight at QN5 must be forced away from its control of White's QR6.

1. ________ ________
2. ________ ________
3. ________ **mate**

DIAGRAM 247

ALEKHINE — BERSEN

Copenhagen, 1925

White Mates in Two Moves

ANALYSIS

One of the marks of a grandmaster is the frequency with which he makes surprise moves that succeed because of his familiarity with mating patterns. Alekhine often tried to defeat weaker opponents in the opening. In this game he sees that a check with a Bishop at KN6 is mate. How does he force the opening of the diagonal to permit that check and mate?

1. ________ ________
2. ________ **mate**

The key to a Boden Mate is the placement of your Bishops. Once you recognize that your opponent's King can be mated after the diagonals have been opened for these Bishops, your goal becomes the discovery of moves that will open these lines. A Boden Mate therefore calls for the consideration of sacrifices that justify your strategy of placing your Bishops on squares bearing on your opponent's King position.

DIAGRAM 248

White Mates in Two Moves

ANALYSIS

Black has committed the error of snatching at Pawns while White was placing his pieces on squares that now make a Boden Mate possible. Perhaps this chapter should be subtitled: *Sacrificing the Queen to Force a Boden Mate!*

1. ________ ________
2. ________ **mate**

DIAGRAM 249

HARRWITZ — HEALEY

London, 1865

Black Mates in Two Moves

ANALYSIS

Even masters make the mistake of letting one objective dull their awareness of a threat. In this game a lesser known club player defeated a master who had neglected his development to advance a passed Pawn he hoped could become a second Queen. The punishment was another Queen sacrifice forcing a Boden Mate.

1. .... ________
2. ________ ________ **mate**

Playing in a Simultaneous Exhibition

One of the features of a chess club's activities is the visit of a well-known master who meets twenty or more opponents in an exhibition of simultaneous play.

The master usually takes White on all boards and moves around within a rectangle of tables. Great tensions develop as players defend carefully and seek threats they hope the master will overlook. He must finish his exhibition in two or three hours, which means he can take only a few seconds to decide on his move at each board. Yet he knows so much more than his opponents that he still wins all or most of the games, sometimes producing several brilliant checkmates in the process. They occur because his strategy is to place his pieces on squares where they can assist in the later attack on an opponent's King position. Sometimes the tactical onslaught is made possible by a trap—an offer of material that, once taken, opens the lines needed for the checkmate. The South American master Canal demonstrated such a satanic offer in a simultaneous exhibition in which he gave away two Rooks and then a Queen to force a Boden Mate!

White	**Black**
CANAL	MARIO

Italy, 1934

1.	**P—K4**	**P—Q4**
2.	**P × P**	**Q × P**
3.	**N—QB3**	**Q—QR4**
4.	**P—Q4**	**P—QB3**
5.	**N—KB3**	**B—N5**
6.	**P—KR3**	**B × N**
7.	**Q × B**	**P—K3**
8.	**B—KB4**	**QN—Q2**
9.	**B—K2**	**0—0—0**
10.	**P—R3**	**B—N5?**

DIAGRAM 250

Black thought his Bishop was safe at N5, for Canal would lose two Rooks if he took the Bishop. True, but taking the Rooks means the Black Queen will no longer defend the Black King position. Black has failed to see that Canal's pieces are ready for a Boden Mate. The master made his remaining moves in a second or two apiece—seeming to fly past the board. Do you see White's threat?

11.	**P × B!**	**Q × Rch**
12.	**K—Q2**	**Q × R**
13.	**Q × Pch**	**P × Q**
14.	**B—R6 mate**	

DIAGRAM 251

Black Mates in Three Moves

ANALYSIS

A battery is most effective when it attacks along an open line. Then one or more pieces can be sacrificed to open the enemy position for a mating attack. In this position White has neglected his defenses while advancing his KNP. The lack of escape squares for the White King therefore permits a Boden Mate.

1. .... ________
2. ________ ________
3. ________ ________ **mate**

DIAGRAM 252

Black Mates in Four Moves

ANALYSIS

This is another example of a Boden Mate following a well-timed sacrifice. White has just played R—R1 in an effort to exchange Rooks. But a pair of checks forces his King to KB1. The solution then becomes obvious, for there is then a way to get the Bishops into the criss-cross final position that means mate.

1. .... ________
2. ________ ________
3. ________ ________
4. ________ ________ **mate**

REMEMBER!

1. As a part of your opening strategy, try to place your Bishops on squares that permit them to bear on your opponent's castled King position.

2. Recognize the general enemy King formation that permits a Boden Mate—limited escape squares; your Bishop dominating one or two squares adjacent to the King; the possibility of getting the other Bishop to a square where it cuts off the last escape squares and mates.
3. Be ready to sacrifice to open the diagonal needed for the mate!

CHAPTER 14

Long Diagonal Mates

How to Drive a Chess Player's Family Crazy

So much has been written about chess that no one person can hope to master all of it. Yet each chess player sooner or later makes the attempt—and begins by building a personal chess library. It begins with HOW TO PLAY books that become well-used friends. Then the player discovers chess magazines (about 200 chess periodicals are available in English and many more in other languages). Of course, it is silly to throw away anything related to chess, for each book or magazine has something of lasting value in it. The collection begins to grow, fed by occasional purchases, magazines arriving every month, and soon the discovery that foreign publications can be ordered in the United States. The chess library requires a bookcase or two—perhaps a corner of a room. But what about the thousands of games, collections, and tournament books that are available, many in inexpensive paperbacks? Perhaps a few chess prints will improve the appearance of what has by now become a chess room. Then again the player may want a chess table and some extra wall space to hold the special chess sets that have been added to the library. Friends and relatives discover that chess-related purchases make perfect birthday and holiday gifts. The chess library has become the master of the house. The player may never use filing cabinets to file tens of thousands of games (as the Yugoslavian grandmaster Gligoric does) or compile hundreds of notebooks containing game scores and notes about them (as the Russian grandmaster Boleslavsky did for years). But once the idea of a personal chess library takes hold a player finds a lifetime interest and another family becomes burdened with the problem of finding room for a collection that can only grow larger.

The Yugoslavian publication *Chess Informant,* with its articles in six languages for world-wide distribution, is one of the best library items available. It uses an international system of chess notation that identifies pieces by chess symbols. Published twice a year, it gathers little dust, for it contains games and positions with notes by the world's best players. Most of it is grandmaster chess, but sometimes it includes games or positions by nonmasters. It is each chess player's dream to see his best effort in print, and *Chess Informant* like most other chess publications includes moments of insight and inspiration by hitherto unknown players. One such position in a 1973 issue demonstrated a brilliant mate by a Canadian player who had gained firm control of a long diagonal.

DIAGRAM 253

DZERA — SHAHAR
Canada, 1973

White Moves and Black Resigns!

ANALYSIS

It appears that Black must win a Rook for his Bishop. But the position contains a hidden attack based on the power of the White Bishop at QN2. White played 1. N—B5! and Black resigned. Let's see why.

a. On 1. N—B5 White threatens mate by 2. Q—N7. If Black tries 1. . . . . B × Q; 2. N × B mate!

b. The only possible defense is a move that protects Black's KN2. Thus, 1. N—B5, B—B3; 2. R—R3, R—K1; 3. Q × RPch, K—B1; and White can mate by 4. Q—R8ch, B × Q; 5. R × B mate!

The various mates possible when the long diagonal is con-

DIAGRAM 254

DIAGRAM 255

Black Mates in One Move

trolled as in Diagram 254 have been given names reflecting players who first used or wrote about them. It is simpler to call all of them Long Diagonal mates.

Long Diagonal mates share several characteristics. In all of them the enemy King is unable to leave its first rank when a check by a Queen or a Rook mates. There is usually a hole in the enemy position created by the advance of a Pawn—most often the KNP. A Bishop supports the mating piece or prevents escape by the opponent's King. In most cases the long diagonal is open. The key to the final mating move is the opening of a file for the invasion of a Queen or a Rook. In some cases, as in Diagram 255, the file is not opened until the mating move.

ANALYSIS

The mate is obvious. 1. . . . . Q × RP is mate because the Bishop on the long diagonal supports the Queen. Since few opponents fail to see one-move mate threats, it is most often necessary to sacrifice a piece or a Pawn to reach such a mating position. Diagram 256 illustrates the basic technique.

DIAGRAM 256

Black Mates in Two Moves

ANALYSIS

Black has prepared for a Long Diagonal mate, with his Queen and Bishop attacking White's KR2 square. White's Knight defends against the mate threat, but White can remove this Knight with check and mate on the next move. Note that Black has followed the strategy of placing his pieces on squares where they attack the enemy King position. Now he must remove a defender.

1. .... _______
2. _______ _______ **mate**

DIAGRAM 257

White Mates in Two Moves

ANALYSIS

The removal of defenders is a frequent necessity in Long Diagonal mates. Here White has three pieces bearing on the mating square, KR8. Black has only two defenders, a Bishop and a King. This justifies the immediate sacrifice of the Queen, for mate follows the removal of Black's defending Bishop.

1. ________ ________
2. ________ **mate**

The study of Long Diagonal mates really began with the work of Juan Bautista Lolli, who explained in 1763 that control of the long diagonal plus the invasion by a Rook or Queen on an open Rook file can force checkmate. He presented a study to illustrate the steps in moving from a dominating position to the final checkmate. His final position is often called the Lolli Mate.

DIAGRAM 258

White Mates in Five Moves

ANALYSIS

Black's P—N3 has helped White gain control of the long diagonal. The mate will depend on control of the KR file.

STEP 1: *Control the KR file*

1. **Q—R6** **Q—B1**

For otherwise 2. Q—N7 mate.

STEP 2: *Open the KR file*

2. **Q × RPch** **K × Q**

STEP 3: *Use the KR file to mate*

3. **R—R1ch** **Q—R3**

For 3. . . . . K—N1; 4. R—R8 mate.

4. **R × Qch** **K ×R**

And again 4. . . . . K—N1; 5. R—R8 mate.

5. **R—R1 mate**

A Long Diagonal mate can occur without a Bishop if a Pawn has been advanced to KB6 when the enemy has played P—N3. Control of the diagonal then means only control of the KN7 square, preventing the enemy King from escaping when checked at its R1 or supporting a mate by a Queen at KN7. Diagram 259 illustrates such a mate.

ANALYSIS (Diagram 259)

White has two Rooks and a Pawn for a Queen, ordinarily enough to win. But Black threatens mate at once by:

1. . . . . **P—B6**
2. **P—N3** (preventing 2. . . . . Q × P mate)

DIAGRAM 259

Black Mates in Three Moves

Now whatever White does Black mates in two more moves.

2. . . . . ______
3. ______ ______ **mate**

Mate also occurs when a Pawn at KB6 combines with a Rook check on the eighth rank. There is something inexorable about the win in Diagram 260.

DIAGRAM 260

Black Mates in Five Moves

ANALYSIS

If not for the blocked position of his King, White would have an easy win. Yet there is no way to avoid the mate that results once Black has placed a Rook battery on the open Rook file.

1. .... ______
2. ______ ______
3. ______ ______
4. ______ ______
5. ______ ______ **mate**

DIAGRAM 261

BLACKBURNE — SCHWARTZ

Berlin, 1881

White Mates in Six Moves

ANALYSIS

Note the keys to a possible Long Diagonal mate: a King unable to leave the corner of the board; a Bishop controlling a long diagonal; a battery of Rooks on the KR file ready to open the file and then mate at R8. Black's Knight is in the way. It checks White's King and, if the King moves, the Black Knight still protects the KRP. This would prevent White's R × P to open the KR file. The solution? Do whatever is necessary to remove that Knight! Then all Black can do is to delay the mate a bit by throwing away some material.

1. ______ ______
2. ______ ______
3. ______ ______
4. ______ ______
5. ______ ______
6. ______ **mate**

Want to Play in an International Chess Tournament?

You too can play in a tournament in which some contestants are world-famous grandmasters. They are called open tournaments, a United States invention that attracts hundreds of players at a time, including some grandmasters when the prizes are substantial. One of these stars usually wins, although there have been some upsets. In 1975, for example, an unknown player named Alan Trefler suddenly became a recognized master when he tied for first in the New York World Open ahead of a number of internationally famous chess masters. It could happen to you too!

Somehow United States open events are not as exciting as a truly international Chess Congress. The best known of these, dating back to the 1890s, is played Christmas–New Year's week at Hastings, England. A number of tournaments are played concurrently, one for each level of playing ability. Doing well in a lower rated event means that next year you will be admitted to a higher rated tournament. Given enough trips to England and improvement in your play, you work yourself up to the Master's Reserve Tournament, whose winner gets into the next Hastings International Master's Tournament. A dream? Some of the greatest players in chess history gained their first important success at Hastings. Most spectacular of all was the first place won by Harry Nelson Pillsbury of the United States in 1895. For the rest of his playing career Pillsbury remained a chess giant welcome at the most important international grandmaster tournaments. His popularity also grew with his many successful attacks leading to or threatening checkmate. Long Diagonal mates were one of his specialties, as he demonstrated in a game that won the brilliancy prize at a tournament in Monte Carlo in 1903.

DIAGRAM 262

PILLSBURY — WOLF

Monte Carlo, 1903

How Does White Threaten Mate in Four?

ANALYSIS

This was the position after Pillsbury's twenty-sixth move, B × P! Consider his threats.

a. If Black plays 1. . . . . N × B; 2. R × Nch! and now:

— 2. . . . . RP × R; 3. R—R4 and 4. R—R8 mate

— 2. . . . . BP × R; 3. Q—B8 mate

— 2. . . . . K—B1; 3. Q—R8 mate

b. Suppose Black doesn't take the Bishop and tries for play by 1. . . . . P—B6. White then mates in four moves by:

(1) clearing the Rook file

(2) checking on it

(3) mating at R8

Given the first move, can you see the rest of the attack? (Diagram 262 with the Black Pawn at QB6.)

1. **B × RPch!** ________
2. ________ ________
3. ________ ________
4. ________ **mate**

There is a curious postscript to the story of Pillsbury's brilliancy prize game. In the position of Diagram 262 Wolf played 26. . . . . R—N3 and Pillsbury won with a second-best move. He played 27. Q × R(N6), for he wins Rook and Pawn for a Bishop after 27. . . . . Q × Q; 28. B× RPch, N × B; 29. R × Q. Yet Pillsbury could have kept his threatened mate alive if he had answered 26. . . . . R—N3 with 27. P—K6! The brilliancy prize was awarded anyway because of the brilliancy of B × P(N6) which led to Diagram 262.

Long Diagonal mates like the one Pillsbury threatened but failed to complete can be attempted when three conditions are recognized:

1. The enemy King cannot escape from the corner of the board. This usually means one of its own pieces is at B1 and a Pawn at B2.
2. You have absolute control of the long diagonal or its critical squares, such as N7 and R8. Such control is possible even when an enemy Bishop is also on the diagonal but must move back to its R1 when you check there with a Rook or a Queen.
3. You must control the file along which you will enter to mate. This usually means you need a battery that permits a sacrifice to open that file.

The eight positions that follow illustrate Long Diagonal mates. Each involves some special sequence of moves to open a file, gain control of a diagonal, or force the final mate. Recognition of the three basic conditions for a Long Diagonal mate should make them easy to solve.

DIAGRAM 263

TARTAKOWER — VIDMAR
Vienna, 1906

White Mates in Two Moves

ANALYSIS

Tartakower was an outstanding grandmaster whose love of a

good joke sometimes interfered with his progress. He would play a move like 1. N—KR3 to open a game against a weaker opponent. Then, when his superior skill led to victory, he would claim his new opening idea had made it possible. Tartakower loved to attack and lost many games when his joy in attacking was not justified by his position. He even seemed pleased when he lost to a sound attack. In this position he had a surprise ready that his more serious opponent did not enjoy—a Long Diagonal mate aided by an advanced Pawn at K6.

1. ________ ________
2. ________ **mate**

DIAGRAM 264

ALEKHINE — STERK
Budapest, 1921
White Moves and Black Resigns

ANALYSIS

White already had a won game, being a piece ahead. He nailed it down with a simple move that forced a Long Diagonal mate. All Black could then do was to sacrifice his Queen and Rooks in a series of "spite" checks—checks given to prolong the game. Instead, Black resigned after White's first move. What was that move? What was its unanswerable threat?

1.________, with ________ to follow.

DIAGRAM 265

White Mates in Three Moves when Black Accepts a Queen Sacrifice

ANALYSIS

Bishops should be placed on the long diagonals when there is an open Rook file and a loosened enemy Pawn position near the King. In this position White has a battery on the open KR file and could mate if the long diagonal were open—which means the removal of the Pawn at Black's KB3. A splendid Queen sacrifice does it!

1. **Q×P** **P×Q**
2. ________ ________
3. ________ **mate**

DIAGRAM 266

Black Mates in Three Moves

ANALYSIS

This type of Long Diagonal mate depends on the fact that a Bishop pins the White KBP. It is called the Mayet Mate. What must Black do to force a Long Diagonal mate?

a. open the Rook file
b. occupy the long diagonal
c. mate at R8

The three moves Black makes achieve those objectives in that order. What is the only move that opens the Rook file? Find that and the rest is obvious!

1. .... ________
2. ________ ________
3. ________ ________ **mate**

DIAGRAM 267

BENZIGER — HENNIG
Germany, 1932

Black Mated in Four Moves

ANALYSIS

A Bishop on a long diagonal must sometimes move closer to the enemy King to make a mate possible. In this position it belongs on KB7 to prevent escape at White's KN3. The attack and final mate are common and should be learned by every player.

1. .... **Q—K8ch**
2. **K—R2**

White could have delayed the mate one move by playing 2. Q—B1.

2. .... B—N8ch
3. K—R1

And now placing the Bishop on its best square meant mate in two.

3. .... ______
4. ______ ______ mate

DIAGRAM 268

Black Mates in Four Moves

ANALYSIS

White's Queen is out of play and cannot aid in the King's defense. Black's goal is the opening of the long diagonal, an aim achieved by first an exchange and then a Queen sacrifice. The result is the ideal Long Diagonal mate by a Rook supported by a Bishop.

1. .... ______
2. ______ ______
3. ______ ______
4. ______ ______ mate

DIAGRAM 269

SPIELMANN — HONLINGER
Vienna, 1929

White Mates in Four Moves

ANALYSIS

Rudolf Spielmann, famous for his ability to find and execute sacrifices, worried his opponents into playing cautiously. But Spielmann could not always be denied and often found he could still carry through mating attacks when he placed his pieces on open lines. Here his Bishops hold the long diagonals. A mate may be possible if he can:

a. clear the long diagonals
b. open the Rook file
c. get a Queen or Rook to KR8

The attack begins with:

1. N—K7ch! Q × N

If 1. . . . . K—R1 the continuation would be unchanged.

2. Q × RPch! K × Q

And now mate in two follows because White's Bishop at Q3 prevents any move by Black's KNP. How does White force a Rook to KR8?

3. ________ ________
4. ________ mate

DIAGRAM 270

BELSITZMAN — RUBINSTEIN
Warsaw, 1907

Black Mates in Three Moves

ANALYSIS

In this game Rubinstein had delayed castling to gain control of the long diagonals and prepare the opening of the KR file. Now opening the file could mean mate. But White could block the mate after 1. . . . . P × P by 2. N—Q5 dis ch, K—Q1; 3. BP × P. Rubinstein's solution was to sacrifice his Queen and then use a double check to force the White King back to N1 where a Rook check meant mate. This attack has won dozens of tournament games in which similar opportunities arose.

1. . . . . ________
2. ________ ________
3. ________ ________ mate

REMEMBER!

To achieve Long Diagonal mates you must:

1. Gain control of the long diagonal or key squares on it.
2. Make certain the enemy King is locked in its corner.
3. Find a way to get a Rook or Queen to the mating square, usually R8 where it is supported by a Bishop on the long diagonal.
4. Be ready to sacrifice to open the file on which your Queen or Rook will advance to mate. This often requires a battery on that file.
5. Watch for moves by your opponent that create a hole in his King position—the most weakening often being P—KN3 when there are also Pawns at KB2 and KR2.

CHAPTER 15

The Greco and Damiano Mates: Typical Wins Against an Open King Position

Know Any Chess Prodigies?

A familiar scenario describes the discovery of chess prodigies—boys and girls twelve or younger with incredible natural talent. The youngster learned to play by watching others or from a parent or an older brother or sister. An accidental opportunity results in victory over some experienced player. Excitement follows and leads to a public performance such as a game with an established master. The prodigy wins and is suddenly a local or even a national hero. Paul Morphy (United States), Samuel Reshevsky (Poland and then the United States), José Raoul Capablanca (Cuba), Bobby Fischer (United States), Arturito Pomar (Spain), and Enrique Mecking (Brazil) were all grandmasters while still teen-agers. The prodigies remain important as players rather than as writers or theorists, although all but Morphy, sometimes working with collaborators, have produced books of their games and perhaps some basic instructional materials. Only the first prodigy of modern times, Alexander Petroff of Russia, St. Petersburg's best player at age ten in 1804, became a chess theorist and scholar. He played less as he grew older, immersing himself in chess theory and beginning the Russian tradition of intense analysis of openings and typical middle game positions. Petroff developed the Petroff Defense (1. P—K4, P—K4; 2. N—KB3, N—KB3), one of the most complex of all opening systems. Among his interests was the attack leading to checkmate when the enemy King position is open.

DIAGRAM 271

HOFFMAN — PETROFF
Warsaw, 1844
Black Mates in Four Moves

ANALYSIS

Petroff's target is White's KB2, for his researches had taught him a typical mating attack based on the open long diagonal and an open Rook file.

1.	**R × P !**
2. **Q × Q**	

White would be lost after 2. Q × R, B × Qch; 3. K × B, Q—N3ch; 4. K moves, Q × P and 5. . . . . Q × N.

2.	**R—B4 dis ch**
3. **K—R1**	**N—N6ch!**
4. **P × N**	**R—R4 mate**

For the Black Bishop prevents escape to KN1!

Petroff had found another way to force a mating position first described by the early chess author Greco in 1612. Called the Greco Mate, it depends on opening the enemy King position by the capture of the KBP, controlling the resulting open diagonal with a Bishop and then mating on an open Rook file when the enemy King has been forced to its R1 square. Greco's attacking idea remains important today, especially with the tendency of so many players to advance their K–side Pawns in efforts to attack or to weaken an opponent's defenses.

DIAGRAM 272

THE GRECO MATE — 1612
White Mates in Three Moves

ANALYSIS

The immediate attack by 1. Q × Nch, K—B1; 2. Q—R8ch, K—K2; 3. Q × P would win. But instead there is a mate in three moves—by opening the diagonal for the white-squared Bishop, forcing the Black King to its R1, opening the Rook file with a sacrifice, and then mating with the Queen. Find the continuation after:

1. **Q × Pch** **K—R1**
2. ________ ________
3. ________ **mate**

Open lines around the enemy King permit the occupation of files, diagonals, and key squares near the King. Several standard mating attacks then become possible. They are successful when the opponent lacks defenders that can otherwise interpose or protect the mating square. The Greco Mate in its several forms depends on control of a diagonal after the opponent's KBP has been advanced or removed. Then, with the enemy King forced to its R1, a sacrifice or a direct attack on the open file leads to mate. KB2 can be controlled (cutting off escape) along the long diagonal or from KN6. Diagram 273 illustrates a final resulting position.

DIAGRAM 273

ANALYSIS

Black is mated, his King trapped whether it is at B1, N1, or R1. We examined such positions briefly in our study of mate with a Rook and a Bishop, but the general necessity to sacrifice to force such a position calls for further examination of winning methods.

DIAGRAM 274

DARSNIEK — RAKITIN
Riga, 1975
Black Mates in Two Moves

ANALYSIS

A player unaware of mating patterns would play 1. . . . . B × N? But there is a mating threat by . . . . R—Q8 if the White Queen can be forced to give up its protection of Q1. A check against a King that is in the open and lacks escape squares will have to be met by a capture or an interposition. Each of

White's possible replies to this check permits mate.

1. . . . . ______
2. ______ ______ **mate**

DIAGRAM 275

KOLTANOWSKI — MEYERS
Blindfold Exhibition, Sacramento, 1941

White Mates in Two Moves

ANALYSIS

The typical Greco Mate position is easy to recognize and exploit. The enemy King is forced to R1; your Bishop controls the open diagonal, preventing escape by the King to N1; the KR file is opened and a Queen or Rook checks and mates along it. Problem: how do you force that file open? Answer: sacrifice!

1. ______ ______
2. ______ **mate**

DIAGRAM 276

Forcing the Greco Mate

ANALYSIS

Sometimes a Greco Mate must begin by opening the long diagonal to the opponent's KB2 and KN1. This position is typical. White can mate in four by 1. B × Pch, R × B; 2. Q × Rch, K—R1; 3. Q—K8ch, B—B1; 4. Q × B mate. But the mate can also be accomplished in three moves after 1. B × Pch, K—R1. Look at Diagram 275 to see the method.

1. **B × Pch** **K—R1**
2. ______ ______
3. ______ **mate**

Note again the method of forcing the mate. Check to make certain your opponent's King lacks escape squares. Be certain you control the long diagonal with a Bishop to keep the King locked in at its R1. Be certain you can open the Rook file and can then check and mate along it.

DIAGRAM 277
MARDLE — GAPRINDASHVILI
Hastings, 1975
Black Mates in Two Moves

ANALYSIS

Nona Gaprindashvili, the best woman player in the world, is the equal of many male grandmasters. Beginning as a prodigy, she quickly advanced in playing strength. Most of her play has been in matches against other women seeking to capture her title. When she plays in tournaments with male masters and grandmasters she does much better than Vera Menchik ever did. There is no Gaprindashvili Club as there was a Menchik Club, partly because of her known ability and perhaps because it is at last recognized that women giving equal time and devotion to chess can master it as well as men can. In this game she had permitted the capture of her KR. Instead of recapturing at her KB1, she played a second sacrifice that forced a Greco Mate.

1. .... _______
2. _______ _______ **mate**

DIAGRAM 278
Black Mates in Three Moves

ANALYSIS

The opening of the enemy King position can also occur as the final move of a mating attack. Examine this position. It will be transformed into that of Diagram 273 by a surprise Bishop move following two sacrifices. The first move is the key, opening the path for the Queen sacrifice so common in achieving the Greco Mate.

1. .... _______
2. _______ _______
3. _______ _______ **mate**

DIAGRAM 279

THE DAMIANO MATE

White Mates in Two Moves

ANALYSIS

Given the advantage of a Queen and a Bishop, as in this position by the Italian player Damiano in his 1512 treatise on chess, any player should be able to mate quickly. Mate in two moves is possible here by 1. Q—N4, Q—N6, Q—B7 or Q—Q5 and then 2. Q × NP mate. But Damiano, illustrating a general attacking idea, preferred the mate by 1. Q × Pch, K—N1 (for the Bishop pins the NP); 2. Q × P mate. The general attack based upon such a pin and ending in mate is called the Damiano Mate. His analysis is further elaborated in Diagram 280.

DIAGRAM 280

White to Play
Mates in Three Moves
and Black to Play
Mates in Four Moves

ANALYSIS

White to Play—This is one of the most common mating procedures in chess. The Black King position is open and lacks defenders. The mate occurs on Black's KB2 after a discovered check by the Bishop and two Queen moves. To what square must the Bishop move to support the mate on White's B7?

1. ________ ________
2. ________ ________
3. ________ **mate**

Black to Play—Black plays 1. .... Q—K6ch.

a. If 2. R—B2, R × Pch; 3. K—R1, Q—K8ch; 4. R—B1, Q × R mate

b. If 2. K—R2, R × NPch; 3. K—R1, R—N5 dis ch; 4. K—

R2, Q—N6 mate. (or 3. . . . . R—N8 dbl ch; 4. K—R2, Q—N6 mate).

c. Now review the Damiano Mate suggestion in Diagram 279. Then find the mate if:

1.	**Q—K6ch**	
2. **K—R1**	_______	
3. _______	_______	
4. _______	_______	**mate**

Consider this chapter an introduction to the five chapters that follow, all of which will examine the use of sacrifices to force an enemy King to a square where, its escape cut off and its defenders pinned or absent, it is mated. The preliminary to any mating attack is familiarity with basic mating positions. The tactics needed to achieve these positions can be learned, for most of them involve the opening of lines that make a King vulnerable to attack. The positions that follow illustrate some of the ways players have achieved such basic mates as the Greco and the Damiano, in each case utilizing open lines or forcing them open while controlling escape squares.

DIAGRAM 281

SANTASIERE — GABLE
Buffalo, 1956

White Mated in Four Moves

ANALYSIS

Anthony E. Santasiere became a chess star as a teen-ager and remained a leading American master for forty years. An accomplished painter, poet, and musician, he preferred to be known as a chess romantic, one who urges others to play daringly and to attack with joy. He did so himself in this game, one of his scores of brilliant wins.

The mate depends on the power of the White Pawn at N6. Like a Bishop it interdicts Black's escape to his KR2 or KB2. Santasiere saw that the entry of his Rook into Black's position would lead to mate.

1. **N—K7ch**	**K—R1**
2. **R—N4!**	**B—B3**

Black tries to create an escape square for his King at N2. But mate follows anyway.

3. **R—R4ch** **K—N2**
4. **R—R7 mate**

Black had another defense which would have delayed the mate.

1. **N—K7ch** **K—R1**
2. **R—N4** **N—B3**
3. **R—R4ch** **N—R4**
4. **R × Nch** **B—R3**
5. **R × Bch** **K—N2**
6. **R—R7 mate**

Such open King positions can be a proper source of joy—for the attacker!

DIAGRAM 282

MENCHIK — THOMAS
London, 1932

White Mates in Three Moves

ANALYSIS

Sometimes even strong players become so involved with their own attacking plans that they fail to see simple threats. Sir George Thomas, long one of England's leading masters, had dreams of mating on the QR file. Meanwhile Miss Menchik's Queen and KBP threatened mate at KN7. Thomas defended with R—N1, and was suddenly lost. His King has no escape squares against a check on the open R file!

1. ________ ________
2. ________ ________
3. ________ **mate**

DIAGRAM 283

TRYLSKI — ZALEWSKI
Warsaw, 1974

White Mates in Three Moves

ANALYSIS

Black has committed two serious errors. He has advanced his KBP to open the diagonal for White's Bishop; he has concentrated his forces on the Queen side when his opponent's strength is on the King side. With White's Rook on its third rank, a Greco Mate is quickly forced.

Remember!—with the Bishop controlling the diagonal, sacrifice and then mate on the Rook file!

1. ________ ________
2. ________ ________
3. ________ **mate**

DIAGRAM 284

A. KARPOV — A. POMAR
U.S.S.R. vs. Spain,
Nice Olympiad, 1974

White Mates in Six Moves

ANALYSIS

Spanish chess fans hoped their onetime prodigy would beat the young Russian grandmaster who one year later was declared world champion by the FIDE. Although a Pawn ahead, Pomar is lost in this position because his King is exposed. Karpov wins by forcing the Black King to R3, where it lacks escape squares and cannot avoid mate.

1. **R—B8ch** **K—N2**
2. **R—N8ch** **K—R3**

For White's Bishop controls Black's QB2.

3. **B—Q2!**

Now the threat is 4. P—N5ch!

3. .... **R—N6ch**
4. **K—B2** **Resigns**

Why? All Black can try is 4. .... P—N4. How does White then mate in two more moves?

5. ________ ________
6. ________ **mate**

DIAGRAM 285

ALEKHINE — YATES
Carlsbad, 1923

Black Mates in Three Moves

ANALYSIS

Alexander Alekhine, Russian chess prodigy who at fifteen began a tournament career that led to the world championship, was the most successful attacking player of his time. Yet he too fell victim to standard attacks when he opened lines to his King position. In this game a British grandmaster forced a mate "from the rear," driving Alekhine's King to KR3 where it no longer had any escape squares.

1. .... ______
2. ______ ______
3. ______ ______ **mate**

DIAGRAM 286
TSCHEPURNOFF — APSCHENEEK
Paris, 1924
Black Mates in Three Moves

ANALYSIS

Given open lines for attack and sacrifice (the KN file, Bishops on the long diagonals), all Black needs is the correct sequence of moves. He finds a Queen sacrifice leading to a Greco Mate that also utilizes Damiano's idea of a pinned piece at N2. Obviously, the Black Knight must be sacrificed along the way to open the diagonal. Try the Queen sacrifice first.

1. .... ______
2. ______ ______
3. ______ ______ **mate**

DIAGRAM 287
ERNSTEEN — BERCHEM
Holland, 1975
White Mates in Seven Moves

ANALYSIS

The chessboard itself seems to dictate moves to prodigies even when they do not know the theory that calls for such moves. This intuitive recognition of winning lines marks the truly talented player. In this game a rising Dutch star automatically sacrifices his Queen, for his opponent's King will then stand naked against two Rooks, a Bishop, and a strong Pawn. Mate must lie ahead!

1. **Q × Nch!** **K × Q**
2. **R(1)—B6ch** **K—R4**

On 2. . . . . K—N4; 3. R—N7ch, K—R4; 4. B—N4 mate

3. **R—B5ch**	**K—N3**
4. **R(B7)—B6ch**	**K—R2**

If 4. . . . . K—N2; 5. R—N5ch, K—R2; 6. B—B5 mate.

Now White mates in three more moves, his win based on forcing the Black King to its R2 where it is mated by a Bishop.

5. ________ ________
6. ________ ________
7. ________ **mate**

DIAGRAM 288
CAPABLANCA —
EMANUEL LASKER
Havana, 1921
(World Championship Match)
White's Attack Led to Mate in Six Moves

ANALYSIS

Capablanca, from his early days as a prodigy, was called a "chess machine." The Cuban made few errors, playing logically to turn small advantages into winning attacks. Here he envisioned a standard mate by Rook and Bishop based on the removal of a defender.

1. **B—Q3ch**	**K—R3**

1. . . . . P—B4 would have held out longer, but would still lose after 2. B × Pch! The analysis is too complex to be considered here, but play through this possible line: 1. B—Q3ch, P—B4; 2. B × Pch, K—B3; 3. R—B7, Q—N5; 4. R—B5!, P × R; 5. Q × N mate.

2. **R—B7**	**R—R8ch**
3. **K—N2**	**Q—Q3**
4. **Q × Nch**	**Resigns**

For on 4. . . . . Q × Q; R × P mate. Problem: How does White mate in two after 4. Q × Nch, K—R4?

5. ________ ________
6. ________ **mate**

REMEMBER!

1. The Greco and Damiano mates are examples of attacks possible against an open King position that lacks defenders. Such mates require that you gain control of a diagonal and

a file, with mate usually achieved through invasion on the file.

2. Exchanges and sacrifices should be considered to remove defenders when the enemy King position is open. But do not attempt sacrifices unless you recognize a typical mating position to follow, with your pieces then controlling possible escape squares and open lines available for the entry of your pieces.

CHAPTER 16

The Magic of the Double Check

TERM TO KNOW

Double check—Attacking a King with two pieces at the same time, thus forcing it to move, for it is impossible to make any single move that will interpose against two checks or a move that captures two pieces.

The double check is one of the most effective weapons in chess. It forces an attacked King to move. If that King lacks an escape square, then the double check mates it. Since the double check usually means the control of several squares near the King, its escape is limited—often to only one square. If one of the two pieces that were involved in the double check can then attack the King while supported by the other piece, mate may and often does result. Diagrams 289 and 290 illustrate the final mate positions most often reached after double checks in the early part of a game. In these cases Rook and Bishop combine to mate.

DIAGRAM 289

ANALYSIS

Black is checkmated. There is no escape from the check by White's Bishop, for it controls the diagonal to Black's QN3. At the same time the White Rook at Q1 supports the Bishop while preventing escape on the open Queen file.

DIAGRAM 290

ANALYSIS

Black is checkmated. There is no escape on Black's first rank or to Black's Q2. The White Bishop supports the Rook and also prevents escape to Black's K2.

DIAGRAM 291

White Mates in Three Moves

ANALYSIS

This is the typical mating position that can lead to the mates examined in Diagrams 289 and 290. Black has wasted time snatching at Pawns while White prepared for his mating attack. Note White's advantages:

1. He controls the open Queen file.
2. His Queen, Bishop, and Rook are on that file.
3. He will have a double check followed by mate if he can force Black's King to its Q1.

Therefore:

1. **Q—Q8ch!** **K × Q**
2. **B—N5ch**

This is the desired double check—by the Rook and by the Bishop.

2. .... **K—B2**
3. **B—Q8 mate** (as in Diagram 289)

or:

2. .... **K—K1**
3. **R—Q8 mate** (as in Diagram 290)

Such double checks occur often, and become effective in forcing mates when you know how to use them. Here is a short game that illustrates the effective use of double checks to force a quick win. It is a variation of the opening called the Giuoco Piano. Black's error is his fourth move, which permits a killing invasion by White's Queen.

1.	**P—K4**	**P—K4**
2.	**N—KB3**	**N—QB3**
3.	**B—B4**	**B—B4**
4.	**P—Q3**	**KN—K2?**
5.	**N—N5**	**O—O**
6.	**Q—R5!**	

Suddenly White threatens mate by 7. Q × RP. He also attacks the Black KBP three times. Black must defend against the mate first.

6.	**. . . .**	**P—KR3**
7.	**N × P**	**Q—K1**

DIAGRAM 292

Black tries to save his pieces. On 7. . . . . R × N; 8. Q × Rch would have permitted White to gain a Rook and a Pawn for a Knight—a decisive advantage.

Now let's follow White's thoughts as he plans his finish.

1. Any move by the Knight at KB7 will discover a check by the Bishop at B4.
2. This means N—Q6 dis ch can win Black's Queen. Is there anything better?
3. N × RP will be a double check by Bishop and Knight. The Black King will then have to move. It can go to R1 or R2. But then N—B7 will either be a double check (if Black's King is at its R1) or a discovered check (if Black's King is at its R2). In either case the Black King will be forced back to its N1 and the Rook file will be open for a mate!

8.	**N × RP dbl ch**	**K—R1** or **K—R2**
9.	**N—B7 dbl ch** (or just ch if the Black King is at R2)	**K—N1**
10.	**Q—R8 mate**	

DIAGRAM 293

There it is. The Black King has no escape squares. The White

Knight supports the Queen; the White Bishop supports the Knight. Double checks have led to mate.

DIAGRAM 294

White Mates in Three Moves

Adolf Anderssen—Master of the Double Check

The idea of matching the world's best players in international tournaments did not take hold until 1851, when the first such event in London was won by Adolf Anderssen of Germany. Anderssen (1818–79) was the most brilliant attacking player of the middle 1800s, his superiority unchallenged until he lost a match to Paul Morphy in 1858. Among the early giants of chess, Anderssen seemed invincible to his lesser opponents because he so often produced sudden attacks leading to smashing victories. He succeeded because of his superior comprehension of chess strategy and his ability to prepare positions based on mating patterns such as those you have been examining in this book. One of his most memorable wins has joined the small list of chess games called "immortal" by chess writers. It occurred in a game played against Dufresne in Berlin, 1853. Anderssen had just sacrificed a Queen and a Rook to obtain this position:

ANALYSIS

The double check was one of Anderssen's favorite weapons and he had prepared for it in this position. Black threatens mate in one move at his KN7, but White wins because his Rook and Bishop on the open Queen file can deliver a double check. Anderssen played:

1. **B—B5 dbl ch**

a. Double check forces a King move. If Black plays 1. . . . . K—B3, how does White mate in one more move?

2. ________ **mate**

b. Black therefore played **1. . . . . K—K1.** Now White mates in two more moves. Note the Bishop at QR3.

2. ________ ________
3. ________ **mate**

In the end Anderssen mated with two supported Bishops. A double check had forced his opponent's King to a square where one of the standard mates became possible. This happens often in double check positions. For example, the mate with Rook and Bishop illustrated in Diagram 290 is common and easy to carry through once its possibility is recognized.

DIAGRAM 295

KOLISCH — MACSZUSCKY

Paris, 1864

White Mates in Three Moves

ANALYSIS

Again we have an open file containing Queen, Bishop, and Rook. Black's King is still at its K1. If it can be forced to its Q1, then a double check would take us right into the position of Diagram 290. The only way to get that King to its Q1 is to play as Kolisch did:

1. Q—Q8ch K × Q

And now double check followed by mate!

2. ________ ________

3. ________ **mate**

You can execute such double check mating attacks if you recognize the basic conditions that permit them. A file (and sometimes a diagonal) must be open. The enemy King must be on that file (or diagonal), or you must have a sacrifice that can force it there. Then you move one piece to a square where it checks, meanwhile uncovering a second check by your other piece. The two checking pieces must at this time be able to co-ordinate their attack on a single square adjacent to the enemy King—on which one of the two checking pieces then mates while being supported by the other.

Let's apply these conditions to two positions in which a double check led to mate.

DIAGRAM 296

SCHULTEN — HORWITZ
London, 1846

Black Mates in Three Moves

ANALYSIS

a. The key file is the KB file.

b. Black wants to force the Black King to its KB, placing it on the key file.

c. The only way to do that is to sacrifice the Black Queen.

d. Then a Bishop move by Black leads to a double check that controls the mating square—KB8.

1.	**Q—B8ch**	
2. **K × Q**	______	
3. ______	______	**mate**

DIAGRAM 297

KOLTANOWSKI — DUNKELBLUM
Antwerp, 1931

White Mates in Three Moves

ANALYSIS

Here is our typical mate again.

a. The key file is the Queen file.

b. A sacrifice forces the Black King to that file.

c. A double check follows, and permits mate by the White Rook.

If you see the pattern then you should find the mate in seconds!

1. ______	______
2. ______	______
3. ______	**mate**

For Those Who Want Something Different!

None of it is especially recommended, but you ought at least to be familiar with some of the aberrations of chess that seem to make some players happy. Perhaps because they are bored with the normal game and perhaps because they enjoy self-torture, some players turn to two-move chess. Each player makes two moves at a time—unless the first of them is a check, in which case it alone is permitted. Others like a variety often called "put and take." Any captured piece must at once be placed somewhere on the board, the only restriction being that Bishops must remain on opposite colored squares. Some weird positions result, such as a King so surrounded by its own Pawns that a smothered mate may finish the game. The variations of speed chess seem most likely to destroy the sense of concentration that leads to success in the normal game. First there is "blitz" chess, in which players must move in a second. Then there is two-minute and three-minute chess played with a clock that soon succumbs to the pounding it receives. Five-minute speed chess is popular in Europe, each player having that much time on his clock. One of the variations made popular at New York's Manhattan Chess Club requires a special clock. It sounds a buzzer every ten seconds, followed by a bell three seconds later. If a player has not moved between the buzzer and the bell, he forfeits.

Herman Helms, chess journalist for more than seventy years and known as the dean of American chess, was an inveterate speed player. He was one of the most practiced users of the Manhattan Chess Club's special clock. One of his favorite opponents, a master like Helms, was the beloved Oscar Tenner, who for years gathered a crowd of onlookers whenever he played his favorite rapid transit games. Diagram 298 is the critical position in one of the ten-second games between Helms and Tenner. Helms, then approaching eighty, saw the possibility of a mate based on a double check. He electrified his audience and placed another incredible win in chess history.

DIAGRAM 298

HELMS — TENNER

New York, 1942

White Mates in Two Moves

ANALYSIS

Black threatens to take White's Queen. White not only allows it but forces it by **1. N × QP dis ch.** Then, after **1. . . . . N × Q; 2. N—B6 mate!** Examine the final position:

a. The Black King is checked by a Knight and a Bishop. A double check means the King must move.

b. But the King cannot move. The White Bishop at R3 cuts off escape to KB1 or K2!

Suppose Tenner had not taken the Queen. How would White have mated on 1. . . . . N—K3?

2. ________ **mate**

DIAGRAM 299
MEEK — AMATEUR
Mobile, 1859
White Mates in One Move

ANALYSIS

Mates by a Knight and a second piece (Queen, Rook, or Bishop) are most common in the opening when the enemy King is still at its K1 and the King file is open. This is a typical example. Although the White Queen is attacked, it cannot be captured if White plays a Knight move resulting in a double check. The only problem is to decide the square on which the Knight not only checks but also prevents the escape of the Black King to its Q2.

1. ________ **mate**

The advantage of the player able to administer a double check is that his opponent must then make a King move. Mate may not follow at once, but at least the King has been forced to a square where some other punishment may follow. For example, a Knight can be on a long diagonal with a Bishop behind it and your pieces otherwise set for a Long Diagonal mate. The Russian master Gusev showed how effective a double check can be in such a position. His win illustrates a useful technique that can lead to a quick finish when other threats already exist.

DIAGRAM 300

GUSEV — POLOVODIN
Soviet Union, 1976
White Plays and Wins

ANALYSIS

Gusev's Rook and Bishop are set for a Long Diagonal mate—if the Rook file can be cleared. The Russian master saw that a Knight check at B6 would be followed by a double check that could lead to mate. He played 1. N—K4! and Black resigned. Let's examine White's chief threats.

a. On 1. . . . . B × Q; 2. R—R8 mate.

b. On 1. . . . . B—N2; 2. N—B6ch, B × N; 3. Q × B with the threat of mate at R8 or at N7 if Black plays 3. . . . . Q—N2.

c. On 1. . . . . K—R2 (to hold the Bishop); 2. N—B6ch, K—R1; 3. R × Bch, K—N2; 4. N—K8 or R5 dbl ch, K—N1; 5. R—R8 mate.

TERM TO KNOW

Smothered mate—Mate by a Knight when the enemy King is completely surrounded by its own pieces and therefore has no escape squares.

The smothered mate occurs frequently, usually following a pattern illustrated by a position composed by Ercole del Rio in 1750. He used it to illustrate how a double check followed by a smothered mate can save what appears to be a hopeless game. Play through the moves following Diagram 301 for an introduction to a tactical finesse that is certain to save more than one game for you during your chess career!

DIAGRAM 301
White Plays and Mates in Seven Moves

ANALYSIS

White is in trouble. Black threatens to exchange Queens or

to capture the White Knight. But White is saved by a double check!

1. **Q—K5ch** **K—R1**

Here and later Black must avoid K—B1 because of White's Q—B7 mate.

2. **N—B7ch** **K—N1**
3. **N × R dis ch**

Removing the Rook that prevented White's Queen from leaving the King file.

3. .... **K—R1**
4. **N—B7ch** **K—N1**
5. **N—R6 dbl ch** **K—R1**
6. **Q—N8ch!**

This beautiful sacrifice is the goal of White's attack. Black's only reply is to take the Queen—thereby locking in his King.

6. .... **R × Q**
7. **N—B7 mate**

Ercole del Rio's position with its amazing winning method depends on an open diagonal for the Queen and a Knight that can check at B7 and again at R6 to finally mate at B7 after the Queen sacrifice. The attack can occur on either side of the board. It is common enough so that every player should understand it and **use it**—as the American grandmaster Pal Benko did in an important game from the United States Championships of 1968.

DIAGRAM 302
BENKO — HOROWITZ
United States Championship, 1968
White Mates in Two Moves

ANALYSIS

Pal Benko, a onetime chess prodigy, a chess problemist, and one of the most imaginative players in the world, often plays combinations and attacks that make chess seem so logical and so easy. Here he had forced the Black King to its R1 and was ready for the sacrifice that leads to a smothered mate. Check the Ercole del Rio position if you do not see the mate at once.

1. ________ ________
2. ________ **mate**

DIAGRAM 303

CAPABLANCA — TORRES
Barcelona, 1929

White Mated in Three Moves

ANALYSIS

This time the mate depends on a different way of forcing Black to smother his King. First White forces the Black King to its R1. Then he invades with his Queen to threaten mate on the eighth rank. To avoid this mate Black moves his Rook to KN1 and is answered by a smothered mate. Black could have avoided the mate by surrendering his Queen, but many players prefer being mated to trying to struggle on a Queen behind.

1. ________ ________
2. ________ ________
3. ________ mate

DIAGRAM 304

White Mates in Two Moves

ANALYSIS

The Black Queen in this position is overburdened. It prevents two mates at once—by Strangely, the defense against one mate will permit the other. What move will take the Black Queen away from its protection of White's KB7 and still leave the Black King hemmed in by its own pieces?

1. ________ ________
2. ________ mate

The six positions that follow illustrate mates following a double check. They are easy to solve if you remember the key advantage of the double check—that it forces your opponent's King to move. The mates to follow then leap into your mind, for double checks often permit mates with which you are already familiar.

DIAGRAM 305

MUNCK — STRAUSS

Germany, 1914

White Mates in Three Moves

ANALYSIS

A double check can involve a rank as well as a file. The winning continuation here requires understanding of mate with a Rook and a Knight. Your first move is a sacrifice that forces Black to open his second rank. Then a move by the White Knight results in a double check that forces the Black King to a square where it is mated by Rook and Knight.

1. ________ ________
2. ________ ________
3. ________ **mate**

DIAGRAM 306

MICHELSON — AMATEUR

Brussels, 1912

White Mates in Three Moves

ANALYSIS

This is a typical position, following as it does a Queen check at R5 and the capture of a KNP that has interposed. Black then attacked the White Queen with his Knight. White, with both Queen and Knight attacked, wins with a double check that forces the Black King to a square where mate will follow. The White Pawn at Q4 plays a critical role in the final position.

1. ________ ________
2. ________ ________
3. ________ **mate**

DIAGRAM 307

KATALIMOV — MIKHIN
Soviet Union, 1976

White Mates in Three Moves

ANALYSIS

This is another mate by a Rook and a Knight, made possible by a Queen sacrifice. Suppose the Black King were at its Q1. How could a double check then force mate? What can be done about Black's hope to escape to his K2? See that and the correct moves force themselves upon you.

1. ________ ________
2. ________ ________
3. ________ **mate**

DIAGRAM 308

Black Mates in Five Moves

ANALYSIS

A discovered check takes Black into the Ercole del Rio position with a smothered mate to follow. Once learned, the attack moves like clockwork. On what square will the Knight mate? How?

1. .... ________
2. ________ ________
3. ________ ________
4. ________ ________
4. ________ ________
5. ________ ________ **mate**

DIAGRAM 309

White Mates in Four Moves

ANALYSIS

This is another smothered mate, ready as soon as the long diagonal can be cleared for the combined action of Queen and Knight. What move does that before Black can carry out one of his own mate threats?

1. ________ ________
2. ________ ________
3. ________ ________
4. ________ **mate**

DIAGRAM 310

FALKBEER — SIMPSON

London, 1860

White Mates in Three Moves

ANALYSIS

No, this is not a smothered mate. And if you cannot see how a well-placed sacrifice leads to a double check and mate, then it would be best for you to go back to the beginning of this chapter and start again!

1. ________ ________
2. ________ ________
3. ________ **mate**

REMEMBER!

1. Double checks leading to mate usually occur on an open file following a sacrifice that forces the enemy King to the square where the double check is possible. But do not sacrifice just for the joy of

administering a double check. Make certain the mate can be forced!

2. Smothered mates are most common when the enemy King is in the corner of the board and, perhaps with a Queen sacrifice as in the Ercole del Rio position, you can check and mate with a Knight when the King is surrounded by its own pieces.

CHAPTER 17

Queen Sacrifices Leading to Checkmate

Let's assume you have been committing the checkmate ideas in the first sixteen chapters of this book to memory. Are you therefore ready to recognize and utilize all the opportunities to checkmate that may occur in your future play? After all, you have examined so many positions in which other players did find mates. You are beginning to understand what they did, and in similar positions you too may may make the brilliant moves that change an advantage into an attack and that attack into a checkmate. Yet you may not be ready to become that ideal player who somehow always knows what moves will lead to victory. Understanding specific mating attacks cannot win unless you also have an approach to chess analysis that leads you from the possible attack to the final mate.

There are some practical steps —call them a method of thinking —that should be followed as your game develops. Let's list them with what can at this point only be a preliminary explanation.

1. *Recognizing the possibility for a standard mate.*

You must know the standard mates presented in previous chapters so well that the one that may be possible in a given position simply leaps into your mind. This calls for the study and restudy of the positions we have been analyzing. Know them! Overlearn them! You cannot use them unless they are recognized automatically and have become part of your total chess thinking.

2. *Understanding barriers to possible standard mates.*

Suppose that a standard mate may be possible in a given position. Perhaps a Rook threatens mate on the eighth rank. Perhaps a Long Diagonal mate is waiting to be forced. But in most situations there will be a barrier to achieving that mate. A Pawn or piece may be in the way; a rank, file, or diagonal may have to be opened; a defender may have to be removed. Your goal then becomes the removal of that barrier. With the standard mate as your final aim, you then concentrate on removing whatever impedes it. This becomes your target.

3. *Accepting material gain when a mate cannot be forced.*

Do not forget that each of your moves is answered by a move by your opponent. You may have an overpowering attack that should lead to checkmate. But your opponent can often avoid that mate by surrendering material—anything from a Pawn to a Queen. Learn to accept such material. Your goal then changes from the drive for an immediate mate to the winning of a game through exchanges or the search for a new mating attack that utilizes your material advantage. In the end a checkmate will be possible anyway.

4. *Understanding the reasons for sacrifices during mating attacks.*

Much has been written about the nature of sacrifices in chess, and each writer has developed his own nomenclature intended to describe or classify sacrifices. In this book, with its emphasis on the practical achievement of given mates, our approach has been functional—that is, the search for the *reason* for a sacrifice. The sacrifices we have examined have served one or more of four chief functions:

a. *opening a line* (rank, file, or diagonal) *for a mate*
b. *opening the enemy King position.*
c. *removing a defender*
d. *gaining time* to move one or more pieces to the square(s) where they are needed to achieve mate.

Except in these positions where an opponent is helpless against the series of moves that result in checkmate, it is necessary to make forcing moves—checks and sacrifices—that change enemy weaknesses into checkmates. This chapter differs from those that have preceded it, for its purpose is to search for the *reasons* for a specific type of sacrifice. Its analysis of positions, therefore, will first set forth the goal a given Queen sacrifice should attain. It will then illustrate how that goal was achieved. Finally, it will where possible show what can happen when the opponent proves ready to surrender material to avoid the mate. Organized thinking about checkmate patterns is only about two hundred years old. But from its beginning it has searched for answers every chessplayer should know. The Queen sacrifice—hardest of all for an opponent to answer—is an ideal introduction to the key questions and their answers.

Sire de Légal Opens the Door

The Café de la Régence in Paris, gone today but a world-famous chess center for more than two hundred years, was long the only place in France where one could be certain to see chess masters at play every day. Paris, always the center of French intellectual life, had several cafes—really restaurants—where gentlemen and the nobility would gather to talk, play cards, and perhaps enjoy chess. In the mid-1700s M. de Kermur, Sire de Légal, made the Café de la Régence his second home. Légal was one of the first chess players to record his games. The games have little to recommend them, for Légal, champion of the club formed at the cafe, was so much better than the gentlemen who dared to challenge him that he won most games quickly. But he did teach them and the rest of the world some basic lessons about the opening. Develop your pieces; do not waste time on senseless Pawn moves; be ready to attack as soon as your pieces have been placed on good squares; do not be afraid to sacrifice if checkmate can result. The Légal Mate, really an opening trap, was first recorded about 1750. It is a perfect example of the speed with which poor play can be punished, and was the first of several Queen sacrifices in the opening to make the rounds of chess practice and play all over Europe.

	White	**Black**
	LEGAL	MONSIEUR X
1.	**P—K4**	**P—K4**
2.	**N—KB3**	**P—Q3**
3.	**B—B4**	**B—N5**
4.	**N—B3**	**P—KN3?**

DIAGRAM 311

Strangely, Black is already lost, his inferior opening play having invited a Queen sacrifice. Wasting time on Pawn moves in the opening often permits an opponent to attack and win material or mate before many moves have been made!

5. **N × P!**

The exclamation point may not be deserved in the 1970s, but in 1750 most players were just beginning to realize the many ways in which mate could be forced. If Black now plays 5. . . . . P × N he remains a Pawn behind after 6. Q × B. It would then have been White's task to make that Pawn advantage the basis of a win later on. But gentlemen did not refuse challenges in eighteenth-century France, and Black took the Queen instead of submitting to the loss of a Pawn.

5.	**B × Q??**
6. **B × Pch**	**K—K2**
7. **N—Q5 mate**	

Sire de Légal had opened the door to a flood of opening traps —moves which win material or mate when an opponent grabs at some offered Pawn or piece. Petroff, some thirty years after Légal had died, suggested another Queen sacrifice in the opening he had invented, mating in a somewhat different way on the eighth move.

PETROFF DEFENSE

1. **P—K4**	**P—K4**
2. **N—KB3**	**N—KB3**
3. **N × P**	**N—B3**
4. **N × N**	**QP × N**
5. **P—Q3**	**B—QB4**
6. **B—N5?**	

Black had given up a Pawn for superior development. Now White plays an inferior move that returns it.

DIAGRAM 312

6.	**N × P!**

This Queen sacrifice is even stronger than Légal's. It leads to mate or the win of White's Queen. It permits us to emphasize the question that should be answered about all sacrifices other than those that force a move by the enemy King. *What happens if the sacrifice is refused?* In this case if White plays 7. P × N Black wins a Queen by 7. . . . . B × Pch and on 8. K × B, Q × Q. White is also lost on 8. K—K2, B—N5ch; 9. K × B, Q ×Q. Mate in two follows White's acceptance of the sacrifice.

7. **B × Q**	**B × Pch**
8. **K—K2**	**B—N5 mate**

Note also that (from Diagram 312) 6. . . . . N × P; 7. B—K3, B × B; 8. P × B, Q—R5ch; 9. P—N3, N × NP wins easily.

These two examples of Queen sacrifices in the opening (and you can find dozens more in books on opening traps) can introduce the methods of anlysis needed to evaluate any sacrifice. They can be summarized through the answers to four questions.

1. *What mate position do I hope to achieve?*

   In other words, can you visualize the pieces on the squares they will occupy when your opponent is mated?

2. *What defenders must I remove to obtain that position?*

   The most common reason to sacrifice is to remove a defender, a key aspect of destroying the barriers to your desired mate.

3. *How does the sacrifice help change the position so that the mate can be achieved?*

   Remember the several key reasons for a sacrifice—to open a line, to open the enemy King position, to remove a defender, to gain time for moves by other pieces.

4. *What advantage will I have if my sacrifice is refused?*

   Many an attack has failed because a player did not realize one of his moves was not forcing. That is, his opponent was able to refuse the sacrifice and make an attacking move of his own instead. A sacrifice is called *sound* if it gains material or achieves a better position even if it is refused. It is sound if it leaves you with an advantage even though your planned mate does not occur.

The positions analyzed in this chapter will illustrate the answers to such questions as they apply to Queen sacrifices that led to mate or to some significant advantage when the sacrifice was refused. Our analysis will include two approaches, the continuation when the sacrifice is accepted and the alternatives when it is refused. As you will see, not all "mating attacks" lead to checkmate.

DIAGRAM 313

LUNDVALL — SCHAUWECKER
Switzerland, 1975

Black Mates in Three Moves

(A Queen sacrifice to open a line)

ANALYSIS

Goal: mate by two Rooks.

Barrier: White's KNP.

Mate should be possible if the KR file can be opened with a check. This would occur only if the White King were on that file. Then Black could play . . . . P × P discovering a check by his Rook. A Queen sacrifice is the only way to force White's King to its KR file.

a. 1. . . . . **Q—R7ch!**
2. **K × Q** _______
3. _______ _______ **mate**

b. But how does Black win if White refuses the Queen sacrifice?

1. . . . . **Q—R7ch!**
2. **K—B1** _______ **mate**

DIAGRAM 314

JENS — MEES
Holland, 1975

White Mates in Five Moves

(A Queen sacrifice to open a King position)

ANALYSIS

Goal: mate by Rooks and Bishops.

Barrier: Black's KNP.

This time the Black King lacks defenders and mate by the Rook aided by other pieces would be possible if the Pawn at Black's KN2 were gone. Method: open the Black King position, force the King to the KR file, and mate it at its KR5. A sacrifice is needed, then, to open the Black King position. It cannot be refused. A King hunt then follows.

1. **Q × Pch** **K × Q**
2. ________ ________
3. ________ ________
4. ________ ________
5. ________ **mate**

DIAGRAM 315

MANDOLFI — KOLISCH

Paris, 1858

Black Mated in Four Moves

(A Queen sacrifice to gain time for moves by another piece)

ANALYSIS

Goal: mate after . . . . N—K7.

Barrier: three moves needed to bring the Knight from KB3 to K7.

The White King lacks escape squares and would be mated if Black could bring a second Knight to bear on his K7 square. How can the Knight get there? Its path is K5—N6—K7!

a. 1. . . . . **N—K5**
2. **B × Q** **N—N6!**

For White cannot take the Knight without permitting Black to mate at once after 3. P × N, N—K7 dbl ch and mate! Meanwhile, 3. . . . . R—R8 mate is also threatened!

3. **N—B6 dis ch**

Now how does Black achieve his mate?

3. . . . . ________
4. ________ ________ **mate**

b. How would Black have won in this variation after White refuses the Queen sacrifice?

1. . . . . **N—K5**
2. **P × N** **Q × B**
3. **P × P** **Q—N6!**

With the threat of mate at the square ________.

c. And, to complete the analysis, how does Black then win after:

4. **N × BP dis ch** **K—B1**
5. **N × R** ________
6. ________ ________ **mate**

DIAGRAM 316

ALEKHINE — NESTOR
Exhibition, 1938

How does White Force a Quick Win?

(A Queen sacrifice to remove a defender)

ANALYSIS

Goal: to remove the Black Rook.

Barrier: the Black Queen can defend the Black Rook.

The Black King lacks escape squares and would be mated by a Rook or Queen that controlled White's eighth rank. White threatens such a mate at once.

a. 1. **R—B8**
How does White now mate in two if Black plays 1. . . . . Q × QP?

2. ________ ________
3. ________ **mate**

b. So Black must play 1. . . . . R × R. Now 2. P × R(=Q)ch, Q × Q leaves Black ahead. But White has a move that removes the defender, the Black Queen!

(From Diagram 316)

1. **R—B8** **R × R**
2. **Q—K7!**

Now the win is simple. On 2. . . . . Q × Q; 3. P × R(=Q)ch, Q interposes; 4. Q × Q mate. And on 2. . . . . Q—QB3; 3. P—Q8(=Q)ch, R × Q; 4. Q × Rch, Q—K1; 5. Q × Q mate.

But what happens on 1. R—B8, R × R; 2. Q—K7, R—KN1, refusing the sacrifice?

3. ________, with a winning advantage.

DIAGRAM 317

BREYER — ENGLUND
Scheveningen, 1913

White Mates in Two Moves

(A Queen sacrifice to remove a defender)

ANALYSIS

Goal: mate on the eighth rank.

Barrier: the Black Queen prevents R—Q8 mate.

White sees that placing a Queen or Rook on the eighth rank will be mate. Suppose the Black Queen defended its Q1 square from its K2 instead of its QB2. Why would it then be unable to capture a Rook at its Q1? If you see that, then a Queen sacrifice means mate in two.

a. 1. ________ ________
2. ________ **mate**

b. But suppose Black tries to avoid the mate by refusing the Queen. He would still be mated on the second move after:

1. ________ ________
2. ________ **mate**

DIAGRAM 318

KOTOV — BONDAREVSKY

Soviet Union, 1957

Black Mates in Four Moves

(A Queen sacrifice to remove a defender and to gain time for an attacking move)

ANALYSIS

Goal: to mate the White King at its Q3.

Barrier: White's bishop at Q4 and his Knight at K5 must be removed.

Try to visualize the possible mate. The White King can be forced to its Q3, where its escape is blocked by its Queen and Pawns and the power of Black's Knight at K5. What will be needed to mate it when it already lacks escape squares? Answer: a check by Black's Knight now at Q2. Where can that Knight check? Answer: at K4 or B4. Problem: the White Bishop at its Q4 is a defender against such a check. Solution: remove that defender!

1. .... **Q—B7ch**
2. **K—Q3** **Q × Bch**
3. **K × Q**

a. How does Black now mate in two more moves?

3. .... ______
4. ______ ______ **mate**

b. Suggest a move that would have prevented the mate if Black had played:

1. .... **Q—B7ch**
2. **K—Q3** **B—B4**

(Threatening 3. . . . . Q × B mate or 3. . . . . N × Nch; 4. B × N, Q—K6 mate, or on 3. B × Q, N × N mate)

3. ______ prevents the mate

DIAGRAM 319

ALEKHINE — AMATEUR

Blindfold Exhibition, 1942

White Mates in Three Moves

(A Queen sacrifice to open a line)

ANALYSIS

Goal: mate by Rook and Bishop or Rook and Knight.

Barrier: the Black KRP must be removed.

This time the Queen sacrifice is the means of opening a file. The position cries out for an Anastasia Mate—a Rook check on the KR file while the Knight at K7 cuts off escape squares. Note the Bishop at White's QB4. It can aid in a second kind of mate, for if both the diagonal to KN8 and the KR file were open, a Rook check on the file would be mate even if White's N at K7 were gone. That means the White Knight at K7 is available for sacrifice. What move rips the Black Pawns away?

1. **Q—N6!**

A new threat exists—Q × NP mate! If Black plays 1. . . . . RP × Q, then 2. R—R3 mate.

a. 1. .... **BP × Q**

How does White now open the Rook file and mate?

2. ______ ______
3. ______ **mate**

b. How would White have still mated on his third move if Black had refused the Queen sacrifice and played:

1. Q—N6 R—N1
2. ________ ________
3. ________ mate

DIAGRAM 320

CAPABLANCA — FONAROFF
New York, 1918

White Mates in Six Moves or Wins Black's Bishop

(A Queen sacrifice to win material by threat of mate)

ANALYSIS

Goal: to mate on the eighth rank or win a piece.

Barrier: the eighth rank is protected by a Queen and occupied by a Rook.

Not all attempts to mate succeed. Sometimes your opponent can prevent the mate by a ruinous loss of material. This position will demonstrate one way of turning a mate threat into a material advantage. White has two problems to solve.

a. Get the Queen away from its Q1.

1. N—R6ch K—R1
2. Q × B! Q × Q

b. Make the Black Rook leave its rank.

3. N × Pch Resigns

On 3. . . . . K—N1; 4. N × Q White is a Knight and two Pawns ahead and wins easily. But what is the mate after 3. . . . . R × N?

4. ________ ________
5. ________ ________
6. ________ mate

Horatio Alger at the Chessboard

Some stories never die; there is always a new generation of listeners to enjoy them. Horatio Alger proved this with a succession of tales that were largely variations on the same theme. A young person surprises the successful world about him by pulling off some magnificent coup that brings him fame and fortune. The chess world has such stories too. Edward Lasker, a young man in his twenties and a budding German chess master, came to London in 1912. He visited the city's leading chess club and was able to try his skill against England's leading player, Sir George Thomas. It was a casual game, but the young Lasker was able to announce mate in eight—one of the best-known examples of a King hunt in chess literature. It began with a Queen sacrifice followed by a double check that drove Sir George's King forward. A series of checks followed until the Englishman's King had move from its first rank to its eighth—where it was mated by a quiet discovered check. This was not a tournament game, but it still helped make Lasker's reputation secure. He had given the world a model of mating technique. Diagram 321 gives the position at the point where Lasker announced his mate.

DIAGRAM 321
(A Queen sacrifice to open a King position)

ANALYSIS

The position cries out for a sacrifice to bring the Black King into the open. Once Lasker saw that the King could not then return to its first rank, he was able to see his way clear to the mate.

1.	**Q × Pch!**	**K × Q**
2.	**N × B dbl ch**	**K—R3**

On 2. . . . . K—R1; 3. N—N6 mate by two Knights!

3.	**N(K5)—N4ch**	**K—N4**
4.	**P—R4ch**	**K—B5**
5.	**P—N3ch**	**K—B6**

Every Black move has been forced. Now White has a mate in three, based on forcing Black's King to its KN8.

DIAGRAM 322
White Mates in Three Moves

6. ________ ________
7. ________ ________
8. ________ **mate**

There you have it. We've examined positions illustrating the four chief reasons for sacrificing material—the Queen in this chapter. We've also seen that a sacrifice is "sound" when it leads to mate or, when it is refused, to some definite advantage in material or position. Our analysis in this chapter has been deeper than in the earlier ones, and it should have prepared you for the thinking needed to find the wins in the six positions that follow. We'll spell out the goals; you'll have to see the barriers and how to overcome them yourself.

DIAGRAM 323

SHAMKOVICH — ERVIN

California, 1975

White Mates in Three Moves

ANALYSIS

Goal: to drive the King into the open.

Do you recognize the possibility of mate with Rook and Knight in this position? Assume the Rook file is open and the Black King at its KN2. Where should the White Rook and Knight then be to force mate?

1. ________ ________
2. ________ ________
3. ________ **mate**

DIAGRAM 324

WATERMAN — FELL

Australia, 1975

White Mated in Three Moves

ANALYSIS

Goal: to gain time for a mating attack.

The Légal Mate turns up in many forms. In this case White threatened it and Black permitted it.

a. 1. **N—K5** **B × Q??**
2. ________ ________
3. ________ **mate**

b. What simple reply would have left Black with a good game after 1. N—K5, P × N; 2. Q × B?

2. .... ________

DIAGRAM 325

HULT — COLLETT
Stockholm, 1946

White Mates in Three Moves

ANALYSIS

Goal: to open a line for a mate.

With the Knight at KB6 and a Rook ready to check and mate, all White needs is an open KR file. He offers his Queen to get that line.

1. Q—N5! R—N1

On 1. . . . . P × Q; 2. R—R3 mate. Although he refused this Queen sacrifice, Black still had to answer the threat of 2. Q × NP mate. He couldn't try 1. . . . . P—N3 because of 2. Q × RP mate. Now an Arab Mate is forced—as soon as the KN file is pried open.

2. ________ ________
3. ________ **mate**

DIAGRAM 326

SPIELMANN — L'HERMITE
Germany, 1927

White Mates in Five Moves

ANALYSIS

Goal: to open a line for a mate.

White has four pieces bearing on a Black King that is trapped in the corner by its own pieces. The King position must be opened, for a mate on the eighth rank can be forced!

1. Q × RP!

With the immediate threat of 2. Q × P mate. Black cannot refuse the sacrifice. On 1. . . . . N × B; 2. Q—R7ch, K—B1; 3. Q—R8 mate. And if 1. . . . . P—B3; 2. Q—R7ch, K—B2; 3. B—N6ch, K—B1; 4. Q—R8 mate. And on 1. Q × RP, P—B3; 2. Q—R7ch, K—B1; 3. Q—R8ch, K—B2; 4. P—N6 mate.

1. . . . . P × Q
2. P × P dis ch K—B1

Now 3. P—R7 gets another Queen, but the Black King might escape after 3. . . . . Q—B4; 4. P—R8(=Q)ch, K—K2. So a Rook sacrifice is needed to keep Black's King trapped.

3. ________ ________
4. ________ ________
5. ________ **mate**

DIAGRAM 327
WOSTYN — FREDRICKSEN
Sweden, 1973

Black Mates in Four Moves or Wins a Bishop and Three Pawns

ANALYSIS

Goals: to open a line and remove a defender.

Black sees a possible mate on the eighth rank if he can force White's Rook to leave that rank. A Queen sacrifice does the job, leading to mate or an advantage in material.

a. 1. . . . . **Q × Pch!**
2. **R × Q**

Accepting the sacrifice in this way permits Black to mate in four more moves—with a Rook on the eighth rank!

2. . . . . **R—Q8ch**
3. ________ ________
4. ________ ________
5. ________ ________ **mate**

b. Alternately, White can avoid the mate—but at too great a cost.

1. . . . . **Q × Pch!**
2. **K × Q** **B × Pch**
3. ________ ________
4. ________ ________
5. ________ ________

and Black has won a Bishop and three Pawns.

DIAGRAM 328
PANFILOV — NOVOCENIN
Soviet Union, 1975

White Mates in Four Moves

ANALYSIS

A sacrifice can have several goals at the same time!

Goals: to remove a defender; to open a King position; to open lines.

Note that Black has made a second Queen. He now threatens mate in three with 1. . . . . Q—N8ch; 2. Q × Q, Q × Qch; 3. K moves, Q—N4 mate. But it is White's move, and he has prepared a mate with his own Rook and Bishop. It requires R × BPch, now prevented by the Pawn defender at Black's KN2. Mate will be forced once that Pawn is gone.

1. **Q—R6ch!** **P × Q**
2. **R × Pch**

Black has two replies to this check, each permitting White to mate.

a. 2. . . . . **K—R4**
3. ________ **mate**

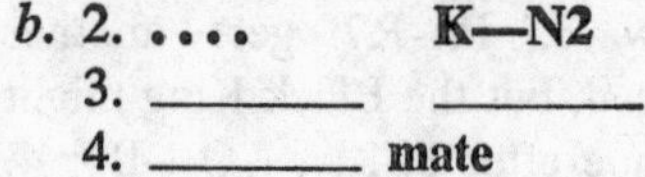

b. 2. . . . . **K—N2**
3. ________ ________
4. ________ **mate**

Remember:

1. A Queen sacrifice is the most dramatic way to open a line, remove a defender, open the enemy King position or change a strong position into a standard mating attack.
2. Always evaluate the position when a Queen sacrifice is refused as well as planning your attack if it is accepted.
3. Follow the method of analysis suggested in this chapter. How do you want to change the position to make your attack possible? What barriers to the attack must be removed? How? The Queen sacrifice is often the key to changing a positional advantage into a checkmate.

CHAPTER 18

Rook Sacrifices Leading to Mate

A Musical Chess Tale

Chess has long fascinated artists and musicians. François André Philidor, a leading French operatic composer, was also a famous chess master who wrote the first modern chess book in 1749—*Analysis of Chess*. Marcel Duchamp, a pioneer of modern art, startled the world in the 1920s with his announced abandonment of art for chess. He spent most of the next forty years proving his right to be known as a chess master. Perhaps the most unusual mixture of chess and the arts appeared in a family of brilliant Swiss musicians—the Johners. Hans Johner, leading artist of the Zurich Tonhalle Orchestra for forty-two years, was Swiss champion eleven times. His older brother Paul, also a musician, was occasionally active and successful in international tournaments. And the four younger brothers, all musicians, were also talented chess players. Each brother married a woman of a different nationality, upon which each learned six languages just to remain on speaking terms with the rest of the family! Since they couldn't always find suitable opponents when busy in the concert world, all six became prominent composers of chess problems.

Hans was the best player in the family, his entries into international tournaments adding many examples of what has been called the "Johner imagination" to chess literature. In a game played during a tournament in Frankfurt, Germany, in 1907, he offered two Rooks to his opponent, Abraham Speyer of Holland, later that country's national champion. Speyer simply missed the theme, threatening a mate himself only to be crushed by the sudden appearance of a Queen sacrifice that led to a familiar mate with Knight and Bishop!

DIAGRAM 329

Johner, playing Black, sacrificed a Rook.

1. .... **R × P!**
2. **B × R**

The Dutch master simply had no idea of what Johner was planning or he would not have accepted the Rook—which turns out to be a Greek gift from a Swiss musician!

2. .... **Q—B6**
3. **B × R**

Speyer saw a way to threaten mate in one. He must have reasoned that Johner would have to play 3. . . . . K × B to prevent 4. Q × P mate. But the Swiss master was ready with a surprise that showed his ability to make use of his thorough knowledge of the standard mates!

3. .... **Q—R8ch!**
4. **K × Q**

DIAGRAM 330

Black Mates in Two Moves

ANALYSIS

White's King is on the long diagonal controlled by Black's Bishop. All Black needs is the correct move with his Knight—a double check that leads to mate. Johner has given away two Rooks and a Queen to achieve a familiar mate!

1. .... ______
2. ______ ______ **mate**

Johner's win illustrates one of the four reasons for which Rooks can be sacrificed in the search for mate or the decisive win of material.

1. *To gain time for attacking moves by other pieces.*
2. *To open a line*
   a. needed by your own pieces—or
   b. needed to create a standard mate position.
3. *To remove a defender.*
4. *To open the enemy King position* by
   a. forcing the enemy King to a vulnerable square—or
   b. creating a hole that becomes pivotal in the attack that follows.

Johner's Rook sacrifice gained time for his 2. . . . . Q—B6. Had White then played 3. R—Q1 to make KB1 available as an escape square, Johner would have played 3. . . . . N × NP. This would have won by a Long Diagonal mate (. . . . Q—N7 mate) or a different kind of mate with Bishop and Knight (. . . . N—K7 mate).

As we have seen repeatedly, the key to any mate is that the enemy King be on a *vulnerable* square—one on which it lacks escape squares or defenders. Sometimes a Rook sacrifice that forces a King to such a square is simple and direct. The sacrifice is obvious. It cannot be refused. A simple standard mate follows at once. Here are two positions demanding such a Rook sacrifice. You can find the correct sequence of moves if you are familiar with standard mating patterns.

DIAGRAM 331

White Mates in Four Moves

ANALYSIS

White's goal: to mate by a supported Queen at KN7.

Barriers: Black's King must be forced to its KN1; the Rook defender at Black's KN3 must be removed.

Solution: Attack the King and then sacrifice a Rook at White's KR8!

1.	**Q × Pch**	**R—R3**
2.	________	________
3.	________	________
4.	________	**mate**

DIAGRAM 332

Black Mates in Two Moves

ANALYSIS

Black's goal: to mate by attack on two adjacent files.

Barrier: the White Pawn at KR2 must be removed to open the KR file.

Solution: Remove the White KRP!

1. .... ______
2. ______ ______ mate

Unfortunately for the player who likes wins to come with great ease, positions like those of Diagrams 331 and 332 are not very common. Deeper analysis is usually needed before you can decide a Rook sacrifice is justified. Consider the rest of this chapter an introduction to the kind of thinking that can first indicate that a Rook sacrifice should be considered and then shows whether or not it is correct.

Queen sacrifices are easier to understand than most other sacrifices because the Queen can control so many squares that it severely limits the possible responses to its invasion of a King position. This makes your decision-making easier, for there are few variations needing examination—often only one. But a Rook, a Knight, or a Bishop does not control so many squares. Your opponent can often refuse the sacrifice of one of these pieces, even though such refusal may mean the loss of a Pawn or a piece. If your opponent can ignore your sacrifice and make an attacking move instead, you may find yourself with a lost game. It is therefore necessary to have an immediate second threat attached to your sacrifice. With the Rook, for example:

1. You may be checking when your Rook reaches the square at which the sacrifice is offered. Such a check may mean the acceptance of the sacrifice is forced.
2. If the Rook offer is a clearance sacrifice (opening a line for the completion of one of the standard mates), your opponent must first prevent that mate. This means the Rook can attack or capture at will.

3. A Rook sacrifice can so clearly open up an enemy King position that the subsequent pileup of pieces to force a standard mate is obvious—especially when the King lacks defenders.

Rook sacrifices are most successful when one or more of these conditions exist:

1. You have an open file along which you can attack the King position with other pieces after the Rook has been sacrificed.
2. You threaten an immediate mate once the capture is accepted.
3. You win material or threaten mate even if the sacrifice is refused.
4. Your opponent's pieces are not available to help defend the King position.

How do you know that the time is ripe for a Rook sacrifice? The positions that follow illustrate such sacrifices in positions frequently met in chess practice. Note that the analysis takes a somewhat new course, examining alternate lines of play in greater detail to help you learn to consider possibilities when sacrifices are refused. Pay special attention to these "if" situations—the kinds of decisions you must face during any mating attack.

DIAGRAM 333

Black Sacrifices a Rook and Mates in Six Moves

ANALYSIS

What conditions should make you consider a Rook sacrifice? You have a Rook on a half-open file. The Rook can capture with check. The Black Queen, Rook, and Bishop then bear on an open King position. White's pieces are on the other side of the board.

Black's goal: to open the King position.

Barrier: the White KNP.

Solution:

1. .... R × Pch!

a. Suppose White refuses the sacrifice by playing 2. K—R1. Find the mate threat if Black then plays 2. . . . . Q—R2.

3. . . . . _______ mate

b. Now find the mate if White plays (from Diagram 333):

1.	R × Pch	
2. K—R1	Q—R2	
3. K × R	______	
4. ______	______	
5. ______	______	mate

Therefore, White must accept the sacrifice.

1. .... **R × Pch**
2. K × R **R—N1ch**

c. Find Black's mate in one after

3. K—B3 ______ mate

Then White must play

3. K—R1 **Q—K5ch**
4. P—B3 **Q—K7**

DIAGRAM 334

Black Forces Mate in Three Moves Beginning with Q–K7

d. Find the mate in two if White tries to prevent Black's threatened 5. . . . . Q—N7 mate by

5. R—N1 ______
6. ______ ______ mate

e. And show how mate in two is still forced after

5. **R—B2**
6. ______ ______ **mate**

DIAGRAM 335

Black Mates in Four Moves

ANALYSIS

Again the conditions are ripe for a Rook sacrifice. A Rook is on a half-open file. Its sacrifice threatens an immediate mate. Enemy pieces cannot defend the King position.

Black's goal: to open the King position.

Barrier: the White KRP.

Solution:

1. .... **R × P!**

Mate is threatened by 2. . . . . Q—R7. White can try three moves to prevent that mate—each of which fails.

a. 2. KR—K1 (to create an escape square)

2. .... ______ **mate**

b. 2. P × R (permitting a standard mate by a supported Queen)

2. .... ______

3. ______ ______

4. ______ ______ mate

c. 2. P—N3 (permitting mate at once)

2. .... ______ mate

DIAGRAM 336

White Mates in Three Moves

ANALYSIS

Once you see that the enemy King lacks escape squares, seek an effective check that may lead to mate. All White needs here is a move that opens the diagonal for a Queen check.

White's goal: a Queen check at KN6.

Barrier: a Black Pawn keeps the diagonal closed.

Solution: Because it is offered with check, a Rook sacrifice forces the opening of the diagonal—with mate to follow.

1. ______ ______

2. ______ ______

3. ______ mate

DIAGRAM 337

White Mates in Two Moves

ANALYSIS

This is a Rook sacrifice to open a line for a simple mate with Queen and Bishop. If the Rook were not on the board, mate in one would follow.

White's goal: to gain time for Q × P mate.

Barrier: the White Rook blocks the diagonal.

Solution: Find a move with the Rook that does not permit Black to find time for a defensive move like .... P—B3 or .... P—KN3.

1. ______ ______

2. ______ mate

DIAGRAM 338

White Wins a Knight or Mates

ANALYSIS

One of the most common Rook sacrifices is the move R × N to open a Knight file when other pieces can then threaten a Long Diagonal mate or a mate by Queen and Rook on open files. R × N wins material more often than it forces mate.

White's goal: to open the KN file and the long diagonal.

Barrier: the Knight is protected; the White Pawn at Q4 blocks the diagonal.

Solution: Remove the Knight and sacrifice the Pawn.

1. **R × N!** **P × R**

Otherwise White can move the Rook away and remain a piece ahead.

2. **Q—N4ch** **K—R1**

And now White forces the mate.

3. **P—Q5** **Q × P(B7)**

Other Black moves do not prevent the mate.

4. **B × P mate**

Find the mate on 3. . . . . R—KN1

4. ________ ________
5. ________ **mate**

The move R × N in such positions can lead to a mating attack even when your opponent refuses the sacrifice and attempts a counterattack. Play through this analysis from Diagram 338:

1. R × N, KR—K1; 2. Q—N4, Q × BP; 3. QR—KB1, Q × B (Black has regained his piece but is now subject to a mating attack that includes another Rook sacrifice); 4. R × BP (threatening 5. Q × P mate), P—KN3; 6. R × RP! (for on 6. . . . . K × R; 7. R—B7ch, K—R1; 8. Q—R4ch, K—N1; 9. Q—R7 mate). Q—QB7; 7. Q—R4 and Black has no reply to the threat of 8. R—R8ch, K—N2; 9. Q—R7 mate. All Black could do in this line is to delay the mate a bit by giving up his Queen and Rook in a series of spite checks.

The rule to follow when R × N is possible is to make certain you can then bring two or more other pieces to bear on the opened King position when it lacks defenders. Queen and Rook or Queen and Bishop often suffice to then mate or gain material.

There we have it—Rook sacrifices that win material or lead to mate when they are accepted. The positions that follow are further illustrations of the five ideas we have examined.

1. The Rook sacrifice with check to open a King position.
2. The Rook sacrifice that introduces new mate threats.
3. The Rook sacrifice to open a line.
4. The Rook sacrifice to force a King to a vulnerable square.
5. The Rook sacrifice that wins material because accepting the sacrificed Rook permits mate.

DIAGRAM 339
ZAMBELLY — MAROCZY
Hungary, 1897
Black Mates in Five Moves

ANALYSIS

Black's goal: to force the White King to its fifth rank to permit attack by the Queen at KR6.

Barrier: White is a Rook and a Bishop ahead. Given time, the White pieces will go into action and end Black's attack.

Solution: Maroczy played

1.	....	**R—R4ch!**
2.	**K × R**	**Q—R6ch**
3.	**K—N5**	

And now Black mated in three more moves by forcing the White King to its K5 with a pair of Pawn checks. A Queen move then mated.

3.	....	______
4.	______	______
5.	______	______ **mate**

All made possible by a Rook sacrifice that gained time for the critical Queen check at R6!

DIAGRAM 340

KOLTANOWSKI — AMATEUR
Blindfold Exhibition, Dallas, 1941

White Mates in Three Moves

ANALYSIS

White's goal: to remove the Black KNP and thus threaten mate.

Barrier: a Rook defends the Pawn.

Solution: Offer a Rook sacrifice to threaten two mates at the same time.

1. **R × Pch!** **R × R**
2. **Q—R8 mate**

This was the actual finish of the game. It is mate in three after

1. **R × Pch!** **K—R2**
2. ________ ________
3. ________ **mate**

Note how the Rook sacrifice removed a defender (the Black Rook defended both KN3 and KR1) and, when refused, left the Black King vulnerable to mate by the Queen and Rook. Rook sacrifices often serve more than one purpose.

DIAGRAM 341

KAPLÁN — HEINRICH
New York, 1974

White Mates in Three Moves

ANALYSIS

White's goal: to open the diagonal for his Bishop while forcing the Black King to a square where it will have no escape squares.

Barrier: the White Rook is on the diagonal.

Solution: Julio Kaplán, one-time child prodigy, later World Junior Champion, and today an active International Master, knows how to take advantage of a mate opportunity. He forces the Black King to its KB1 with a double check, sacrifices his Knight, and mates with his Queen. All of which illustrates a Rook sacrifice to force a King to a vulnerable square.

1. ________ ________
2. ________ ________
3. ________ **mate**

DIAGRAM 342

SCHUMOV — JAENISCH
St. Petersburg, 1914

Black Mated in Five Moves

ANALYSIS

Black's goal: to open Black's King position for a mating attack based on control of the KN file.

Barrier: the White KNP

Solution: Open the file with a Rook sacrifice. First check the continuation if the sacrifice is accepted, as it was in the game.

1.	....	**R × Pch**
2.	**K × R**	**Q—N3ch**
3.	**K—R1**	**B—Q4ch**
4.	**P—B3**	

a. And mate follows quickly because the White Rook at KB1 cannot protect the KBP and still prevent mate at his KN1.

4.	....	______
5.	______	______ **mate**

b. Refusing the sacrifice also loses.

1.	....	**R × Pch**
2.	**K—R1**	**R × Pch**
3.	**K × R**	

For a mate in three follows

3.	K—N1	______
4.	______	______
5.	______	______ mate

c. Therefore, after 1. . . . . R × Pch; 2. K—R1, R × Pch; 3. K × R, Black plays

3.	....	**Q—R5ch**
4.	**K—N2**	**Q—R6ch**
5.	**K—N1**	

And mate in two follows.

5.	....	______
6.	______	______ **mate**

d. In this line, White can try 4. K—N1, when Black mates with 4. . . . . R—N1 ch, 5. B—N5, R × N mate.

DIAGRAM 343

SCHMID — ROSSOLIMO
Heidelberg, 1949

Black Sacrifices Two Rooks and Wins

ANALYSIS

Sometimes an opponent can ward off mate by giving up material. In this position the only defense to a mate leaves Black a Queen ahead—which means a mate will follow anyway in a few more moves.

Black's goal: to open the White King position to permit the long diagonal to be opened later.

Barrier: White's King is behind its Pawns, while the White Bishop prevents the advance of the Black KP necessary to open the diagonal.

Solution: Open the King position and the diagonal by two Rook sacrifices!

1. .... **R × Pch!**

a. Obviously White cannot refuse the sacrifice, for on

2. K—R1 _______ mate

2. **K × R** **R × Pch**

b. Now if White refuses the sacrifice he is mated in two moves.

3. K—N1 _______
4. _______ _______ mate

So he plays:

3. **B × R** **P—K6ch**

c. Find the mate in one if White plays

4. K—N1 (or K—R2) _______ mate

4. **R—Q5** **Q × Bch**
5. **K—R1** **Q × Rch**
6. **K—N2** **Q—B7ch**
7. **K—R1** **Q—B6ch**
8. **K—N1** **B × R**

And the threat of mate at KN7 or KN8 forces White to resign or give up his Queen.

d. Find the mate after

9. **Q × B** **Q × Q**
10. **K—R2** _______
11. _______ _______
12. _______ _______
13. _______ _______ **mate**

DIAGRAM 344

BEST — MUIR
Correspondence, 1975
Black Mated in Three Moves

ANALYSIS

Rook sacrifices are often the preludes to lethal discovered checks.

Black's goal: to open the White position for a series of checks.

Barrier: the White KRP and the White Rook preventing . . . . P—B7.

Solution: Sacrifice the Rook at R7!

1. . . . . R × Pch!

a. How does Black mate if White refuses the sacrifice?

2. K—N1 R—N1ch
3. K × R ________ mate
or
3. K—B1 ________ mate

b. Or White can try to prevent the mate by giving up material. 1. . . . . R × Pch!; 2. K—N1, R—N1ch; 3. B—N5, R × Bch; 4. Q × R, Q × Qch; 5. K × R, Q—R5ch; 6. K—N1, Q—N6ch; 7. K—B1. But what Black move now forces the win of a Rook a few moves later?

7. . . . . ________

c. So White had to take the Rook.

1. . . . . R × Pch
2. R × R P—B7ch
3. ________ ________ mate

DIAGRAM 345

TAUBENHAUS — JANOWSKI

Paris, 1903

White Mates in Four Moves

ANALYSIS

Again we have a Rook sacrifice to force a King to a vulnerable square. Note that there are no Black defenders near his King.

White's goal: to open the King position, gaining time for a Queen check.

Barrier: the Black KRP.

Solution: Capture the KRP with check.

1. R × Pch!

a. How does White mate in two moves if Black refuses the sacrifice?

1. . . . . K—N1
2. ________ ________
3. ________ mate

b. And how does White use his Queen and Rook to force mate in three more moves after Black accepts the sacrifice?

1. .... **K × R**
2. ________ ________
3. ________ ________
4. ________ **mate**

DIAGRAM 346

AMATEUR — JANOWSKI
France, 1921

Black Mates in Two Moves

ANALYSIS

Sometimes a mate awaits only the removal of a defender. If that can be done with a check, so that the opponent does not have time to bring up another defender, the mate is immediate.

Black's goal: mate by Q × RP.

Barrier: White's KNP defends the KRP.

Solution: Remove the defender!

1. .... ________
2. ________ ________ mate

Let's close our examination of the Rook sacrifice with a position in which the persistent offer of a Rook—refused again and again—finally led to a forced mate.

DIAGRAM 347

KOLTANOWSKI — DUNKELBAUM
Blindfold Exhibition, Antwerp, 1929

A Rook Sacrifice Forces Mate

ANALYSIS

White hopes to mate by driving the Black Queen away from the defense of its Knight. To do this he first sacrifices a Pawn and a Knight, and then makes the first of three offers of a Rook.

White's goal: to remove a defender.

Barrier: the Black Queen defends the Black Knight.

Solution: Drive the Queen away!

1. R—Q1!

a. Begin by examining 1. . . . . Q—K1. How does White then mate in two more moves?

1. R—Q1 Q—K1
2. ________ ________
3. ________ mate

So Black decides he must remove the White Knight, thereby freeing Black's KB2 as an escape square.

1. R—Q1 Q × Pch
2. K—B1! Q × N

The White King moved to B1 to avoid later checks by the Black Queen. Now White makes his first Rook offer.

3. R—Q5

b. Find White's mate in two after

3. R—Q5 Q × R
4. ________ ________
5. ________ mate

Since the Rook cannot be captured, the Black Queen seeks a square from which it can still defend the Knight.

3. . . . . Q—R5
4. R—R5!

The same mate threat (as in *b.*) exists if the Rook is captured now.

4. . . . . Q—B3
5. R—KB5! Resigns

For there are no longer any squares on which the Queen can protect the Knight.

c. Find the mate after

5. . . . . Q × R
6. ________ ________
7. ________ ________
8. ________ **mate**

REMEMBER!

1. Consider a Rook sacrifice when you have open lines and your opponents's King lacks defenders.
2. Rook sacrifices succeed when you can bring two or more pieces—especially a Queen and a second piece—to bear on the opened King position.
3. Your opponent may decline the sacrifice. Make certain you have a mate threat or a forced gain of material, should that occur.
4. Since a Rook sacrifice should be the preliminary to the forcing of one of the standard mates, make certain you see that mate as a possibility before you consider the Rook sacrifice.

CHAPTER 19

Sacrificing the Bishop to Mate or Win Material

Too Bad He Lived in India!

About 1820 a brilliant young player named John Cochrane caused a sensation in the chess clubs that made London a national chess center. There were then only a few dozen European players we would today call masters, and Cochrane seemed ready to become the equal of any of them. But young men need careers, and Cochrane found his in India. He spent his entire adult life in Madras except for the "vacations home" he received every few years. Cochrane would spend part of each leave in London's chess clubs, where his reputation brought two results. Amateurs clamored for a game with him; England's best players stayed away—some say because they feared the results of play against John Cochrane. Only a handful of Cochrane's games against the leading players of his time remain in chess literature. It's a pity, for we can never know how well he might have done had he had a concentrated chess career. Yet he still left a number of brilliant reminders of his dangerous attacking skill against opponents of all kinds.

Cochrane's readiness to sacrifice is illustrated by a game played during his 1842 visit to London. He chose an opening in which a Knight is sacrificed to gain time for quick development. He then gave up a Rook for further development. After only eleven moves he was able to sacrifice a Bishop in a position where a later Queen sacrifice forced mate.

White	Black
COCHRANE	AMATEUR

MUZIO GAMBIT

1. P—K4	P—K4
2. P—KB4	P × P

The King's Gambit Accepted, an opening most dangerous for Black when, as in this game, he neglects his development in order to hold on to his extra Pawn.

3. N—KB3	P—KN4
4. B—B4	P—N5
5. O—O	P × N
6. Q × P	

DIAGRAM 348

This is the Muzio Gambit. White has sufficient compensation for his Knight with three pieces bearing on the Black King position. The opening is rarely played today because Black can obtain an equal game by refusing to accept the gambit—instead playing such moves as 2. . . . . B—B4, 2. . . . . P—Q4 or 2. . . . . P—Q3.

6.	Q—K2
7. P—Q4	B—N2
8. B × P!	

Cochrane's goal is development. This move served to prepare the later attack along the KB file.

8.	B × Pch
9. K—R1	B × P?

Black's play provides a case study of how to lose by neglecting your development.

10. N—B3	B × R
11. N—Q5	Q—B4

DIAGRAM 349

White Mated in Four Moves

ANALYSIS

With five pieces in play and a Black King position without defenders, all White needs is a move that clears the KB file. He offers his Bishop as a clearance sacrifice. Black accepts it as he has everything else.

1. **B—Q6!** **Q × B**
2. **Q × Pch** **K—Q1**
3. ________ ________
4. ________ **mate**

Black could have prolonged the game with 1. . . . . N—KR3, but would then have been lost after 2. B × Q, B—K4 (to protect his QBP); 3. Q—R5! White will win another piece or mate.

The earlier chapters have included many Bishop sacrifices as parts of mating attacks. But there are three special kinds of common positions in which the Bishop sacrifice alone makes the mate possible.

1. As in Cochrane's game, a Bishop sacrifice can *clear a line* for a mating attack. Such a sacrifice wins when the mate threat can be forestalled only by leaving an attacked piece where it is. Thus, if the Bishop sacrifice involves a capture or an attack on another piece, and that piece cannot be moved without mate following, then the Bishop has won or will win material.
2. Bishop sacrifices can win by *forcing the enemy King to a vulnerable square* . . . one on which it can be attacked with gain of time. If the King lacks defenders and the Bishop sacrifice leads to the entry of two or more of your pieces—usually a Queen and a piece that supports it on the square where it will mate—then the sacrifice is called "correct." Of course, if defenders prevent the entry of your pieces, then the sacrifice is incorrect. Thus, check to make certain you *can* invade before attempting the sacrifice.
3. Bishop sacrifices, like any other sacrifices, can *open the enemy King position.* But such an opening must be followed by the entry of other pieces to force mate whether or not the Bishop is captured. Often such a sacrifice wins material when the opponent finds it necessary to sacrifice in return to prevent mate.

The positions analyzed in this chapter illustrate these three kinds of Bishop sacrifice, in each case leading to mate or the gain of material. Let's begin with examples of clearance sacrifices of the Bishop to help make a mate possible.

DIAGRAM 350

White Mates in Two or Wins Black's Queen

ANALYSIS

White's real threat: if the White Bishop were not on the board, Q—KB8 would be mate. The diagonal to KB8 must be cleared. What Bishop move opens that line and simultaneously attacks and wins Black's Queen?

a. If the sacrifice is accepted:

1. ________ ________
2. ________ **mate**

b. If the sacrifice is declined:

1. ________ **K—N1**
2. ________, **winning the Queen.**

DIAGRAM 351

KOLTANOWSKI — AMATEUR

Blindfold Exhibition, Switzerland, 1937

White Mates in Six or Wins Black's Queen

ANALYSIS

White's real threat: if the KR file can be opened, White can force mate by a supported Queen along that file. Fortunately for White, the Black Queen has no escape squares against an attack by the White Bishop.

1. **B—N5!**

a. If the sacrifice is declined: on any move other than 1. .... P × B, White will capture the Black Queen.

b. If the sacrifice is accepted:

1. .... **P × B**
2. **P × P** **Q—K2**
3. ________ ________
4. ________ ________
5. ________ ________
6. ________ **mate**

DIAGRAM 352

GRECO'S POSITION, 1619
White Mates in Six Moves

ANALYSIS

This position was published in Greco's *Treatise on Chess,* one of the first chess books. After questionable opening play by Black (1. P—K4, P—K3; 2. P—Q4, N—KB3; 3. B—Q3, N—B3; 4. N—KB3, B—K2; 5. P—KR4, 0—0; 6. P—K5, N—Q4) we reach Diagram 352. The sacrifice demonstrated by Greco has since been one of the most used standard attacks in chess. A Bishop is sacrificed to open a King position lacking defenders when two or more pieces can then be brought into action against that King.

1. B × Pch K × B

Otherwise Black is a Pawn behind with an opened King position.

2. N—N5ch B × N
3. P × B dis ch K—N3
4. Q—R5ch K—B4
5. Q—R3ch K—N3
6. Q—R7 mate

It's important to understand that alternate Black moves would also be followed by mate or some significant gain of material. In each of the following lines, begin by setting up the position of Diagram 352.

a. **1. B × Pch K × B**
2. N—N5ch K—N1
3. Q—R5!

Threatening 4. Q—R7 mate.

3. .... B × N
4. P × B P—B3 or B4
5. ________ ________
6. ________ **mate**

b. **1. B × Pch K × B**
2. N—N5ch K—N3

Now White either mates in two or wins Black's Queen.

3. ________ ________
4. ________ **mate**

or

3. ________ ________
4. ________, **winning the Queen.**

c. **1. B × Pch K × B**
2. N—N5ch B × N

3. **P × B dis ch** **K—N3**
4. **Q—R5ch** **K—B4**
5. **Q—R3ch** **K—K5**
6. ________ **mate**

d. 1. **B × Pch** **K × B**
2. **N—N5ch** **B × N**
3. **P × B dis ch** **K—N1**
4. ________ ________
5. ________ ________
6. ________ ________
7. ________ **mate**

e. And finally, consider:

1. **B × Pch** **K—R1**
2. **N—N5** **B × N**
3. **P × B** **R—K1**
4. **Q—R5** **N × QP**
5. **B—N6 dis ch** **K—N1**
6. **Q—R8 mate**

Now that you have played through the sequence of moves in the Greco position repeatedly, return to Diagram 352. Without looking at the analysis, make certain you understand how to mate or win material in each line that can follow the acceptance of the Bishop sacrifice. Then try the next three positions, each a different example of the mating attack illustrated by Greco so long ago.

DIAGRAM 353

YATES — MARIN
Olympiad, Hamburg, 1930
White Mates or Wins Black's Queen

ANALYSIS

White's goal: mate by a supported Queen at KR7.

Method: sacrifice the Bishop; check with the Knight and then bring in your Queen to force mate.

Reminder: first decide what you can do if the sacrifice is declined.

a. 1. **B × Pch** **K—R1**
2. **Q—R5** **P—KN3**
3. ________ ________
4. ________ **mate**

b. 1. **B × Pch** **K—R1**
2. **Q—R5** **R—Q1**
3. ________ ________
4. ________ ________
5. ________ **mate**

And if the sacrifice is accepted:

c. 1. **B × Pch** **K × B**
2. **N—N5ch** **K—N1**
3. ________ ________
4. ________ **mate**

(Of course, if Black plays Q × N along the way to prevent the mate, then White has won a Queen for two pieces—a decisive gain of material.)

d. Find the win after:

1. **B × Pch** **K × B**
2. **N—N5ch** **K—N3**
3. **N × KP dis ch** **K—R3**
4. ________ ________
5. ________ ________
6. ________ **mate**

The success of the Bishop sacrifice we have been examining (B × Pch) depends on the moves that follow it—usually a Knight check at N5 and then either a Queen check or a move that prepares a Queen check. We can therefore reach a conclusion about this type of sacrifice: do not play such a move unless:

— it forces the enemy King to a vulnerable square to which you can then quickly bring the pieces you need to mate it.
— the opponent lacks defenders of his King position.

If your opponent has time to bring a piece to the defense of his King position, your sacrifice may be in vain. That piece can defend against your threatened mate. Diagram 354 shows the type of position in which B × Pch will not win—unless the potential defender can be forced out of the way. This is done by attacking it or forcing it to a square where it is needed to defend a piece. Once it does that, the mate threat comes alive. And if it tries to remain in position to prevent the mate, then you may win important material even though you do not mate.

DIAGRAM 354
White's Bishop Sacrifice Mates or Wins a Queen

ANALYSIS

White's goal: mate after the moves B × Pch, N—N5ch and the entry of the Queen.

Barrier: the Black Queen can prevent the mate after 1. B × P, K × B; 2. N—N5ch, K—N1; 3. Q—R5, Q—R3.

Solution: sacrifice the second Bishop to get the Black Queen away from the Black King position.

1. **B × Pch** **K × B**

If Black declines the sacrifice by 1. B × Pch, K—R1; 2. B—Q3 or N1 leaves White ready to prepare a new attack against the now open Black King position.

2. **N—N5ch** **K—N1**

a. Remember that White wins the Black Queen after 2. . . . . K—R3 by:

3. ________ ________
4. ________

b. And White mates or wins a Queen after 2. . . . . K—N3 by:

3. ________ ________
4. ________ ________
5. ________ mate

or

3. ________ ________
4. ________ ________
5. ________, winning the Queen.

3. **B × P!** **Q × B**

(And on 3. . . . . Q—Q2; 4. B × R, Q × B; 5. Q—R5 Black must give up his Queen with 5. . . . . Q × N to prevent mate.)

Alternately, 3. . . . . Q—R3; 4. B × R leaves White a piece ahead with an easily won game.

c. 4. **Q—R5** **R—Q1**

5. ________ ________
6. ________ **mate**

DIAGRAM 355

KOLTANOWSKI — O'HANLON

Match, Dublin, 1937

The Bishop Sacrifice Forces the Win

ANALYSIS

White's goal: to open the Black King position—which lacks defenders.

a. White has a winning attack if the sacrifice is accepted:

1. **B × Pch** **K × B**
2. **Q—R5ch** **K—N1**
3. **Q × Rch** **K—R2**
4. ________

and the entry of the White Rook will prove decisive.

b. Therefore, in the game Black tried to defend by declining the sacrifice:

1.	B × Pch	K—B1
2.	B—N6	R—Q1
3.	Q—R5	K—K2
4.	N—Q4	B—Q2
5.	R × N	P × R
6.	B × P	Resigns

Suppose Black had played Q—B1 or the Queen to another safe square. White would then mate in three by:

6. .... Q—B1
7. ________ ________
8. ________ ________
9. ________ mate

A Bishop sacrifice, like any other sacrifice, can be the critical preliminary to a mating attack. The sacrifice is most successful when it is made with check and the enemy King can escape that check only by moving to a square where mate awaits it. Diagram 356 illustrates the kind of position in which a Bishop sacrifice is indeed the only way to continue the game!

DIAGRAM 356
Black Mates in Four Moves

ANALYSIS

Black's Bishop is attacked. Should it move to the "safe" square Q4, White would mate at once by Q—B8. Fortunately, the White King is in the open and a Bishop sacrifice permits Black to mate.

1. .... **B × Pch!**

a. Now there is a mate in two if White accepts the sacrifice:

2. P × B ________
3. ________ ________ mate

b. And a mate in three if White declines the sacrifice:

2. K—K1 ________
3. ________ ________
4. ________ ________ mate

DIAGRAM 357

Black Mates in Four Moves

ANALYSIS

Black's goal: to mate with Queen and Knights.

Barrier: the Queen's entry into the White position is blocked by the Black Bishop.

Solution: sacrifice the Bishop!

1. .... **B × Pch**
2. N × B

a. Find the immediate mate on:

2. K—R1 ______ mate

2. .... **Q—K5ch**

And mate in two more moves must follow:

b. 3. **K—B1** ______ **mate**

or

3. **K—R1** ______ **mate**

And therefore:

3. ______ ______
4. ______ ______ **mate**

There you have it. Bishop sacrifices can lead to mate in the three ways we have demonstrated—by clearing lines for already prepared mating attacks, by forcing a King to a vulnerable square, or by opening a King position. A Bishop sacrifice that has two of these results is of course more dangerous. But it is necessary to remember that the Bishop sacrifice does not always force a mate. You always then need two or more pieces ready to bear on an exposed King. You may have to be satisfied with some gain of material instead of the mate. In all cases, you must see several moves ahead—sometimes all of a forced sequence of six or seven moves.

The six positions that follow review the chief types of Bishop sacrifices. They tend to be longer than most of the attacks previously examined in this book because they usually begin with a Bishop sacrifice and then one or two basic follow-up moves. But because such attacks follow similar sequences of moves, you should soon find it possible to discover a winning attack in a given position of one of these types. Remember that your mating attack can often be stopped by some ruinous countersacrifice of material. In modern play attacks based on a Bishop sacrifice may threaten mates, but more often lead to the win of material instead.

DIAGRAM 358

Black Mates in Four Moves

ANALYSIS

Black's goal: to mate with his Queen at KR6.

Barrier: getting the White KRP out of the way; moving the Queen to KR6 without giving White time to bring his Queen to the defense of his King position.

Solution: use a Bishop sacrifice to gain time to get the Queen to KR6; use a Knight sacrifice to open the KR file.

1. .... B—N7ch!

White's moves are forced in this neat example of a Bishop sacrifice to gain time for a mating attack to succeed.

2. R × N Q—B8ch
3. ______ ______
4. ______ ______ mate

DIAGRAM 359

KOLTANOWSKI — AMATEUR
Blindfold Exhibition, Los Angeles, 1949

White Mated in Four Moves

ANALYSIS

White's goal: mate by a supported Queen.

Barrier: the Black Pawns prevent immediate entry into the King position.

Solution: offer a Bishop to open the King position while threatening mate.

1. **B—KB6!**

a. If Black declines the sacrifice by a move like 1. . . . . P—QB3, White forces mate by:

2. Q—N5 ______
3. ______ ______
4. ______ mate

b. Another mate threat follows

1. .... P—KR3
2. Q—N6 ______
3. ______ ______
4. ______ mate

c. The game concluded with:

1.	....	P × B
2.	**B—K4!**	________
3.	________	________
4.	________	**mate**

Becoming a World Class Grandmaster

The entire world now uses a rating system for chess players first developed by Professor Arpad Elo of the United States. Players gain points by wins and lose them by losses, with more gained by a win or draw against a better-ranked player and more lost by a draw or loss against a lower-ranked player. Moving up with what is usually a 200-point spread for each level, you become a beginner, Class D, C, B, A, and finally an Expert or (in Europe) a candidate-master. This level—from 2000 to 2199 points—is the mark of the ability to beat almost any other player in a given game, but not every time! Once the player has overcome whatever weaknesses cause him to falter against better players, he may move up above 2200, when he receives the designation of master. He may then be ready for international play, gained by invitation or by success in open tournaments.

The International Chess Federation accepts master ratings from national chess federations. Someone doing well in an international tournament approved by the FIDE may achieve a "norm" set for that event. These norms are set for the title of International Master and for Grandmaster. For example, in a given tournament of sixteen players 9–6 may be the IM norm and 11–4 the GM norm. Achieving the IM norm in two events results in the lifetime IM title. An IM who achieves the GM norm in two rated events gains the GM title. In 1976 there were about 110 GMs in the world. Of these a dozen held ratings of 2600 points or more. They are often called World Class Grandmasters. Only Robert J. Fischer of the United States and Anatoly Karpov of the Soviet Union have held ratings above 2700 points—each while he was the world champion.

The Czech star Vlastimil Hort, quiet, learned, rarely making mistakes, and capable of sudden attacks that overwhelm his opponents, is one of the most successful World Class Grandmasters. Like any player of his class, he is a potential world champion. His 1974 game against the Bulgarian grandmaster Radulov demonstrated his ability to perceive unusual mates—in this case the end product of a Bishop sacrifice.

DIAGRAM 360

HORT — RADULOV
Romania, 1974

White Mated in Six Moves

ANALYSIS

Do you recognize the setting for a Bishop sacrifice? There are no Black defenders near his King; White's Queen and Knight can attack at once after the Bishop sacrifice is accepted.

1. **B × Pch! K × B**
2. **N—N5ch K—N3**

a. Of course, on 2. . . . . K—N1 White threatens mate after 2. ________

3. **Q—R3**

b. And now the threat is:

4. ________ mate

3. **. . . . N(B3) × P**
4. **Q—R7ch K—B3**

c. And mate in two moves followed!

5. ________ ________
6. ________ **mate**

DIAGRAM 361

ENDT — BRENNEISEN
West Germany, 1975

White Forced Mate in Seven Moves

ANALYSIS

The ideal position again! B × Pch will be followed by N—N5ch; there are no Black defenders near the King position.

Barrier: the need to keep attacking so that Black lacks time to create escape squares or bring up defenders.

1. **B × Pch K × B**
2. **N—N5ch K—N3**

a. On 2. . . . . K—R3; 3. B—B1, with the threat of ________

3. **P—R5ch K × N**

b. 3. . . . . K—B4 permits mate in two by:

4. ________ ________
5. ________ mate

4. **B—B1ch K—B3**
5. **Q—N4! Resigns**

c. The threat is 6. Q—N5 mate. Find the mate in two after:

5. . . . . P—N3.
6. ________ ________
7. ________ mate

DIAGRAM 362

URZICA — HONFI
Hungary, 1975

White Mated in Three Moves

ANALYSIS

Remember that Bishop sacrifices are useful in removing defenders. In this case White wants to play the killing Q—Q5ch. How does a Bishop sacrifice close the diagonal to Black's Queen?

1. B—K4ch! P × B
2. ________ ________
3. ________ mate

Of course, Black could have delayed the mate by giving up his Queen.

DIAGRAM 363

ILYIN-GENEVSKY — KUBBEL
Leningrad, 1925

Black's Bishop Sacrifice Mates or Wins White's Queen

ANALYSIS

Black's threat: to mate by . . . . Q × P if he can block White's defense of KN2; alternately, to mate by . . . . R × N if the White Rook can be induced to leave the first rank.

Barrier: White's Queen, Rook and Knight (K1) are active defenders.

Solution: a Bishop sacrifice can block White's lines of communication!

1. . . . . B—B7

a. This cuts the Queen off from KN2. If White makes a move like

2. P—N6 Q × Q
3. R × Q ________ mate

b. And if 2. Q × B, Black simply wins that Queen! For:

2. Q × B ______
3. ______ ______ mate

c. And finally: (from Diagram 363)

1. .... **B—B7**
2. **P—N3** ______
3. ______ ______
4. ______ ______ **mate**

REMEMBER!

1. The Bishop sacrifice B × Pch as examined in this chapter succeeds only when your opponent's King position lacks defenders and you can follow the sacrifice with the immediate invasion of your Queen and a supporting piece.
2. Otherwise, Bishop sacrifices fulfill the normal goals of blocking or opening a line, opening a King position, removing a defender, or forcing a King to a vulnerable square.
3. In evaluating a Bishop sacrifice, always consider the continuation if the sacrifice is declined. Unless the sacrifice is also a check, your opponent may have time to bring up a defender or make an attacking move himself.

CHAPTER 20

Sacrificing the Knight to Mate or Win Material

William Lombardy—Technician Extraordinary

Why are some grandmasters better than others? Each of them had to master the same openings, middle game ideas, and ending technique. All study regularly and keep up with new theoretical developments. But each grandmaster seems to have some special characteristic that makes his play unique. Some are innovators, ever seeking and finding new ideas in the opening. Others are tacticians who complicate games and then find brilliancies where others might play safely. A few are technicians—a term meriting definition. Such players seek a small advantage early in the game, usually based on their great knowledge of recent play in the openings they prefer. They then nurse that advantage with care, making exchanges or using it as the basis for an attack. Their great knowledge of endings helps them reach simplified positions with few pieces remaining on the board where their tiny advantage (an open file; an advanced Pawn; a hole in the enemy King position) is magnified and becomes the basis for a win. The strongest grandmasters are always technicians, their success also involving a touch of the innovator or tactician as well.

Father William Lombardy, the only clergyman in modern chess history to be a grandmaster, is an unusually gifted technician. He left the church in 1976 to devote himself fully to chess. Born in New York City in 1937, World Junior Champion in 1957, a grandmaster since 1960, he is a prolific chess writer and teacher. His play demonstrates the ability to launch attacks ten moves or more deep beginning with a sacrifice and successful because he has seen some final position in which mate or the gain of material is assured. He showed the value of studying the openings in his victory against the Argentine grandmaster Miguel Quinteros during the Manila Tournament of 1973. Lombardy had studied this new line of play reached after thirteen moves of a Sicilian Defense. But he still spent more than an hour before playing the Knight sacrifice that began a winning attack. The sacrifice opened a key diagonal whose control later helped win the game. His victory also gave him the $1,000 Brilliancy Prize, until then the largest such award ever offered in a chess tournament!

DIAGRAM 364

LOMBARDY — QUINTEROS

Manila, 1973

A Knight Sacrifice Leads to Victory!

ANALYSIS

White's development is better than Black's. He has greater control of the center of the board. The Black King, still on its K1, cannot be brought to safety by castling, for both Black Rooks have moved. A winning attack is possible if Black can be prevented from completing his development.

1. **N × KP!**

The Knight is sacrificed to open a line—the diagonal KR5—K8. Black accepts the sacrifice because otherwise he has lost a Pawn and his King position has been weakened.

1.	**P × N**
2. **Q—N6ch**	**K—Q1**

Better than 2. . . . . K—B1; 3. P—K5, P × P; 4. P—B5 with the later forced opening of the King-side and mate threats at White's KB7.

3. **P—K5**	**P × P**
4. **P—B5!**	

The point of White's play is that, beginning with the Knight sacrifice, he has been opening lines around the Black King position.

4.	**P × P**
5. **B × N**	**B × B**
6. **N—Q5**	

This is the technician at work. Compare this position with that of Diagram 364:

1. Black's King is on an open file dominated by a White Rook.
2. All five White pieces are active while Black is still undeveloped.
3. Black will be able to make only defensive moves as White attacks.

6. .... **Q—B3**

For White was threatening to win a Bishop by 7. N × B.

7. **R × P!**

Again threatening to win the Bishop, for Black cannot recapture at his KB3 with a Pawn because White's Queen would then take the Black Rook at KN1.

7. .... **R—B1**
8. **B—N4**

DIAGRAM 365

Now all five White pieces have joined in the attack. Can you see White's reply to 8. . . . . B—N4ch?

a. 8. .... B—N4ch
9. ________ winning the Bishop

8. .... **R—N3**
9. **R × B** **P × R**

b. If:

9. .... R × R
10 Q × NP R—K3
11. B—R5! threatening (on 11. . . . . R—K1)
12. ________ ________
13. ________ mate

10. **Q—N7** **R—N2**

c. Rather than play on in a hopeless position, Black permits the mate. Had he tried 10. . . . . R—K1; 11. B—R5, R—K3; 12. Q—N8ch, N—B1; 13. Q × Nch, K—Q2; 14. N—N4 dis ch, Q—Q3; 15. R × Qch, R (K3) × R; 16. B—N4ch, K—B2; 17. Q × B mate (epaulettes!) is one of several ways for White to win. After 10. . . . . R—N2 White won at once by:

11. ________ **mate**

This was a "grand" game in more ways than one!

Knight sacrifices are often part of sustained attacks like Lombardy's in his brilliancy prize game. More often, they are the critical element in a simple forced mate. Like other sacrifices, they serve the purpose of:

— opening a line neded by another piece;
— opening the enemy King position;
— forcing the enemy King to a vulnerable square;
— removing a defender;
— threatening mate whether or not the sacrifice is accepted.

You may never have the opportunity or the ability to produce as farsighted an attack as the one you have just examined. But any future efforts in such a direction must begin with an understanding of the kinds of position in which Knight sacrifices work. They don't always lead to mate, but a sound Knight sacrifice will either make a mate easier to achieve or win important material. We'll look at seven simpler positions and then at another one where it becomes clear that Knight sacrifices are an integral part of some attacks built on the possibility of the standard mates you already know.

DIAGRAM 366

Black Mates in Two Moves

ANALYSIS

Black's goal: to open the KR file.

Why the Knight sacrifice wins: the White King has no escape squares; a Black Rook is ready to force mate if the KR file can be opened.

Solution: sacrifice the Knight to force the opening of the KR file!

1. . . . . ______
2. ______ ______ **mate**

DIAGRAM 367

KOLTANOWSKI — AMATEUR
Blindfold Exhibition, Omaha, 1940
White Mates in Three Moves

ANALYSIS

This position is similar to the previous one, except that first the Black King must be driven to its R1.

White's goal: to open the KR file.

Why the Knight sacrifice wins: the White King will have no escape squares and no interpositions against a check.

Solution: use a Bishop check to force the Black King to R1; then sacrifice the Knight to open the KR file. Here again we see that a Knight sacrifice with check must be accepted when a King lacks escape squares!

1. B × Pch K—R1

On 1. . . . . R—B2; 2. B × Rch wins the Rook.

2. ________ ________
3. ________ **mate**

DIAGRAM 368

KOLTANOWSKI — CAVERLY
California, 1948
White Mated in Six Moves

ANALYSIS

White's goal: to force the Black King to a vulnerable square.

Why the Knight sacrifice wins: the Knight must be offered twice, and must be taken the second time. The White Pawn on B6 controls Black's KN2 and makes the attack along the open KR file fatal.

1. N—N5ch K—R1

a. Find White's threat after:

1. . . . . P × N
2. Q × P KR—Q1
3. P × P dbl ch K—N1
4. ________ ________
5. ________ mate

2. N—B7ch Q × N

b. For on:

2. . . . . K—R2
3. ________ mate

3. **Q × RPch** **Q—R2**
4. **P × P** **R—B2**

c. And mate follows by:

5. ________ ________
6. ________ mate

DIAGRAM 369

Black Mates in Two Moves

ANALYSIS

The existence of two or more mate threats can permit a Knight sacrifice that removes a defender and makes one of the threats become a mate.

Black's goal: to mate by Q—K6 if the White Knight no longer defends that square; to mate by Q—Q5 if the White Pawn on its QB3 no longer defends that square.

Why the Knight sacrifice wins: White's King lacks escape squares; therefore, White must capture Black's Knight if it checks.

1. .... ________
2. ________ ________ mate

DIAGRAM 370

PLATZ — GOLDMAN

New York, 1948

A Knight Sacrifice Forces Black to Resign at Once!

ANALYSIS

Already two Pawns ahead, White clinches the win with a move that threatens two mates. His victory can be delayed but not avoided!

White's goal: to threaten mates at KR7 and KB8 at the same time.

1. **N—N5** **Resigns**

a. White mates at once after:

1. .... B × N
2. ________ mate

or

1. .... R × R
2. ________ mate

b. In an effort to prevent the mate Black might play 1. . . . . P—N3. Find the mate after:

2. Q × P   R—B2
3. Q—R6ch   K—N1
4. ________   ________
5. ________ mate

DIAGRAM 371

A Knight Sacrifice Wins!

ANALYSIS

This attack is common when Black has not yet castled and White has occupied a half-open file with a Queen supported by a Rook.

White's goal: to open the Black position, with a mating attack to follow.

Why the Knight sacrifice wins: Black must take the Knight or lose a Rook.

1. **N × P!**   **K × N**
2. **Q × Pch**   **K—B1**

a. Find the mate after:

2. . . . .   K—K1
3. ________   ________
4. ________ mate

b. The winning move after 2. . . . . K—B1 is:

3. ________, forcing Black to lose his Queen.

DIAGRAM 372

White Wins by Forcing Black to Accept a Knight Sacrifice!

ANALYSIS

Always search for a possible standard mate. The trapped Black King in this position cries out for a mate by Knight and Bishop.

White's goal: to place a Knight at KB6 without fearing its capture.

Barrier: the Black Queen defends that critical square.

Solution: get two Knights to bear on KB6!

1. **N × N!** **B × Q**

a. Find the mate if Black plays:

1. .... P × N
2. ________ ________
3. ________ mate

b. And now White has a forced mate after 2. N—Q7!

2. **N—Q7** **Q × N**
3. ________ **mate**

or

2. **N—Q7** any move other than **Q × N**
3. ________ ________
4. ________ **mate**

DIAGRAM 373
ALEKHINE — FREEMAN
Blindfold Exhibition, New York, 1924

White Mates in Four Moves

ANALYSIS

The recognition of a standard mate permits a Knight sacrifice that leads to mate. The Black King has no escape squares against a Rook or Queen on its first rank.

White's goal: to clear lines for a mate on the eighth rank.

Barrier: the Black Queen must be forced away from its defense of its Q1.

1. **R—K8ch** **N—B1**
2. **N—R6ch** **Q × N**

For 2. .... K—R1; 3. R × N mate. Now White mates in two more moves—for he has cleared the lines for an unanswerable attack on the eighth rank.

3. ________ ________
4. ________ **mate**

The Most Exciting Annual Chess Event

There are many interesting chess events each year, among them the various national championships, world-famous open tournaments like the United States Open, famous club championships, and traditional tournaments at places like Hastings, England, and the Canary Islands. But by far the most exciting chess activity of them all takes place every spring in the Soviet Union. It is called the Spartakiad, a team competition that involves almost all the masters, grandmasters, and ambitious nonmasters in this most active of all chess communities. With Russian grandmasters about half the world's total, such an event is certain to produce games that go down in chess history.

A dozen or so teams enter a final series of matches. Each team (usually of twelve players) represents a city or region. It must contain two women, sometimes includes two juniors, rewards two or more upcoming candidate-masters, and of course features its IMs and GMs. In a country with millions of players entering tournaments each year, the Spartakiad is seen as the great test of ability for all but the established grandmasters. Do well in this competition and you are certain of national recognition, a higher rating, and perhaps the special aid of some great master as teacher and coach. Thus, the games on the lower boards are fierce struggles. In the Fourteenth Spartakiad in 1976 one such game showed how knowledge of standard mates helped a player produce a brilliancy which, even though it did not end in checkmate, still demonstrated how Knight sacrifices can open lines, maintain tension, and lead to final victory.

DIAGRAM 374

BEREZYOK — IJNIN

Bielorussia-Ukraine Match

1976 Spartakiad, Soviet Union

Knight Sacrifices to Open Lines

ANALYSIS

White has sacrificed a piece to open the Queen side and to make Black lose the time that would otherwise have enabled him to castle into relative safety. The Black King now has no escape squares. That means Black will have no time for developing moves if his King is attacked.

White's goal: to open the King file.

1. N—B7ch! Q × N

Black had no other move. The White Knight was sacrificed to pull the Black Queen away from its defense of its K3.

2. N × P! Q—K4

a. Mate by a supported Queen would have followed:

2. . . . . P × N
3. ________ ________
4. ________ mate

3. N—B7ch! Q × N

Again the only move. The sacrifice of the two Knights has opened the King file.

4. Q—K2ch N—K4

b. Mate by a Rook and a Bishop would have won if:

4. . . . . Q—K4
5. Q × Qch N × Q
6. ________ mate

5. Q × Nch B—K2

c. 5. . . . . Q × Q was impossible because of 6. ________ mate.

6. Q × Q B × Bch
7. K—N1 O—O

d. On 7. . . . . B—QR3 White mates in four by gaining control of the eighth rank.

8. ________ ________
9. ________ ________
10. ________ ________
11. ________ **mate**

8. Q × B, and Black soon resigned.

Knight sacrifices should be part of your play for the same reasons other sacrifices are part of your arsenal. They too can open lines, smash King positions, force a King to a vulnerable square, remove defenders, and be part of a double mate threat. You will find them when you analyze each position in search of one of the standard mates. Its ability to sacrifice itself with check makes a Knight sacrifice hard to ignore, as does its move, which permits it to attack two or more pieces at the same time. Finally, the Knight is an attacking piece against which interposing to block a check is impossible. The six positions that follow will give you opportunities first to make certain you see a way to threaten mate and then see a way to use the Knight as part of the attack leading to mate or some important gain of material.

DIAGRAM 375
Black Mates in Two Moves

ANALYSIS

This is a simple application of the basic rule: *always look for a standard mate!* That mate becomes obvious once you see that the Black Bishop and Rook can force mate if the Black Knight leaves N5.

Solution: Sacrifice the Knight to gain time for the mate!

1. .... ______
2. ______ ______ **mate**

DIAGRAM 377

White Sacrifices a Knight and Wins!

DIAGRAM 376

Black Mates in Three Moves

ANALYSIS

Black appears to be in trouble with two pieces under attack. But he can force a kind of epaulettes mate by driving the White King to its QB3. How? A Knight check begins the road to White's defeat!

1. .... ______
2. ______ ______
3. ______ ______ **mate**

ANALYSIS

The holes in the Black King position, the White Bishop at KR6, and the active Queen combine to make a mate by Queen and Bishop at KN7 a clear goal. How can it be achieved? Only by blocking the Black Queen's defense of its KB3. A Knight sacrifice, because it is a check, forces the win.

1. **N—K7ch!**

a. Find the win after:

1. **N—K7ch** **R × N**
2. ______ ______
3. ______ ______
4. ______ **mate**

b. And find the win after:

1. **N—K7ch** **Q × N**
2. **R × Q** **R × R**
3. ______ ______
4. ______ **mate**

c. The easiest win follows:

1. **N—K7ch** **K—R1**
2. ________ **mate**

DIAGRAM 378

ALEKHINE —VAN MIDENS
Exhibition, Holland, 1933

White Mated in Four Moves

ANALYSIS

The position is ripe for a mate by two Rooks on the open KR file. But White cannot hold the Pawn at KN6 that would make such a mate possible by locking in the Black King. Instead, he finds a Knight sacrifice that gives his Queen control of the long diagonal to Black's KN1. Black must then occupy the key escape square at his KB2, making the mate possible after all!

1. **N—K5** **P × N**

If Black declines the sacrifice White doubles Rooks on the KR file and mates by R—R8.

2. **QR—R1** **Q × P**
3. ________ ________
4. ________ ________
5. ________ **mate**

(In the game Black was mated in four moves because he did not interpose his Bishop to delay the mate.)

DIAGRAM 379

SIEGERS — AMILIBIA
Correspondence, 1973

Black Mates in Five Moves

ANALYSIS

White's King has no escape squares. It will be mated if the Q file can be opened for Black's Rook. Then mate by a supported Queen will follow.

Black's goal: to open the Queen file.

Barrier: a Bishop is in the Rook's way; a Knight blocks the Queen file; a White Pawn is on White's Q2.

Solution: two sacrifices do the job! They can be played in either order.

a. 1. .... _______
2. _______ _______
3. _______ _______
4. _______ _______
5. _______ _______ **mate**

b. Black also wins with 1. . . . . Q × NP; 2. R—K1, Q—B6ch; 3. R—K2, N—B5; but the mate takes more than five moves because White can now create an escape square by 4. _______.

DIAGRAM 380
HORT — RADULOV
Germany, 1974

White Mated in Three Moves

ANALYSIS

Think this through as Hort did.

1. Q—R7 mate is a clear goal.
2. The Black Knight at his KB3 defends the mating square.
3. The goal is first to remove that defender.
4. A Knight sacrifice will attack Black's Queen and hit at the defender.

1. **N—Q5!** **KP × N**
2. **B × N** **Q × B**
3. **Q—R7 mate**

a. Black could not have played:

1. N—Q5 N × N
2. _______ mate

b. And 1. . . . . Q—Q1 would lose by:

2. _______ _______
3. _______ mate

REMEMBER!

1. Knight sacrifices are often useful in helping force one of the standard mates. They can clear lines, open the enemy King position, force a King to a vulnerable square, and sometimes aid in threatening two mates at once.
2. When you use a Knight sacrifice to open an enemy position, be certain you have enough material bearing on that position to take immediate advantage of whatever weakness your sacrifice has created.
3. Especially in tense positions, a Knight sacrifice that does not have to be accepted can be a critical loss of time. Your

opponent can make an attacking move instead of accepting the sacrifice. Your reply to that attacking move may mean that your goal in making the sacrifice can no longer be achieved. Diagram 381 illustrates the kind of error awaiting you.

DIAGRAM 381
Why does the Knight Sacrifice 1. N × P Fail?

ANALYSIS

1. N × P fails and could even lead to a mate by Black. In playing 1. N × P White hoped for:

1. N × P	**P × N**
2. Q × B	**Q × Q**
3. R × Q, with a better game.	

Instead, Black wins by:

1. N × P?	**P—N4**
2. Q—R5	**P × N**

And now White has lost a piece, for he cannot play:

3. R × B?	**Q × R!**
4. R × Q	**R—N8ch**
5. Q—Q1	**R × Qch**
6. R—K1	**R × R mate**

As with all other sacrifices, always consider the key question: *What happens if my sacrifice is refused?*

CHAPTER 21

Understanding Pawn Promotion

Query: A Fish or a Comer?

It's always fun to talk chess with grandmasters, and to observe how neatly they categorize all possible opponents. Someone of the master's own strength is referred to as a "match" or a "problem." Someone the master feels he can beat most of the time is called a "pretty good player." Anyone who has been defeating other grandmasters is labeled a "comer." One of expert or weak master strength is dismissed as a "club player." And the rest of the chess world, in the words of one international master who was never so happy as when visiting chess clubs and playing at odds, fit into the categories of "woodpusher" (someone who doesn't know much chess theory), "fish" (falls for traps that anyone ought to recognize and avoid), and "potzer" (a fumbler to whom you can give odds of a Queen or a Rook and win brilliantly every time).

An outstanding characteristic of the improving player is his ability to use his Pawns wisely, placing them on squares where they become part of an over-all plan, exchanging them when an advantage can result, and above all shepherding them forward with the threat of promotion on the eighth rank. Pawn promotion is the most common goal of endgame play, and whatever advantage develops in the earlier parts of the game is often realized only when the promotion of a Pawn changes the balance of forces and aids in a mating attack.

It is not the function of this book to teach the complete details of endgame play, but bear in mind that most examples of

Pawn promotion do occur in the endgame. Such a promotion is often the decisive moment of a chess game, and it is important to realize what goals and understandings combine to make Pawn promotion an effective tool in your drive toward checkmate.

1. The promotion of a Pawn justifies sacrifices, and you may give away anything from a Pawn to a Queen or more to force the Pawn forward.
2. Queening a Pawn does not always mean you will then have a decisive material advantage. There are times when you Queen a Pawn and lose the new Queen at once—to draw an important defender out of position or to break up an enemy attack.
3. Sometimes Queening a Pawn does not serve to force a checkmate. Instead, it can leave you with a comfortable material advantage. At this point you must apply your knowledge of mating techniques to utilize that advantage and move toward the mate.
4. Pawn promotion is not necessarily to a Queen. The special characteristics of a position may demand a Rook, Knight, or Bishop instead.

To begin with, you must be certain of the technique of promoting a single Pawn to a Queen in the classical position illustrated by Diagram 382. Every player meets this type of position many times. If you understand the concept of "the opposition," and your Pawn is *not* a Rook Pawn, then you can promote the Pawn to a Queen and later use your King and Queen to force a mate on the edge of the board.

TERM TO KNOW

Opposition—Being able to place your King two squares away from your opponent's on the same rank, file, or diagonal. This forces his King to move back, or to the side, in either case taking him "out of opposition." You are said to "have the opposition" when you have achieved such a position and it is your opponent's turn to move.

DIAGRAM 382

White Takes the Opposition and Wins: If He Advances His Pawn At Once He Can Only Draw

ANALYSIS

No player can move beyond the lowest levels without mastering this position.

a. If White permits Black to take the opposition, a draw results.

1. P—N4?, K—N4; 2. K—N3, K—N3; 3. K—B4, K—B3; 4. P—N5ch, K—N3; 5. K—N4, K—N2; 6. K—B5, K—B2; 7. P—N6ch, K—N2; 8. K—N5, K—N1; 9. K—B6, K—B1; 10. P—N7ch, K—N1; 11. K—N6 *stalemate*

b. If White takes the opposition, he Queens his Pawn and wins.

1. K—N4!, K—B3; 2. K—R5, K—N2; 3. K—N5, K—B2; 4. K—R6, K—B3; 5. P—N4, K—B2; 6. P—N5, K—N1; 7. K—N6, K—B1; 8. K—R7, K—B2; 9. P—N6ch, K—B1; 10. P—N7ch, K—B2; 11. P—N8(=Q)ch and White soon mates by forcing Black's King to an edge of the board, bringing his King to opposition near it, and then mating with a supported Queen or by a Queen check when White's King is in opposition to the Black King.

The technique of Queening a Pawn is not essentially the goal of this chapter. It is rather a preliminary assumption. Given an extra Pawn and the opposition, you should win. Given two extra Pawns, the win becomes easier. And given a larger advantage (a piece or more with Pawns still on the board) you should also win easily unless the position contains some special continuation for your opponent.

DIAGRAM 383

NEUSTADT — KOSTRO
Soviet Union, 1970

White Establishes Two Connected Passed Pawns

ANALYSIS

White will win if he can establish two connected passed Pawns, for their advance will give him a Queen or will win a piece.

1. **P—N4!**	**P × P**
2. **P—B5**	**Resigns**

Black cannot prevent the loss of a piece:

2. **. . . .**	**K—B2**
3. **P—B6**	**R—Q1**
4. **P—Q7**	**B × P**
5. **P—B7**	

winning the Rook or the Bishop. If Black tried:

4.	**P—Q7**	**K—K2**
5.	**P—B7**	**R × P**
6.	**P—B8(=Q)**	**R × R**
7.	**Q × RP**	

and White will win because his Queen can prevent any Black counterplay while he advances his QRP to the eighth rank for a second Queen.

DIAGRAM 384

White Queens a Pawn

ANALYSIS

Black's King is too far away from White's Queen side Pawns. How does White force one of them to the eighth rank? He must be ready to sacrifice two of his Pawns to get the third one through!

1.	**P—N5**	**K—B4**
2.	**P—B6**	**P × BP**

a. And White Queens at QR8 or QN8 by either P × RP or P—N6. Show why 3. P × BP is an error.

if 3. P × BP ________

b. White remains a Queen ahead after:

1.	**P—N5**	**P × P**
2.	**P—B6**	**P × P**
3.	**P—R6**	**P—N5**
4.	**P—R7**	**P—N6**
5.	________	________
6.	________	________
7.	________	

DIAGRAM 385

MIESES — JANOWSKI

Vienna, 1896

White Queens a Pawn and Wins

ANALYSIS

Giving up a Pawn or two to get a Pawn to the eighth rank can win. So can giving up a piece or more to promote a Pawn.

1.	**P—Q7**	**P × Nch**
2.	**K × P**	**R—Q7**
3.	**P—Q8(=Q)**	**Resigns**

A Queen against a Rook can win, especially when White can soon promote his QBP!

Had White not advanced from his Pawn and brought his Knight to safety:

1. **N—K5** **R × Pch**
2. **K—R3** **P—QR4!**

and Black threatens 3. . . . . R × Pch; 4. K—N3, R(N7)—N7 mate. White could have defended by a move like Q—N1, but why even consider such an inferior line when 1. P—Q7 is so clearly a win?

DIAGRAM 386

E. MEYER — FINKELSTEIN
New York, 1965

Black Promotes a Pawn and Wins

ANALYSIS

This win against a "comer" who later became a leading American master was made possible by Black's advanced KRP, which now becomes a Queen. Giving up a Rook and receiving a Queen is a winning bargain!

1. . . . . ________
2. ________ ________
3. ________ ________
4. **Resigns**

for Black will now have a Queen against a Rook.

DIAGRAM 387

KERES — MECKING
San Antonio, 1972

White Moves and Black Resigns

ANALYSIS

Pawn protections also play a key role in some mating attacks. In this position Keres played 1. P—Q7 and Mecking resigned. Let's see why.

a. If Black takes the Pawn:

1. **P—Q7** **Q × P**
2. ________ wins a Rook!

b. If Black moves his Rook away:

1.	**P—Q7**	**R—R1**
2.	________	________
3.	________	________
4.	________	**mate**

DIAGRAM 388

IVKOV — LOMBARD
Yugoslavia, 1972

White Moves and Black Resigns

ANALYSIS

As a general rule, when there are both White and Black Pawns on both sides of the board, a Queen wins against a Rook. This means that promoting a Pawn can be far more important than keeping a Rook. A Yugoslav grandmaster demonstrates how it is done in this win against one of Switzerland's chess stars.

1.	**P—K6**	**Resigns**

a. White gains the advantage of a Queen against a Rook on:

1.	**P—K6**	**K × R**
2.	________	

b. And also promotes quickly on:

1.	**P—K6**	**P × P**
2.	________	

c. While Black loses if he too attempts to promote a Pawn:

1.	**P—K6**	**R × Pch**
2.	**K—N4**	**P—QR4**
3.	**P × P**	**P—R5**
4.	**P—B8(=Q)**	**P—R6**
5.	________	________
6.	________	**mate**

DIAGRAM 389

MEDINA — ENEVOLDSEN
Madrid, 1951

White Mates in Two Moves

ANALYSIS

The usual goal of Pawn promotion is to make a Queen. That Queen can sometimes play an immediate role in forcing checkmate. Note that Black's King lacks escape squares in this position. A check on the diagonal means mate.

1. ________ ________
2. ________ **mate**

DIAGRAM 390

LJUBOJEVICH — MILICHEVICH
Yugoslavia, 1974

White Moves and Black Resigns

ANALYSIS

A Queen is also far superior to two pieces when both players still have Pawns on both sides of the board. The Queen then uses its great mobility to pick off one or more Pawns. Then it helps one of its Pawns through to make a second Queen or win an enemy piece. The problem here is to find the one move that guarantees White will have and retain a Queen.

1. ________ ________
2. ________

and White has a Queen against a Knight and a Bishop, with the Black Queen-side Pawns an easy target.

DIAGRAM 391

RADULOV — ROSSOLIMO
Yugoslavia, 1972

White Promotes His KP or Wins a Rook

ANALYSIS

A passed Pawn supported by a Rook when no enemy piece is able to block its advance must reach the eighth rank. What temporary sacrifice won in this game? Remember that the advantage of a Rook in the ending is usually decisive.

1. ________ ________
2. ________

and White will be a Rook ahead. Always be ready to sacrifice to get a Pawn to the eighth rank.

DIAGRAM 392
LOBIGAS — MICHELI
Olympiad, 1972

White Moves and Black Resigns

ANALYSIS

The presence of a Pawn on the seventh rank invites considerations of whatever sacrifices are necessary to promote it to a Queen. White's goal in this position is to promote his KNP or mate if Black takes the Pawn. The key to the win is the fact that opening the KR file will permit that mate, and so will the opening of the KN file!

1. Q × RP! Resigns

a. Now White mates in two more moves on:

1.	K × P
2. ________	________
3. ________ mate	

b. And he mates in three more moves if Black accepts the sacrifice:

1.	P × Q
2. B—R7ch	K × B
3. ________	________
4. ________ mate	

c. Finally, if Black tries to defend with:

1.	R—KR5
2. Q × P	B—Q2
3. ________	________
4. ________ mate	

Other defenses are equally hopeless.

DIAGRAM 393
KLOVAN — DEMENTJEV
Soviet Union, 1972

A Double Queen Sacrifice Wins!

ANALYSIS

It is important to realize that a promoted Pawn can be sacrificed to remove a defender when a standard mate awaits completion. White's Queening square (Q8) is controlled by a Black Bishop. But that Bishop is overloaded, for it must also defend Black's KB1.

1. **B—Q6! Resigns**

a. If Black captures the Bishop:

1. .... **B × B**
2. ________ ________
3. ________ ________
4. ________ **mate**

b. If Black takes the White Queen:

1. .... **Q × Q**
2. **P—Q8(=Q)ch B × Q**
3. ________ **mate**

c. If Black creates an escape square:

1. .... **P—KR4**
2. **Q × Q** **B × Q**
3. ________

and White's Pawn will Queen—one of several possible winning continuations.

DIAGRAM 394

LEVENFISH — ALATORTSEV

Soviet Union, 1947

A Pawn Promotion to Open a Line

ANALYSIS

Gregory Levenfish, a world class grandmaster for more than thirty years, had sacrificed a piece to advance his Pawns. Now he promotes (and loses) his Pawn because he sees a Rook at K7 can force mate in a few more moves.

1. **P × B(=Q) R × Q**
2. **R—K7 Resigns**

a. If it were now White's move, what would be his mate in one?

3. ________ **mate**

b. White also mates after:

2. .... **P—N5**
3. **P × QNP** **P × P**
4. ________ ________
5. ________ **mate**

c. As well as after:

2. .... **P—Q5**
3. **P × QP** **K—Q4**
4. **Q—K5ch** **K—B5**
5. ________ ________
6. ________ **mate**

We have reviewed the chief uses of an advanced Pawn that can be promoted to a Queen:

1. To leave you with a material advantage,
2. To draw away a defender and then force a standard mate,
3. To clear a line or open a key square for a mating attack.

But there are times when promoting a Pawn to a Queen does not win. Sometimes you can promote a Pawn and still be mated by an opponent whose attack is not affected by your extra Queen. At other times, especially in the ending, the presence of a Queen can place your opponent in stalemate. Let's examine the kinds of position in which promotion to a piece other than a Queen is essential in saving or winning a game. Such positions can arise in the opening when your opponent plays poorly and permits the steady advance of a Pawn. Such things happened often a hundred years ago, when few players understood the theories of chess as well as even weak club players do today.

White	**Black**
AMATEUR	ALPHONSE GOETZ

Strassburg, 1880

1. **P—K4** **P—K4**
2. **P—KB4** **P × P**
3. **P—QN3?**

Of course, most players now know they must avoid moves that invite enemy pieces to attack and chase Kings so early in the game.

3. **. . . .** **Q—R5ch**
4. **P—N3** **P × P**
5. **P—KR3** **P—N7 dis ch**
6. **K—K2** **Q × Pch**
7. **K—B2**

DIAGRAM 395

Black Mates in One Move!

ANALYSIS

Normally a Pawn reaching the eighth rank is promoted to a Queen. But you are also permitted to take a Rook, Bishop, or Knight. Black would have an easy win on 7. . . . . P × R(=Q). But what piece at Black's KR8 makes it mate in one?

7. **. . . .** ________ **mate**

Unexpected promotions are rare in the opening, for few players permit themselves to be attacked as quickly as White was in Goetz's easy victory. But most players know a few opening traps in which an unexpected Pawn promotion leads to a win. Let's look at one in which promotion to a Knight (with check) gains time for a winning attack.

ALBIN COUNTER GAMBIT

1. **P—Q4** **P—Q4**
2. **P—QB4** **P—K4**

3. P × KP	**P—Q5**
4. P—K3?	**B—N5ch**
5. B—Q2	**P × P!**

White's best move is now 6. P × P, when his position remains full of holes. The trap that follows is much worse.

6. B × B?	**P × Pch**
7. K—K2	

Of course, 7. K × P, Q × Q is equivalent to resignation.

7.	**P × N(=N)ch**

DIAGRAM 396

The Knight check makes all the difference. On 7. . . . . P × N(=Q); 8. Q × Qch, K × Q; 9. R × Q White can hold the game. But instead he must reply to a check.

a. 8. R × N, B—N5ch wins the White Queen.

b. 8. K—K1, Q—R5ch; 9. K—Q2 leaves Black a piece ahead with such immediate attacking moves as 9. . . . . N—QB3; 10. . . . . B—N5 and 11. . . . . R—Q1 threatened. On 9. P—N3, Q—K5ch; 10. K—B2, Q × R. The attack wins for Black, and White never has the time to capture the Black Knight.

Always consider the possibility of promoting to a piece other than the Queen. Many important games were won by promotion to a minor piece, with the Knight the most dramatic.

DIAGRAM 397

UTUMEN — GAPRINDASHVILI

Soviet Union, 1971

Black Wins By Promoting to a Knight

ANALYSIS

The exchange of a Queen for two Rooks leaves Black a Knight ahead—enough to later force a win. Promotion to a Queen would have meant a draw.

1.	**Q—B7ch**
2. R × Q	**P × Rch**
3. K—N2	**P × R(=N)ch**
4. K—R3	**R—K2**

With Rook, Knight, and Bishop against a Queen, Black won in a few more moves.

Can you find White's draw by perpetual check after:

3. . . . . P × R(=Q)
4. ________ ________
5. ________ ________
6. ________

and Black cannot escape the Queen's checks.

DIAGRAM 398

White Promotes to a Knight and Wins

ANALYSIS

This time promotion to a Queen loses.

a. 1. **P—B8(=Q)** ________
2. ________ ________ **mate**

b. But promotion to a Knight wins.

1. **P—B8(=N)ch** **K—K1**
2. **N—Q6ch** **K—K2**
3. ________ ________
4. ________ wins Black's Queen.

White can then play to Queen one of his remaining Pawns.

DIAGRAM 399

PEDRAG — MLIMARIC

Yugoslavia, 1970

White Wins by Promoting a Pawn to a Knight!

ANALYSIS

White loses if he promotes to a Queen! One possible line is:

a. 1. **P—K7ch** **K—B2**
2. **R—N7ch** **K × P**
3. **P—K8 (=Q)** **Q—N6ch**
4. **K—Q6** **R—Q5ch**
5. **K—B7** **R—B5ch**
6. **K—Q8** ________
7. ________ ________ **mate**

b. But White mates in four when he makes a Knight!

1. **P—K7ch** **K—B2**
2. **R—N7ch** **K × P**
3. ________ ________
4. ________ **mate**

Chess players have often referred to promoting to any piece

but a Queen as "underpromotion." Perhaps another term is needed, for examples like that in Pedrag's win deserve such a label as "imaginative promotion" or "thoughtful promotion!"

DIAGRAM 400

STERK — MARSHALL
Austria, 1912

White Mated in Four Moves

ANALYSIS

Sterk had given up material to obtain this position. Now a Queen sacrifice reveals a hidden mate that depends on promoting a Pawn to a Knight!

1. **Q × N!** **P × Q**
2. **P × P dbl ch** **K—R2**

a. On

2. .... K—B1
3. ________ mate

b. After 2. . . . . K—R2 (as played)

3. ________ ________
4. ________ **mate**

c. While White would have won quickly had Black refused the Queen sacrifice and played:

1. Q × N Q—Q3
2. ________ ________
3. ________ mate

DIAGRAM 401

White Mates in Six Moves

ANALYSIS

This composed position is solved by two examples of "imaginative promotion." White must demonstrate a mate in six moves.

1. **P—K7** **R—Q1**
2. **P × R(=N)**

For 2. P × R(=Q or R) is stalemate!

2. .... **B × B**

a. Find the mate on:

2. .... B—K4
3. N—K6 B—R7
4. ________ ________
5. ________ ________
6. ________ mate

b. And find the mate on:

3. **P—B7** **B—N1**
4. **P—B8(=B)** **any move**
5. ________ **any move**
6. ________ **mate**

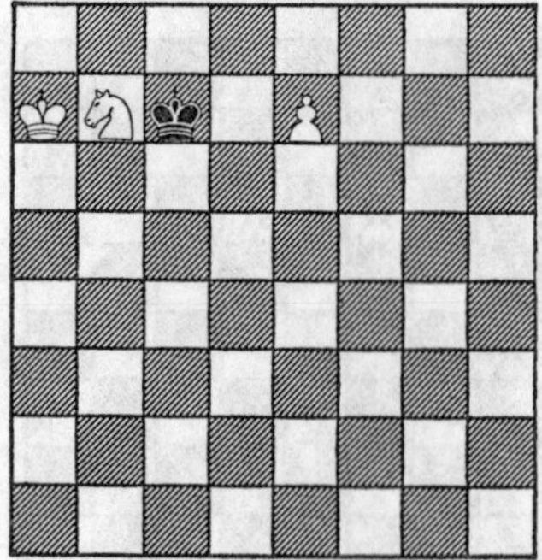

DIAGRAM 402

From an endgame study by W. Shinkman (U.S.A.)

White Mates in Six Moves

ANALYSIS

This study illustrates the technique of mating with Knight, Bishop, and King against a lone King. Mate depends on forcing the enemy King to a corner square of the same color as your Bishop. You should memorize this position and its solution, for sooner or later you will have to demonstrate your mastery of this type of mate over the chessboard!

1. **P—K8(=B)**

Promotion to a Knight creates an ending (N, N and K *vs.* K) you cannot win; promotion to a Rook would require more than six moves for the mate; promotion to a Queen is stalemate.

1. **....** **K—B1**
2. **K—N6** **K—N1**
3. **B—Q7** **K—R1**
4. **N—B5!** **K—N1**
5. ________ ________
6. ________ **mate**

Our discussion of Pawn promotions ends with a review of one of the best-known of all endings, one in which a Pawn must be promoted to a Rook to win. It is called the Saavedra Position, the subject of analysis in England a century ago!

DIAGRAM 403

THE SAAVEDRA POSITION

White to Play and Win

ANALYSIS

White is in check. He must escape checks by the Black Rook so that he will have time to promote his Pawn. Black will draw by giving up his Rook for the Pawn. Thus 1. K—N7, R—Q2; 2. K moves, R × P will draw. So White must work his way back on the QN file.

1. **K—N5**	**R—Q4ch**
2. **K—N4**	**R—Q5ch**
3. **K—N3**	**R—Q3ch**
4. **K—B2**	**R—Q5**

Had White played his King to the QB file earlier, Black would have had time for R—Q8, followed by a check and the capture of the Pawn or Queen on the QB file. Now Black hopes to draw on:

5. P—B8(=Q) R—B5ch
6. Q × R stalemate!

That means the White Pawn cannot be promoted to a Queen. Only a Rook will do:

5. **P—B8(=R)**

a. White's threat is now:

6. ________ ________
7. ________ **mate**

So Black makes the one move that prevents that mate.

5. .... **R—R5**

b. And White makes the one move that threatens another mate and also attacks Black's Rook!

6. ________

REMEMBER!

1. A Pawn reaching the eighth rank normally becomes a Queen. But always ask yourself whether a piece other than a Queen will:
   a. force the win in fewer moves;
   b. prevent an enemy attack;
   c. prevent a stalemate.
2. Be ready to offer or force a temporary sacrifice if it helps you advance and promote a Pawn, with resulting material advantage.
3. Always pay special attention to the possibility of promoting to a Knight with check or with resulting control of a key escape square needed by your opponent's King.

CHAPTER 22

Drawing: Half a Point Is Better than Losing!

The Draw as a Kind of Victory

Face it. There will be times when your best strategy does not do the job. Your opponent will defend well, and there will be no way to win. Or your attack may be rebuffed so skillfully that you are then faced with a probable loss. At such times finding a way to draw—and thus to receive half a point—is a kind of victory. Arthur Bisguier, former United States champion, proved that in one tournament for the national title when he drew every game he played, some of them aggressively handled by both sides. There is no ignominy in accepting a draw, and there is often honor when you find a way to turn a difficult position into a forced draw!

Drawing requires technique just as mating does. This chapter will examine three of the roads to the draw—the perpetual check, the forced repetition of moves, and stalemate. There will always be players who offer draws because they are too lazy to seek a way to win. And there will be others who draw to protect their reputations when they fear an opponent is too strong. But the draws we will illustrate are fighting weapons designed to save games that might otherwise be lost. As such, they are an intrinsic part of the technique of every player who tries to get the most out of each position that develops in his chess career.

There are three principal ways to force a draw.

1. You obtain a position in which you force perpetual check. This makes the game a draw by repetition of moves.
2. With few pieces left on the board, you sacrifice whatever pieces can still move and gain

the draw by being stalemated. That is, your King has no moves and you are not in check when it is your turn to move.

3. You force your opponent to repeat moves because otherwise he will be checkmated or lose material. He may have much more material than you do, or have definite mate threats, but your own threats are so great that all he can do is to make the same moves over and over—which leads to a draw.

In considering the draw, you should be aware of two rules that will not be considered in this chapter except for their mention now. A game is drawn if fifty moves have been made without a capture or a Pawn move after one of the players has given notice of the application of this rule. A game is also drawn when a position has been repeated three times with the same player to move. Such a draw must be claimed at once, for if an additional move is made that changes the position the claim is no longer valid. In applying this rule, it does not matter whether the threefold repetition has occurred in consecutive moves or at three times during the game—so long as the position has appeared three times with the same player to move.

DIAGRAM 404
White Draws by Perpetual Check

ANALYSIS

Black threatens mate in one move against any White move except a check (1. . . . . Q—R2 or 1. . . . . R—R5). But White has an immediate draw by perpetual check. All he has to do is make use of the key squares Q8 and QR5, and Black cannot find a way to escape from check!

1. ________ ________
2. ________ ________
3. ________

and White draws by repeating these checks!

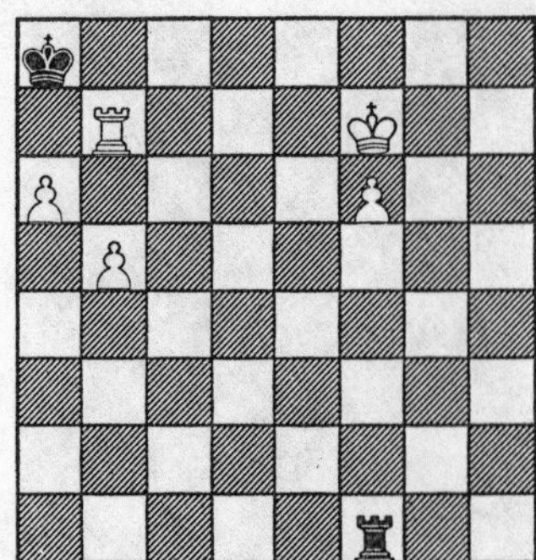

DIAGRAM 405

Black Forces Perpetual Check or Stalemate

ANALYSIS

This is a common perpetual check situation, made possible by the position of Black's King—stalemated if the Black Rook is off the board. So Black seeks moves that invite his Rook's capture. If White refuses the gift, Black continues to check on squares that avoid the interposition of White's Rook (which would free the Black King from its stalemated position).

1.	**R × Pch**
2. **K—K7**	**R—K3ch**

(or 2. . . . . R—B2ch; 3. K—Q6, R × R; 4. P × Rch, K × P and Black can draw because he has the opposition in the King and Pawn vs. King ending.)

3. **K—Q8**	**R—K1ch**
4. **K—B7**	**R—B1ch**
5. **K—N6**	**R—B3ch**
6. **K—R5**	**R × Pch**
7. **K × R** or **P × R**	**Stalemate**

DIAGRAM 406

MUKHIN — MAKARICHEV

Soviet Union, 1975

White Draws by Perpetual Check

ANALYSIS

Black has just promoted a Pawn and has a Queen and Bishop against a Rook—normally enough to win with ease. But White's King has the opposition, and can use it to support a Rook that will force the draw by perpetual check. The defense that gains the half-point succeeds because Black has no way to attack White's King and cannot create new escape squares for his own King.

1. **R—KN8!**	**Any move—say P—R4**
2. ________	________
3. ________	________
4. ________	

and the Black King cannot escape the checks!

DIAGRAM 407

FINKELSTEIN — SOLTIS
New York, 1968

White Draws by Perpetual Check

ANALYSIS

Andy Soltis, international master, chess journalist, and author, and repeatedly champion of New York's Marshall Chess Club, had outplayed White from the opening moves of this game. He is a piece ahead at this point. Suddenly White has a forced draw in a game he should have lost, for a mating threat exists that prevents Black from making a normal-looking capture of a checking Knight!

1. N—R6ch K—R1
2. N—B7ch

How does White mate in two moves on:

2. .... R × N
3. ________ ________
4. ________ mate

So Black had to play 2. . . . . K—N1 and White drew with 3. N—R6ch and perpetual check.

DIAGRAM 408

BROWNE — PLANINC
Netherlands, 1974

Black Moves and Forces the Draw by Stalemate

ANALYSIS

United States champion Walter Browne had gained a three-Pawn advantage in this game, but had made the mistake of placing his Queen on a square where it stalemated Black—if only Black did not have his Queen on the board! Problem: to force the White King to capture that Queen. Method: a check that cannot be ignored.

1. .... Q—R2ch
2. K—B3 Q—K7ch
3. K—N3 ________

For this is the one check that forces White to capture the Queen or lose his own Queen. Result: stalemate!

The positions we have just examined illustrate those bits of luck or planning that permit a lost game to be transformed into a draw. Perpetual check, a draw because of stalemate, and, as we shall now see, a draw by repetition of moves to avoid a threatened checkmate are the three roads to the half-point when a loss seems certain. The games in which such draws occur become worthy of study by other players, for the fascination of observing the escape of the player with the poorer position or less material is a triumph of the imagination to be shared and enjoyed. "After all, it could happen to me, too!" must be the thought of each player as he studies such a game. One of the forced draws that has remained popular among students of chess for more than a hundred years was played in Vienna back in 1872. It remains one of a kind—an amazing proof that miracles can occur over the chessboard!

White	Black
HAMPPE	MEITNER
1. **P—K4**	**P—K4**
2. **N—QB3**	**B—B4**
3. **N—R4**	**B × Pch**

The battle begins at once. Black wants to punish White for his third move, and sacrifices a Bishop to begin an invasion by his lone Queen!

4. **K × B**	**Q—R5ch**
5. **K—K3**	**Q—B5ch**
6. **K—Q3**	**P—Q4**

Now Black threatens 7. . . . . Q × KPch. A reply such as 7. Q—K2, P × Pch; 8. Q × P?, B—B4 wins for Black. White decides to seek safety for his King on the Queen side.

7. **K—B3**	**Q × KP**
8. **K—N3**	**N—QR3**

With the immediate threat of 9. . . . . Q—N5 mate.

9. **P—QR3**

DIAGRAM 409

Black becomes frantic here. He cannot permit the White King to find safety behind its Pawns. Or perhaps he saw the remaining moves in the game and was coolly forcing the draw. We'll never know!

9.	**Q × Nch!**
10. **K × Q**	**N—B4ch!**
11. **K—N4**	**P—QR4ch!**

Three brilliant moves in a row, with Black apparently determined to give everything away. His reasoning soon becomes clear.

DIAGRAM 410

12. **K × N**	**N—K2**

This move was needed to hold the QP, and suddenly White must find an answer to the threat of mate by 13. . . . . P—QN3ch; 14. K—N5, B—Q2 mate.

13. **B—N5ch**	**K—Q1**
14. **B—B6!**	

This is the only move that can prevent the mate threatened by 14. . . . . P—QN3.

14.	**P—QN3ch**
15. **K—N5**	**N × B**

The mate threat is still there. If White now tries to develop a piece by a move like 16. N—B3, Black would win by 16. . . . . B—Q2 and 17. . . . . N—Q5 dbl ch and mate. In the same way Black threatens the immediate 16. . . . . N—Q5ch and 17. . . . . B—Q2 mate. So White must capture the Black Knight.

16. **K × N**

How is Black to continue? White threatens to escape by 17. K × QP. But a perpetual check is there, made possible by the threat of a mate by two Rooks!

16.	**B—N2ch!**

DIAGRAM 411

Consider the possibilities. If Black plays 17. K × B, he will be mated after 17. . . . . K—Q2; 18. Q—N4ch, K—Q3; 19. Q—K6ch, P × Q; 20. ANY MOVE,

KR—QN1 mate. So the Bishop is safe and White has only one other move.

17. K—N5 Drawn

For Black can draw by perpetual check. Black plays 17. . . . . B—R3ch; 18. K—B6, B—N2ch; 19. K—N5, B—R3ch and we have a draw coming by repetition of moves.

ANALYSIS

Why can't White escape by 17. K—N5, B—R3ch; 18. K—R4?

Black would force a mate by a Pawn in two moves!

17. K—N5 B—R3ch
18. K—R4? ________
19. Any Move________ mate

You may be amazed by the Hamppe-Meitner game for a few minutes and then convince yourself it was one of those apparent miracles that came out of the last century—a time when people knew so much less about chess than we do today. Then consider the following game, played by a Spanish master and the Canadian grandmaster Duncan Suttles in our own time. Few players are as unpredictable as the quiet Suttles, who has defeated some of the world's best despite his refusal to play the openings everyone else prefers. Instead, he quickly forces each game into unfamiliar paths built about his trying to gain an advantage by unusual placements of his Pawns. Yet in this game he was lucky to survive at all, for sometimes the unusual is also questionable!

MORA — SUTTLES
1964 Olympiad
IRREGULAR OPENING

1.	**P—K4**	**P—KN3**
2.	**P—KR4**	**B—N2**
3.	**N—QB3**	**N—QB3**
4.	**P—R5**	**P—Q3**
5.	**B—B4**	**N—Q5**
6.	**P—Q3**	**N—R3**
7.	**B × N**	**B × B**
8.	**KN—K2**	**B—N5**

DIAGRAM 412

9.	**P × P**	**RP × P**
10.	**Q—B1!**	**B—R4**

On 10. . . . . B × Q; 11. R × Rch, K—Q2; 12. R × Qch, R × R; 13. R × B White would have won a Bishop.

11. **P—B4** **P—K4**
12. **N × N** **B × P**

It seems that Black has won a Pawn and will remain with a strong attack on the White King. But White has a perpetual check in hand that begins with a Queen sacrifice!

13. **O—O!** **B × Q**

DIAGRAM 413

14. **B × Pch!** **K—Q2**
15. **B—K6ch** **K—K1**

White draws after 15. . . . . K—K2; 16. N—Q5ch, K—K1; 17. B—B7ch, K—Q2; 18. B—K6ch (note that on 17. . . . . K—B1?; 18. N—K6 is mate!).

16. **B—B7ch** **Drawn**

For White wins a piece and the game if Black plays 16. . . . . K—B1; 17. N—K6ch, K—K2; 18. N—Q5ch, K—Q2; 19. N × Q, QR × N; 20. QR × B. To avoid this Black must submit to the perpetual check that follows 16. . . . . K—Q2; 17. B—K6ch, etc.

ANALYSIS

Show the draw after:

16. .... **K—K2**
17. ________ ________
18. ________ ________
19. ________,

with perpetual check

DIAGRAM 414

Black Draws by Perpetual Check

ANALYSIS

White's threats seem overwhelming. He has just played his Queen to R6, and mate at QN7 or QR8 seems inevitable. But Black has a defense that saves the half-point—a perpetual check!

1. .... **R × Pch!**

a. Find the draw by perpetual check on:

2. **P × R** ________
3. ________ ________
4. ________

and White cannot escape the checks!

b. And show how the draw is also forced after:

2. **K—R2** ________
3. ________ ________
4. ________ ________

with the same perpetual check.

DIAGRAM 415

Problem by H. F. L. Meyer London News, 1871

White Draws by Perpetual Check!

ANALYSIS

This amazing old problem is offered as an amusing example of the power of two Knights to force a draw in a position created to demonstrate that even a player with all his pieces still on the board can be held to a draw! After eighteen moves the pieces return to their original position, and a draw by repetition is assured since Black cannot prevent the same position occurring a third time!

1. N—N4ch, K—N3; 2. N—K5ch, K—B3; 3. N—N4ch, K—K2; 4. N—B5ch, K—Q2; 5. N—K5ch, K—B1; 6. N—K7ch, K—N1; 7. N—Q7ch, K—R2; 8. N—B8ch, K—R3; 9. N—N8ch, K—N4; 10. N—R7ch, K—N5; 11. N—R6ch, K—B6; 12. N—N5ch, K—Q6; 13. N—N4ch, K—K7; 14. N—B3ch, K—B7; 15. N—Q3ch, K—N6; 16. N—K4ch, K—N5; 17. N—K5ch, K—B4; 18. N—N3ch, K—B3.

Which is where we began! Draw!

Once you realize that perpetual checks, stalemates, and the forced repetition of moves turn seemingly lost positions into draws, and once you understand the technique of forcing those draws in typical positions, you should be able to convert many a difficult game into half a point. The six positions that follow illustrate more of these basic ways of forcing the draw. In each, the analysis is designed to lead you to the mind-set necessary to find the solution.

DIAGRAM 416

BROND — BRAGA
Argentina, 1934

Black Draws by Perpetual Check

ANALYSIS

Black is in serious trouble. White threatens P × P followed by the capture of the Black Bishop. If Black attempts 1. . . . . R—N4; 2. P × P, B—N5; White will have time to double his Rooks on the open King file and might then mate with his Rooks and Bishop. But Black has a forced draw that begins with a Rook sacrifice!

1. . . . .   ________
2. ________   ________

And the White King cannot escape the checks.

DIAGRAM 417

ROSSETTO — STAHLBERG
Chile, 1947

White Draws by Perpetual Check

ANALYSIS

White's all-out attack on the Black King has been repulsed. Black has accepted and retained a Rook and a Knight offered during the assault. Now White has no winning chances left. But he does have a way to force perpetual check—based on the threat of a mate if Black tries to avoid the checks by heading for his Queen side. A simple repetition of moves forces the draw.

1.	**Q × Pch!**	**K—B2**
2.	**Q—R5ch**	**K—N2**
3.	**Q—R6ch**	**Drawn**

Find White's win on:

1.	**Q × Pch**	**K—B2**
2.	**Q—R5ch**	**K—B1?**
3.	________	**mate**

DIAGRAM 418

BANTER — HARN
England, 1956

Black Forces a Stalemate

ANALYSIS

There's great satisfaction in being able to draw when you have a clearly inferior position. White has four Pawns and a Bishop against a Rook, and threatens to win another Pawn. But Black sees that his King will be stalemated if he gives up his Rook and Queen and in the process forces White to place his Queen at K6!

1.		**R × Pch!**
2. **K × R**		________
3. ________		**Stalemate!**

DIAGRAM 419

Black Forces a Stalemate!

ANALYSIS

Black's inability to meet the threat of White's N—N6 mate makes his position seem hopeless. Yet he sees that he will be stalemated if only he can get his Rooks off the board. So he calmly forces White to capture them and gains an unexpected half-point!

1.	________
2. ________	________
3. ________	________
4. ________	________
5. ________	**Stalemate!**

Compare this position to that of Diagram 405. The basic positions, once learned, bring draws again and again!

DIAGRAM 420

TRINGOV — SCHMID
1964 Olympiad

Black Draws by Perpetual Check

ANALYSIS

The 1964 Olympiad, hard fought by all its teams, featured a number of games in which players quickly accepted draws to keep their teams from falling behind. But other games became draws after deep planning. In this case Black had just sacrificed his Queen at his QB5 to open the White King position. Now the combination of a Rook and a Bishop force the draw by perpetual check.

1.	....	**B—R6ch**
2.	**K—N1**	**QR—N1ch!**
3.	**B × R**	________
4.	________	________
5.	________	________

And draw by perpetual check is forced.

DIAGRAM 421

PORTISCH — PETROSIAN
1964 Olympiad

Black Draws by Perpetual Check

ANALYSIS

Even world class grandmasters are often happy to find a draw by perpetual check. White here threatens mate in one by Q—B8 or Q—K8, and Black escapes only because the White King cannot find a square where it will not be checked by Black's Queen!

1.	....	**Q—N5ch**
2.	**K—B1**	**Q—B5ch**
3.	**K—K1**	**Q—K5ch**

a. The draw is secure if White plays:

4.	**K—B1**	________

b. While on 4. K—Q1 a similar series of checks draws:

4.	**K—Q1**	**Q—N8ch**
5.	**K—K2**	**Q—K5ch**

6.	**K—Q2**	**Q—B5ch**
7.	**K—B2**	**Q—B5ch**
8.	**K—Q1**	**Q—N5ch**
9.	**K—B1**	———

And the checks continue.

REMEMBER!

1. You draw when a position is repeated three times with the same player to move. You also draw when you are stalemated—that is, with no legal moves possible when you are not in check.
2. Learn the typical stalemate and perpetual checks positions presented in this chapter. The half-points gained through draws are the rewards of knowledge rather than luck!
3. Be ready to sacrifice in an inferior position if you can thereby transform it into one of the typical draws based on repetition of moves, perpetual check, or stalemate.

CHAPTER 23

Using the King to Help Checkmate

The King Is a Fighting Piece!

Many players are so concerned with the safety and protection of the King that they develop a fear of using it aggressively. There are times when the King can be an essential part of a mating attack and other times when only the active use of the King can prepare a position for what will soon be a drive toward mate. The endgame is the obvious time to make the King show that its ability to move to any square on the board (better than a Bishop!), to move in any direction (better than a Rook!), or to control an adjacent square (better than a Knight!) makes it an attacking piece whose proper use wins again and again. This chapter illustrates situations in which King moves win games, often acting as the critical factor that closes an escape door for the opponent, completes a mating pattern, helps promote a Pawn, and in such ways turns advantages into victories. In the process, we will review some of the special uses of the King in the endgame and its utility in controlling key squares during a mating attack. Not all of the positions we will examine lead to immediate mates, but we will see what procedure should be followed once a King's activity has helped win enough material to make the coming mate inevitable.

DIAGRAM 422

White Mates in Three Moves

DIAGRAM 423

White Mates in Four Moves

ANALYSIS

This position is typical of the win with two Rooks when an opponent's Rooks are out of play. Black has doubled his Rooks instead of keeping one of them available to interpose against a White check. Now White mates in three moves by cutting off Black's escape square at his KB4—with a King move!

1. ________ ________
2. ________ ________
3. ________ **mate**

ANALYSIS

This position illustrates the win with King and Queen against King and Queen when one King is confined to a corner square. A zugzwang develops after White makes a King move, for Black must then move his Queen.

1. **K—R3** **Q—B7**

Black hopes for a stalemate on 2. Q × Q.

2. **Q—Q1ch** **Q—N1**
3. ________ ________
4. ________ **mate**

DIAGRAM 424

ZESCHKOVSKY — ALBURT
Soviet Union, 1975

White Mated in Four Moves

ANALYSIS

Black is crushed, and all White needs is a way to bring his pieces to their best attacking squares. He begins with a double check that forces the Black King to an exposed square.

1. **P × P dbl ch** **K × P**
2. **R—Q5ch** **K—B5**

a. White mates on:

2. .... N × R
3. ________ mate

3. **K—B2**

This is the decisive move, for it cuts off Black's hope to escape to N6 and thereby delay the mate.

3. .... **Q × Q**

b. Permitting mate in one by:

4. ________ **mate**

3. . . . . Q—Q2 wouldn't have saved Black because of 4. R—K1 and the threat of mate by R—K4 cannot be met.

DIAGRAM 425

ROSSOLIMO — AMATEUR
Paris, 1944

White Mated in Five Moves

ANALYSIS

Chess almost died in France during the German occupation of World War II, except for informal play in which French masters kept in form by playing whoever was available at chess cafes. Rossolimo was one of those whose skill remained very much alive!

1. **Q × Pch!** **K × Q**

a. Find the Arab Mate after:

1. .... P × Q
2. ________ ________
3. ________ mate

2. **R—R1ch** **K—N3**
3. **K—B4!**

Cutting off Black's escape to his KN4.

3. .... **R—K3**

b. White mates with Rook and Bishop on:

3. .... P × N
4. ________ ________
5. ________ ________
6. ________ mate

c. And mated anyway with:

4. **R—R8** **R × P**
5. ________ **mate**

DIAGRAM 426

It Really Happened!

Some chess positions seem so unreal that your first reaction is to assume they were composed by players who had been day-dreaming over the chessboard. Yet this time a bizarre position is the actual finish of a game in which Black made the mistake of taking everything offered to him. After sixteen moves, he found himself a Knight, two Bishops, a Rook, and four Pawns ahead—and checkmated! The game was played in an English postal tournament. The loser's name has been obscured by the winner's good manners (the letters N.N. being chess terminology for an anonymous opponent). Moral—using the King as an attacking piece can be as dangerous as it is sometimes profitable!

EDWARDS — N.N.
England, 1963
KING'S GAMBIT

White, with three days between moves and obviously anxious to test a little-explored attacking line in the Cunningham Defense against the King's Gambit, gets much more than he anticipated when Black makes his King vulnerable to an almost endless series of sacrificial moves.

1. **P—K4** **P—K4**
2. **P—KB4** **P × P**
3. **N—KB3** **B—K2**
4. **B—B4** **B—R5ch**
5. **P—N3** **P × P**

6. **B × Pch**	**K × B**
7. **N—K5ch**	**K—K3?**

White would have a long effort ahead of him to prove the soundness of his attack after 7. . . . . K—B1. But instead Black's King goes wandering.

8. **Q—N4ch**	**K × N**
9. **O—O**	**P × Pch**
10. **K—R1**	**B—B3**
11. **P—Q4ch**	**K × P**
12. **B—K3ch**	**K × B**
13. **P—K5**	**B × P**
14. **R—K1ch**	**K—B7**
15. **Q—N2ch**	**K × R**
16. **N—B3 mate**	

Back to Diagram 426 to check your final position. Beware of King moves that lack a specific goal!

DIAGRAM 427
CAPABLANCA —
EMANUEL LASKER
New York, 1924
The Active King Wins for White

ANALYSIS

The New York 1924 tournament was dominated by the three best players in the world, Lasker (who finished in first place), Capablanca (second), and Alekhine (third). This game clinched second prize for the Cuban world champion. Lasker resigned when Capablanca's next move took away any chance to prevent the mate that would soon follow the Queening of one or two Pawns with the aid of an active King.

1. **P—B6ch**	**Resigns**

Why did Lasker give up the game?

1. **. . . .**	**K—B1**
2. **P—N6**	

(With the threat of: 3. P—B7, 4. K—B6 and 5. P—N7 mate)

2. **. . . .**	**B—K1**
3. **P—N7ch**	**K—N1**

And now the entry of the King forces the Queening of a Pawn. The winning move is:

4. ________

and either the KBP or the QP (or both) will Queen! Mate with Queen and King against King will then follow in a few more moves.

DIAGRAM 428

ROGULJ — ANDRES
Yugoslavia, 1968

Black's King Helps Force Mate

ANALYSIS

This position helps clarify the win with King and Queen against King and Rook when the Rook's mobility is limited by the presence of an active King. White resigned at this point, and it is valuable to examine one way in which Black might have won had White played on.

1.	**R—N2**	**Q—Q5**
2.	**K × P**	**Q—Q8**
3.	**R—N1**	**Q × Pch**
4.	**R—N2**	

a. Black mates in three on:

4.	K—R1	Q—B6ch
5.	R—N2	______
6.	______	______ mate

4.	**. . . .**	**Q—B5ch**
5.	**K—N1**	**K—R6**
6.	**R—QB2**	**Q—N5ch**

b. And Black mates in two by:

7.	**K—R1**	______
8.	______	______ **mate**

Had White moved his Rook to a distant square like KR2 on his sixth move, a series of checks would have picked off that piece. Work it out!

DIAGRAM 429

LARSEN — KAVALEK
West Germany, 1970

White's Active King Forces the Win

ANALYSIS

White's material advantage wins only because his King can invade the Black position and then support a mating attack.

1.	**K—B3!**	**P—KN4**
2.	**K—N4!**	**K—N2**
3.	**K—B5!**	**Resigns**

Why? Suppose Black plays 3. . . . . P × P. One possible win would then be:

4.	B—B6ch	K—R2
5.	B × KP	Q—B4
6.	K—B6ch	K—N1
7.	B—B4ch	K—R2
8.	R—Q7ch	K—R1
9.	________	________
10.	________	________
11.	________	mate

Of course, Black could have given up his Queen along the way—with a lost game and an easy mate to follow as White's remaining pieces close in.

DIAGRAM 430

HODOS — ASATURIAN

Soviet Union, 1970

White's King Helps Force Mate in Four Moves

ANALYSIS

Black is lost because his King has no escape squares and his pieces are unable to come to his King's defense. But White's King must aid in his winning attack.

1.	K—N5!	N—Q1
2.	K—B6!	P—R4

a. 3. ________ ________

4. ________ mate

b. Mate also follows:

1.	K—N5	P—B5
2.	K—B6	B—N5
3.	________	________
4.	________	mate

c. As well as:

1.	K—N5	N—Q5
2.	K—B6	B—K3
3.	R × B	N × R
4.	B—B7ch	K—R1
5.	B × N	R—B1ch
6.	B × R	P—KR4
7.	________	Any move
8.	________	mate

The active King aids in mate, as you have seen, in three important ways.

1. It prevents the escape of an enemy King by taking control of an essential escape square during an attack.
2. It enters the enemy position and supports a piece or pieces that then force mate.
3. By supporting passed Pawns, it aids in promotion to a Queen and then assists that Queen in effecting mate.

The five positions that follow offer further illustrations of such winning tactics. Once you recognize the type of position with which you are dealing, the winning line should become readily apparent. And, in most cases, the win requires more than the two or three moves found in a final sequence during a mating attack. But once the King has been moved to the square where it will be most effective, the mating ideas flow and victory soon follows.

DIAGRAM 431

PADEVSKY — BARCZA
Hungary, 1965

White's Pawns Force the Win

ANALYSIS

White will win if he can Queen a Pawn, and there are several ways to do this. He selects the KRP as his candidate for promotion, and uses his King to help block the long diagonal.

1.	**K—N6**	**B—Q5**
2.	**P—B6**	**K—Q4**
3.	**P—N5**	**K—K3**

Black bites at a stone wall. What is now White's quickest route to a Queen?

a. 4. ________

b. Note that a hasty series of Pawn advances can give Black a draw!

1.	**P—B6**	**B—B4**
2.	**K—N7**	**K—B5**
3.	**P—R6**	**K—N4!**
4.	**P—R7**	________
5.	________	________
6.	________	________

And White can at best draw.

DIAGRAM 432

KELLER — HUG
Switzerland, 1975

Black's King Quietly Aids in the Mate

ANALYSIS

Black's King controls his Q6 and QB6, preventing White's King from escaping to those squares. Result—Black can demonstrate the technique of mating with Queen and Bishop!

1. .... **Q—R5ch**
2. **K—N2** **Q—N5ch**

a. Now White has two ways to lose:

3. **K—R2** ______
4. ______ ______
5. ______ ______ **mate**

b. 3. **K—B2** **B—R5ch**
4. **K—B1** **Q—B6ch**
5. **K—N1** **B—B7ch**
6. **K—B1** ______
7. ______ ______ **mate**

DIAGRAM 433

MATULOVIC — DEZE
Yugoslavia, 1975

Black's King Helps Force Mate

ANALYSIS

Black has just played . . . . P—Q7 and White has resigned. Why?

1. **P—N6** **K—Q6**
2. **P—N7** **K—B7**

a. Threatening 3. . . . . ______ mate

3. **N—K3ch** **K—B8**
4. **N—B4** **B—B4!**
5. **P—R3** **B—N6!**
6. **P—N8(=Q)**

b. And mate in two follows:

6. .... ______
7. ______ ______ **mate**

DIAGRAM 434

MALICH — KNAAK
West Germany, 1975

White Supports His Queen to Force Mate

ANALYSIS

Black, a Pawn behind, cannot afford to exchange Queens, for White would then promote his extra Pawn to a Queen and mate with ease. So all Black can do is to keep checking to try to keep White's King from getting too close to the Black King. He fails, and the combination of King and Queen finally mates.

1. **K—K7!**	**Q—N5ch**
2. **Q—Q6**	**Q—N2ch**
3. **Q—Q7!**	**Q—N5ch**
4. **K—B6**	**Resigns**

a. White wins on:

4.	**Q—N3ch**
5. ________	

and the exchange of Queens is forced.

b. 4.	**Q—B5ch**
5. ________	

and mate will follow on KN7 or KR7.

c. 4.	**Q—B1ch**

5. ________, with the same threat.

DIAGRAM 435
SHASHIN — KORCHNOI
Soviet Union, 1973
White's King Aids in the Mate (Black to Move)

ANALYSIS

Even a world class grandmaster can press an attack too hard. Korchnoi had permitted White to threaten mate while Black's Queen, Rook, and Knight stormed White's King position. But Shashin calmly walked his King out of danger! Korchnoi is now lost, as the next few moves demonstrated.

1.	**P—R3ch**
2. **K—N6**	**N—K5ch**
3. **Q × N**	**R—N8ch**
4. **Q—N5!**	**Q × B**
5. **R × P dbl ch**	**Resigns**

a. For on:

5.	**K—R1** or **K—B1**
6. ________	**mate**

b. And, on Black's other possible line of play from the diagram:

1.	**P—R3ch**
2. **K—N6**	**N—K5ch**
3. **Q × N**	**R—N8ch**
4. **Q—N5**	**R × Qch**
5. **P × R**	**Q—Q6ch**
6. **R—B5 dis ch**	**Q—B5**
7. ________	________
8. ________	**mate**

REMEMBER!

1. The King is an active piece that should be moved toward the center of action in the endgame.

2. The King can perform the important task of blocking escape squares during an attack, can support pieces to complete a mating attack, and can control the squares on the road of a Pawn destined for promotion.

3. However, the use of a King early in the game can expose it to attack. In general, activate your King in the later stages of the game, when few enemy pieces remain on the board to attack it.

CHAPTER 24

How Chess Masters Use Mating Threats

A Kind of Rationale

The five games presented in this chapter illustrate how basic mating ideas can be incorporated into your play. They are in no sense the "best" games ever played, but they are superb models of the utilization of mating threats to win games. Games won by White have been selected because of the greater ease in seeing attacks from the White side of the board when analyzing from a diagram. The comments and analysis are intended to clarify the thinking that keeps an attack moving toward victory.

Not all games end in mate, nor do all of the games in this chapter. But in each case you will observe a similar application of the basic ideas this book has stressed. You cannot utilize mating threats or succeed in mating attacks unless you understand basic checkmate patterns. You cannot execute an attack unless you understand how to open lines, organize batteries, remove defenders, and apply pressure by a superior co-ordination of material against a King position. Finally, you must be ready to accept material gain when mate cannot be forced.

It is suggested that you play through these games more than once. As you gain greater understanding of the tactics utilized by the winners, you will find yourself with that "Of course!" feeling that comes from greater comprehension of when an attack is possible and what must be done to make it succeed.

GAME ONE—
An Attack in the Opening

White	Black
SAX	DONNER

Amsterdam, 1976

FRENCH DEFENSE

What to Watch For:

White offers a Pawn in an effort to open the King side. Black refuses the offer and instead tries to block White's attacking lines. But White uses his control of the center and his superior development to break through. Using mating threats to force Black to make repeated moves with the same pieces, White prevents his opponent from completing his development. Finally, White uses sacrifices to force the win.

1.	P—K4	P—K3
2.	P—Q4	P—Q4
3.	N—QB3	N—KB3
4.	B—N5	B—K2
5.	P—K5	KN—Q2
6.	P—KR4	

DIAGRAM 436

Black can now win a Pawn by 6. . . . . B × B; 7. P × B, Q × P. But, as Alekhine demonstrated in his win against the Swiss master Fahrni in 1914, White gains a strong attack by 8. N—R3, Q—K2; 9. N—B4, N—B1; 10. Q—N4. Black should decline the Pawn offer and play 6. . . . . P—KR3 or 6. . . . . P—QB4. In this game the Dutch grandmaster Donner tries a new method of blocking the lines leading to his King position. His young Hungarian grandmaster opponent smashes a defense that will probably never be attempted in master play again!

6.	....	O—O
7.	B—Q3	P—KB4
8.	P—KN4!	

DIAGRAM 437

8. P—KN4! will force the win. The White Pawn at K5 limits Black efforts to develop. Once White opens lines he will find it easy to bring his pieces to attacking positions.

Examine some of the immediate threats.

1. If Black plays 8. . . . . N—QB3 to develop a piece, he loses a Pawn on 9. P × P, P × P; 10. N × P.
2. On 8. . . . . P × P; 9. Q × P will threaten Q × Pch as well as Q—R5 with mating threats.
3. If 8. . . . . P—KN3; 9. P × P, NP × P; 10. N—R3 and White will prepare a Rook battery on the KN file, play N—B4 and bring his Queen into play on the King side to join in the attack.

In view of such threats, Black decides to counter at once in the center of the board.

8.	**P—B4**
9. **NP × P**	**BP × P**

With hopes of impelling White to move his Knight, when 10. . . . . N × P frees the Black position. But White sees that the loss of a piece is unimportant when compared with the immediate opening of the Black King position.

10. **P—B6!**

DIAGRAM 438

a. Play through this attack from the position of Diagram 438!

10.		P × P
11. B × Pch!		K × B
12. Q—R5ch		K—N1
13. N—B3		Q—K1
14. Q—R6		P × B
15. N × NP		R—B2
16. R—KN1		B—B1
17. ______		______
18. ______		______
19. ______	mate by Queen and Knight	

Return to the diagram, where Black decides to give up material to free his pieces and plays:

10.	**N × BP**
11. **P × N**	**B × P**
12. **Q—R5**	

b. Find the win after:

12.		P × N?
13. ______		______
14. ______		______
15. ______	mate by Queen and Bishop	

12.	**P—KN3**
13. **B × P!**	

For White gains a murderous attack on: 13. . . . . P × B; 14. Q × Pch, K—R1; 15. Q—R6ch, K—N1; 16. N—B3, N—Q2; 17. Q—N6ch, K—R1; 18. R—KN1, Q—K2; 19. N—K5! and White will mate or win material.

13.	**Q—K2**
14. **N—N5!**	

c. Threatening to win a Rook on:

14.	P × B
15. Q × Pch	Q—N2

(On 15. . . . . K—R1; 16. N—B7 still wins a Rook!)

16. _______	_______
17. _______	

14.	**N—B3**
15. **B—Q3**	**P—K4**
16. **N—K2**	

DIAGRAM 439

d. White would keep his extra piece with an easy win after:

16.	P—K5
17. B × B	Q × B
18. _______	_______
19. _______	

16.	**K—R1**
17. **N—B7**	**Q × N**
18. **B × Bch**	**Resigns**

DIAGRAM 440

e. For White mates on:

18.	R × B
19. Q—K8ch	K—N2
20. R—N1ch	K—R3
21. Q—N8!	R—N3
22. _______	_______
23. _______	_______
24. _______	mate

(Can you see both of the final mate possibilities?)

GAME TWO— Using Open Lines to Force a Mate

White	**Black**
HARTLAUB	TESTA

Bremen, 1931

DANISH GAMBIT

What to Watch For:

Openings like the Danish Gambit give you an advantage in development if Black tries to hold the Pawns he gains in the first few moves of the game. That is the case in this sharp win, for the loss of time involved in holding a two-Pawn advantage leaves Black undeveloped and subject to mate threats as early as the twelfth move. Note how control of the long diagonals permits a familiar Rook sacrifice and finally mate with a Rook and a Bishop. This model attack using open lines is important for demonstrating the folly of grasping for material gain at the cost of proper development.

1. **P—K4**	**P—K4**
2. **P—Q4**	**P × P**
3. **P—QB3**	**P × P**
4. **B—QB4**	**P × P**
5. **B × P**	

DIAGRAM 441
AFTER 5. B × P

a. Black can now obtain equality by:

5.	P—Q4!
6. B × QP	N—KB3
7. B × Pch	K × B
8. Q × Q	______
9. ______	______
10. ______	

and the material is even. White will plan action on the King side; Black on the Queen side.

5.	**B—N5ch**
6. **N—B3**	**P—Q3**
7. **N—B3**	**N—KB3**
8. **O—O**	**B × N**
9. **B × B**	**O—O**

Consider the positions of the two sides. White's Bishops control the long diagonals. Black has two extra Pawns.

10. **P—K5!**	**N—K5**

b. What is White's best move on:

10.	P × P?
11. ______,	

with the threat of 12. R—Q1. Then the open file and his complete development should permit White either to pick off Pawns or to attack the Black King position.

11. **B—N2**	**B—N5**
12. **Q—Q4!**	

DIAGRAM 442

c. White threatens 13. Q × N as well as mate on the long diagonal. Thus, on:

12.	B—B4?
13. ______	

opens the diagonal, threatens mate, and at the least regains material.

12. **....**	**B × N**
13. **P × B**	

d. For 13. P × P loses when Black replies:

13.	______

13. **....**	**N—N4**

e. Threatening to win a Queen on:

14. P × P?	______
15. ______	______

14. **K—R1**	**N × P**
15. **Q—Q3!**	**N × P(K4)**
16. **R—KN1!**	

DIAGRAM 443

f. White would now mate with Rook and Bishop on:

16.	N × Q?
17. R × Pch	K—R1
18. ______	______
19. ______	______
20. ______ mate	

16. **....**	**Q—Q2**
17. **Q—Q2**	

g. Now White threatens:

18. R × Pch!	K × R
19. Q—N5ch	K—R1
20. ______	______
21. ______	______
22. ______	______
23. ______ mate by Queen and Bishop!	

17. .... **N—N3**
18. **Q—Q4!**

White still threatens mate on KN7, and Black plays his only defense.

18. .... **N—K4**
19. **R × Pch!**

DIAGRAM 444

h. Black loses whether or not he accepts this Rook sacrifice. The game shows what happened when he took the Rook. Let's see what would have occurred had he refused it.

19. .... K—R1
20. R × Pch! K × R
21. Q—R4ch K—N3
22. R—N1ch K—B4
23. Q—N5ch K—K5
24. ______ ______
25. ______ mate

19. .... **K × R**
20. **R—N1ch** **K—R1**

i. For mate follows:

20. .... K—B3
21. Q—R4ch K—B4
22. Q—N5ch K—K5
23. ______ ______
24. ______ mate

21. **Q × Nch!** **P × Q**

j. And now mate comes after:

22. ______ ______
23. ______ ______
24. ______ **mate by Rook and Bishop!**

DIAGRAM 445

Final Position

This beautiful game has underlined the folly of trying to hold Pawns sacrificed for development in the opening. The double advantage of a half-open KN file and control of the long diagonals led to one mate threat after another!

GAME THREE— Using Mate Threats To Win Material

White	**Black**
TARJAN	HAMMIE

San Francisco, 1976

KING'S INDIAN DEFENSE

What to Watch For

James Tarjan of California, who achieved grandmaster status at age twenty, is an innovator who seeks and finds opening improvements. His best games underline the importance of open lines, and he has developed a style that emphasizes Pawn or piece sacrifices to gain control of the squares around an opponent's King position. Note in this game how his mating threats limit his opponent's choice of replies, thus restricting Black's development. Tarjan's mating threats can be met, but only at the cost of material. Games like this one mark the emergence of a world class grandmaster! After the players have castled on opposite sides of the board, Tarjan is first to open lines.

1. **P—Q4** **N—KB3**
2. **P—QB4** **P—KN3**
3. **N—QB3** **B—N2**
4. **P—K4** **P—Q3**
5. **P—B3**

Tarjan plays the opening with a definite plan. He wants to maintain his Pawn on K4, and also keeps the option of a Pawn advance attack with a later P—KN4 and P—KR4.

5. .... **O—O**
6. **B—K3** **N—B3**
7. **Q—Q2** **R—K1**
8. **N(1)—K2** **R—N1**
9. **P—KR4**

DIAGRAM 446

White, after a series of opening moves that have been played many times, introduces an attacking idea. He threatens to open the Black King position by such moves as P—KN4 and P—R5. This would open the KR file and lay the foundation for an attack along that file.

9. .... **P—KR4**
10. **O—O—O** **P—R3**
11. **B—R6** **B—R1**
12. **P—KN4!** **P × P**
13. **P—R5!**

In Tarjan's style! He has just surrendered a Pawn and now offers a second Pawn to help open Black's King position.

13.	**P × BP**
14. **P × P!**	

DIAGRAM 447

a. White mates after:

14.	P × N?
15. P—N7!	P × R (=Q)ch
16. N × Q	N—KR2
17. P × B (=Q)ch	K × Q
18. B—N7ch!	K × B
19. ______	______
20. ______	______
21. ______	mate by a Queen!

14.	**P × P**
15. **Q—N5**	

b. Threatening mate in two by:

16. ______	______
17. ______	mate by Queen and Bishop

15.	**K—B2**
16. **N—B4**	

c. For mate by a supported Queen looms if White can play:

17. ______

16.	**R—N1**

The point of Tarjan's attacking style is that he first gains an advantage in development and then makes moves that threaten mate. Black can meet these threats in this game, but only by moves that use already developed pieces. Thus the need to defend prevents the completion of Black's development.

17. **P—K5!**	**N—KR2**
18. **Q—N3**	**B—B4**
19. **B—R3**	

Play to remove defenders! Tarjan has also opened a line for his QR to join in the attack.

19.	**N × QP**

Black seeks to remove some of the pressure against his King.

20. **R × N**	**B × P**

DIAGRAM 448

21. **Q × BP!**

d. White mates if Black takes the Rook:

21. .... B × R
22. B × B P × B
23. Q—R5ch K—B3
24. N(3)—Q5ch K—K4
25. _______ _______
26. _______ mate

21. **....** **P—K3**
22. **B × B** **NP × B**

e. Black would lose a Rook and a Knight after:

22. .... KP × B
23. _______ _______
24. _______ _______
25. _______

23. **Q—R5ch**

The lines are open! First Tarjan repeats moves to gain some time on his clock. Then he continues the attack.

23. **....** **K—B3**
24. **Q—R4ch** **K—B2**
25. **Q—R5ch** **K—B3**
26. **R—Q3** **R—N5**

DIAGRAM 449

27. **B—N7ch!** **R × B**

f. White wins a Queen after:

27. .... K × B?
28. _______ _______
29. _______

28. **Q—R6ch** **K—B2**
29. **Q × Pch** **K—B1**
30. **Q × BPch** **R—B2**

g. Black loses on:

30. .... Q—B3
31. N—K6ch K—N1
32. N × R Q × N
33. Q—K6ch K—R1
34. R(3)—R3 B × N
35. _______

and the battery of three pieces bearing on Black's KR2 will force mate.

DIAGRAM 450

31.	**N—K6ch**	**K—K1**
32.	**Q × Rch**	**Resigns**

h. For Black must play:

32.	....	K × Q
33.	______	______
34.	______	

and White's extra Rook forces an early win.

This game clarifies a decision every player must learn to make. When an attack has failed to mate, and a critical gain of material remains possible, take that material!

GAME FOUR— Using Mate Threats in an Open Position

White	Black
TARTAKOWER	SCHLECHTER

St. Petersburg, 1909

KING'S GAMBIT DECLINED

What to Watch For

This game is characterized by repeated sacrifices—each introducing a mate threat or the threat of a significant gain of material. Black makes two questionable Pawn moves in the opening and White quickly gains superior development. He uses it to launch one of the most memorable long-range attacks in chess history. He fails to mate, but gains material and forces his opponent's resignation when mate appears inevitable in a few more moves.

1.	**P—K4**	**P—K4**
2.	**P—KB4**	**B—B4**
3.	**N—KB3**	**P—Q3**
4.	**P × P**	**P × P**

White's goal in the King's Gambit is to attack along the open KB file. Tartakower opens that file as soon as he can.

5.	**P—B3**	**N—KB3**
6.	**N × P**	**O—O**
7.	**P—Q4**	**B—Q3**
8.	**N—B3**	

White cannot hold the extra Pawn. If 8. B—Q3, B × N; 9.

P × B, N—N5; 10. B—KB4, N—QB3 and Black has the better game after 13. . . . . N(5) × KP.

8. . . . . **N × P**
9. **B—Q3** **R—K1**
10. **O—O**

DIAGRAM 451

a. White's first threat appears after the quiet opening. He hopes to play:

11. B × N R × B
12. N—N5 R—K2
13. ______

threatening mate (Q × RPch and Q—R8 mate) and thus winning the KBP after Black's only defense, 13. . . . . P—KR3.

10. . . . . **P—KR3?**

Better is 10. . . . . B—KN5, bringing another piece into play. As you will soon see, the Black Pawn on KR3 becomes a target later on.

11. **N(1)—Q2** **N—KB3**
12. **N—B4** **P—B4?**

Black wants to weaken the White Pawn center, but is again neglecting his development. Better is 12. . . . . N—B3.

13. **N(B3)—K5** **P × P?**

DIAGRAM 452

It is time to consider an attack. White's development is superior; the lines are open for his pieces; the Black King position lacks defenders.

14. **N × P!**

The point of this sacrifice will be apparent in a few moves. However, even at first glance it is obvious that it effectively opens lines in the Black King position!

14. . . . . **K × N**
15. **Q—R5ch** **K—N1**
16. **R × N!**

DIAGRAM 453

b. White wins a piece on:

16.		Q × R
17. ______		______
18. ______		

c. And has a longer-range winning attack after:

16.	P × R
17. Q—N6ch	K—B1
18. B × Pch	K—K2
19. Q—N7ch	K—K3
20. Q—N4ch	K—Q4
21. Q × Pch	K—B3
22. N × B	Q × N
23. ______	

winning a Rook!

16.	**R—K8ch**
17. R—B1	**R × Rch**
18. B × R	**B—B1**

d. For White would win a piece after a developing move like:

18.	N—B3?
19. ______	______
20. ______	

19. B × P!

DIAGRAM 454

e. Accepting this new sacrifice would subject Black to an attack he could not resist. One possible line of play might then be:

19.	P × B
20. Q—N6ch	B—N2
21. R—K1	B—Q2
22. N—K5	Q—K1
23. B—B4ch	K—B1
24. Q—R7!	B × N
25. ______	______
26. ______	______
27. ______	______
28. ______ mate	

19.	**Q—B3**
20. B—N5	**Q—B4**
21. N—Q6!	

White must prevent Black from completing his development, when the extra piece would become decisive. This sacrifice fulfills that need and also opens the QB4 square for White's Bishop.

21. .... **B × N**
22. **B—B4ch!** **B—K3**

f. For on 22. . . . . K—B1, White has:

23. ______ mate

23. **R—KB1** **Q × Rch**

g. Black has no choice. On:

23. .... B—B5
24. ______ wins the Queen.

(While 23. . . . . Q—K4; 24. Q—K8ch, K—R2; 25. B—Q3ch wins Black's Queen or mates)

24. **B × Q** **N—Q2**
25. **B—Q3** **N—B1**
26. **P × P**

The series of mating threats has left White with a Queen and two Pawns against a Rook and a Knight. This material advantage now wins.

DIAGRAM 455

26. .... **B—KB2**
27. **Q—B3** **N—K3**
28. **B—K3** **R—N1**
29. **P—KN4**

With two Pawns against one on the King side, White threatens to advance and Queen a Pawn.

29. .... **P—KN4**
30. **Q—KB6**

h. Threatening to win a Bishop with:

31. ______

30. .... **B—B1**
31. **B—R7ch** **K × B**
32. **Q × Bch** **N—N2**
33. **B × P** **Resigns**

DIAGRAM 456

White has his choice of winning methods. He can advance hs QP and win a piece when it reaches the eighth rank. Or he can advance his King-side Pawns and either mate or win another piece. With a hopeless position, Black has no option but to resign.

GAME FIVE—
Opening the Center to Force a Mating Attack

White	Black
LUCZAK	SZCZEPANIEC

Poland, 1973

SICILIAN DEFENSE

What to Watch For

The Sicilian Defense, one of the most analyzed of openings, remains a verdant field for new ideas. Its complexity invites departures from previously accepted lines, some of which disappear from master play as soon as a crushing novelty proves hitherto accepted play unsound. This game provides such a novelty. In a variation played for many years, White finds a way to open the center and gains open lines that permit him to drive the Black King to a distant square on which a standard mate brings victory. Pay special attention to the sacrifices that create these open lines!

1. **P—K4** **P—QB4**
2. **N—KB3** **N—QB3**
3. **P—Q4** **P × P**
4. **N × P** **N—KB3**
5. **N—QB3** **P—K4**

This move inaugurates the Pelikan Variation (named after a player, not a bird). Black accepts a backward QP because he expects to gain a considerable lead in development.

6. N(Q4)—N5 P—Q3
7. B—KN5 P—QR3
8. B × N P × B
9. N—R3 P—B4
10. Q—R5 P—Q4

DIAGRAM 457

Until this game it was believed Black has equality or better at this point.

11. **O—O—O!** **B × N**
12. **P × B** **N—Q5**

a. Black's general plan, with White's King position open to invasion, has been to form a battery on the QB file. Any White move that permits easy Black development is therefore bad. For example, find the Black reply to:

13. N × P ______

attacking the Knight and vacating QB1 for a Rook.

13. **P × BP!**

Intended to delay Black's development of his Bishop and thus making it harder for Black to build his battery on the QB file.

13. .... **Q—R4**
14. **R × N!**

b. The first sacrifice in White's plan to open the center before Black has castled or developed an attack against the relatively exposed White King. Find White's reply to:

14. .... Q × N
15. ______

14. .... **P × R**

DIAGRAM 458

White has given up a Rook for a Knight to open the King file. How can that file be used? The White Rook belongs on K1, but a Bishop is in the way. Solution? Sacrifice the Bishop!

15. **B—N5ch!** **P × B**
16. **R—K1ch** **B—K3?**

Perhaps 16. . . . . K—Q1 would have been better, but White would then play Q—R4ch and have a strong attack with his Rook, Knight and Queen bearing on an exposed Black King.

c. Of course, White wins on:

16. .... K—B1?
17. ______ ______
18. ______ mate

17. **R × Bch** **K—Q1**

d. For Black is lost on:

17. .... K—B1?
18. ______ ______
19. ______

and mate soon follows on KN7.

18. **Q × BP** **K—B1**
19. **N × QP**

DIAGRAM 459

e. Now White threatens to win a Rook and the game by:

20. R—K8ch R × R
21. Q × Rch Q—Q1
22. ______ ______
23. ______ ______
24. ______

19. .... K—N1
20. Q—N7! Q × Pch
21. K—Q1 R—QB1
22. R—QN6!

f. Threatening:
23. ______ mate

22. .... R—R2

DIAGRAM 460

Black has succeeded in his plan to flee to the Queen side, but is now the target of a standard mating attack ending in a smothered mate! Can you see it?

g. 23. ______ ______
24. ______ ______
25. ______ ______
26. ______ ______
27. ______ **mate**

The moral? Be ready to sacrifice to open lines against an exposed King!

REMEMBER!

1. You can plan and implement a mating attack when your pieces can operate along open lines, you control the center (or block it), and you can obtain an open file bearing on the enemy King position (as in *Game One*).
2. Learn and play gambit openings to gain practice in attacking when you have a lead in development, paying special attention to attacks on weak points, gaining open lines, and using threats of mate or material gain to limit your opponent's choices of moves (as in *Game Two*).
3. Try to be first to open lines when you and your opponent have castled on opposite sides of the board. Bring your pieces to bear on the enemy King position, play to remove defenders, and use threats to mate or win material to make your opponent remain on the defensive. Then, if your at-

tack fails to bring mate, be willing to accept a gain of material (as in *Game Three*).

4. Punish an opponent who makes unnecessary Pawn moves in the opening by placing your pieces in the center of the board, being ready to sacrifice to open the enemy King position or restrict his development during your attack (as in *Game Four*).
5. When your opponent has attacked prematurely and has delayed castling, consider sacrifices to open the center for a direct assault on his King (as in *Game Five*).

CHAPTER 25

You Can Do It Too!

Over the Oceans and a Home at Last!

All of the masters whose wins appear in this chapter share a blessing—migration to the United States of America. They came seeking freedom of opportunity in a free world, and found it in the world of American chess. Much of the game in the United States today reflects the success and influence of a handful of players whose chess training was in other countries. Samuel Reshevsky came from Poland and George Koltanowski from Belgium by way of Spain (during its civil war); Pal Benko fled Hungary's turmoil and Lubomir Kavalek that of Czechoslovakia; Anatol Lein and Leonid Shamkovich are recent arrivals from the Soviet Union. Viktor Korchnoi first settled in the Netherlands and has been invited to live in the United States. Their presence and that of such foreign-born players as Walter Browne and Nicholas Rossolimo—among dozens more for whom we lack room here—have helped American chess prove its universality. Here as in a few other parts of the world a chess master is judged by his ability, not for his religion, race, or politics.

This chapter is a preliminary review of mating ideas from the play of these masters. Even more, it is a special offer of thanks to the American chess community in the name of all those who found a real home within the chess fraternity of the United States. Each of the players mentioned in this chapter has produced enough beautiful wins to fill a book. The large number of positions from George Koltanowski's games presumes no superiority on his part, but are included because, coming from one player's files, they help to illustrate the great variety of mates possible to one who has mastered the ideas contained in this book. You can do it too, for finding a checkmate in a given position is the reward of knowledge—the kind of knowledge you should hopefully have mastered by now!

(The Editors)

DIAGRAM 461

KOLTANOWSKI — AMATEUR
Blindfold Exhibition
Providence, Rhode Island, 1940

White Mates in Three Moves

ANALYSIS

Apply the lessons you have learned. White has a Rook on a half-open file. His Queen and Knight bear on an open King position. His mate depends on being able to play Q—N6. How does he complete the opening of the Black position so that his Queen and Knight can then force mate?

1. ________ ________
2. ________ ________
3. ________ **mate**

DIAGRAM 462

RESHEVSKY — YANOFSKY
1968 Olympiad

White Mates in Three Moves

ANALYSIS

The immigration of the Polish chess prodigy "Sammy" Reshevsky gave the United States a world-class grandmaster who dominated the game in his adopted country for some twenty-five years. Repeatedly active as a mainstay of United States teams, he won this game when he was almost sixty. His Canadian opponent was crushed by Reshevsky's success in achieving three positional advantages—a Bishop preventing any move by the Black KBP, a Rook on an open file, and a Queen ready to force its way to KR7. The only problem is to find a way to force the Black Bishop at Black's KN2 to move!

1. ________ ________
2. ________ ________
3. ________ **mate**

DIAGRAM 463
KOLTANOWSKI —
MRS. MARY HOFFENBERT
Blindfold Exhibition
Oak Ridge, Tennessee, 1947

White Mates in Three Moves

ANALYSIS

Giving hundreds of exhibitions around the United States over more than thirty-five years, George Koltanowski built a national following that made his visits a time of local excitement. One of his regular stops was at Oak Ridge, where he always felt a little smothered by what was still a frightening new power source—atomic energy. And that may explain why he tried so hard for quick wins—as in this case where a double check is the prelude to what by now must be a familiar mate!

1. ________ ________
2. ________ ________
3. ________ **mate**

DIAGRAM 464
KOKKORIS — KAVALEK
Athens, 1968

Black Mates in Seven Moves

ANALYSIS

The year of the Russian invasion of Czechoslovakia, 1968, was also a year of decision for Lubomir Kavalek, then Czechoslovakia's national comer. His grandmaster talent, shown in this finish, has made him one of the highest-ranked American players. With three pieces for a Queen, he sacrifices a Bishop to get White's Rook off its first rank (remove the defenders!). Then he invades with his own Rook.

1. .... **B—B6ch!**
2. **R × B** **N—B6ch**
3. **K—K2** **R—Q7ch**
4. **K—B1**

And now the White King is forced to its KR3 where it is mated by the combined action of a Rook, a Knight, and a Bishop!

4. .... ______
5. ______ ______
6. ______ ______
7. ______ ______ **mate**

DIAGRAM 465

KOLTANOWSKI — AMATEUR

Blindfold Exhibition
Netherlands, 1938

White Mates in Three Moves

ANALYSIS

The life of a professional chess master is a round of travels—to play or to give exhibitions in country after country. It is recommended only to those mad enough to enjoy it—and unable to leave the road that promises a new or old chess puzzle tomorrow. This time it was an old one—the Arab Mate combined with a double check. These two aids to forcing checkmate push the Black King to its corner square and its demise.

1. **R × N(K5)** **N × R**
2. ______ ______
3. ______ **mate**

DIAGRAM 466

RESHEVSKY — POLUGAEVSKI

Palma de Mallorca, Spain, 1970

White Mates in Five Moves

ANALYSIS

Any contest between two world-class grandmasters can become an exciting struggle in which the smallest error is exploited to launch an attack. Black's advance of his King-side Pawns had created holes in his King position. White then invaded with Queen and Knight.

Now he can ignore Black's threatened . . . . Q × Pch as he completes the opening of lines leading to mate.

1. **P × Pch** **K × P**
2. **Q—Q5ch** **Resigns**

All Black can do is interpose his pieces to delay the mate for a few moves! Thus:

2. **. . . .** **N—K4**
3. ________ ________
4. ________ ________
5. ________ **mate**

DIAGRAM 467
KOLTANOWSKI — SOULTANBEIEFF
Hastings, 1927

White Mates in Four Moves

ANALYSIS

Participation in Hastings tournaments was part of George Koltanowski's path to world prominence. In the 1920s the young master often played all-out attacks based on mating patterns glimpsed within complicated positions. When they succeeded, as in this game, they led to interesting mating positions. White has placed his Queen and Knight on critical squares while Black was setting up a mate threat (. . . . Q—N8). But White strikes first against a King position that lacks defenders. Note that the mate would have been impossible without the White Pawn at K5! Try a check!

1. ________ ________
2. ________ ________
3. ________ ________
4. ________ **mate**

DIAGRAM 468
BENKO — HOFFMANN
New York, 1967

ANALYSIS

Pal Benko, a student playing in Iceland when the Russians invaded Hungary in 1956, was one of the thousands of Hungarians who emigrated to the United States. There he became a leading chess writer, a ranking grandmaster, and among the most active and most successful participants in his new country's open tournaments. This is one of his victories in such an event. Note that his opponent threatens mate in one. But Hoffmann resigned after:

1. **B × Pch**

For he cannot escape mate on:

1. .... **K—N4**
2. ________ ________
3. ________ **mate**

DIAGRAM 469

KOLTANOWSKI — AMATEUR

Blindfold Exhibition
Switzerland, 1936

White Forces Mate in Eight Moves

ANALYSIS

George Koltanowski's success in blindfold play has often reflected his understanding of mating patterns which, once recognized, seem to dictate his moves just as clearly as if he had full sight of the board. Can you see an epaulettes-type mate in this position? Watch it appear!!

1. **N—B6ch** **P × N**
2. **R × Nch** **P × R**
3. **Q × Pch** **K—B1**
4. **P × P** **Q—B2**
5. ________ ________
6. ________ ________
7. ________ ________
8. ________ **mate**

DIAGRAM 470

BROWNE — DAMJANOVICH

Venice, 1971

White Mates in Four Moves

ANALYSIS

Walter Browne grew up in the United States, becoming one of a number of rising young chess masters. Seeking a short cut to international play, he returned to his native Australia, became its champion, and was invited to play (and tied for first!) in a major international event in Puerto Rico. Result—he became a grandmaster! Later taking United States citizenship, he became the nation's champion. His carefully prepared attacks have kept him in the forefront of the world's best—as can be seen from the sudden explosion of the position that won this game against one of Yugoslavia's leading players. Suppose the Black Pawn at KN2 were gone. How can mate then follow? A sacrifice prepares the mate by Queen and Bishop.

1. ________ ________
2. ________ ________
3. ________ ________
4. ________ **mate**

DIAGRAM 471
KOLTANOWSKI — AMATEUR
Simultaneous Exhibition
St. Cloud, Minnesota, 1975

ANALYSIS

This position, in an exhibition that was in a sense George Koltanowski's celebration of his election to the presidency of the United States Chess Federation, permitted one of those Queen sacrifices we examined in an earlier chapter. This will be mate by a Rook. It should give you no problems!

1. **Q—R6** **R—KN1**
2. ________ ________
3. ________ **mate**

DIAGRAM 472
A WIN BY SHAMKOVICH IN 1970
White Mates in Two Moves

ANALYSIS

Leonid Shamkovich, after long efforts, was permitted to emigrate from the Soviet Union. He went to Israel and then to the United States. Few players have so quickly become part of the

American chess scene—and with as much immediate success. This position from his earlier play is a simple demonstration of the strength that comes from invading your opponent's position. Do you see the Arab Mate—repeated in this chapter because it is so common in mating practice?

1. ________ ________
2. ________ mate

DIAGRAM 473

KOLTANOWSKI — AMATEUR
Blindfold Exhibition, Spain, 1934

White Mates in Four Moves

ANALYSIS

Perhaps the key lesson American chess masters have learned from those who came from other lands to join them is the importance of precise play. Constant play in European tournaments demands the need to conserve one's energies for the next day's play. An unnecessary drawn-out ending means fatigue, and should be avoided. A bit of extra thinking can finish a game quickly when an advantage is clear. In this position White can win Black's Bishop and then play on to a later mate. But why bother to take a piece when a mate is already possible? Its execution requires forcing Black to play . . . . P—KN4 to lock in Black's King.

1. ________ ________
2. ________ ________
3. ________ ________
4. ________ mate

DIAGRAM 474

LEIN — SAVON
Soviet Union, 1971

White Mated in Five Moves

ANALYSIS

The style of Anatol Lein is certain to affect the play of American masters who must now seek ways to handle the former Soviet champion. Lein often gains points through careful play with his Pawns, whose prepared advance limits an opponent's options. In this game he achieved a mate that began with an apparent piece sacrifice.

1.	**P—B7**	**R × R**
2.	**P—B8(=Q)ch**	**R × Q**

Now Lein could have picked off the second Black Rook—but instead executed a simple mate that again demonstrated the power of a combined Queen and Rook!

3. ________ ________
4. ________ ________
5. ________ **mate**

DIAGRAM 475
KOLTANOWSKI — AMATEUR
Blindfold Exhibition, Brussels, 1953
White Mates in Three Moves

ANALYSIS

This chapter has demonstrated how amateurs and grandmasters alike can be mated by the same kinds of attack. Here is a game in which the two roads to a positional advantage occurred at one time—weak opening moves followed by passive play. No wonder the end came in only fifteen moves, with two ways to mate from the diagrammed position!

1. P—K4, P—K4; 2. N—KB3, P—Q3; 3. P—Q4, QN—Q2; 4. B—QB4, P—KR3?; 5. P × P, P × P; 6. B × Pch, K × B; 7. N × Pch, K—B3; 8. Q—Q5, N—K2; 9. Q—B7ch, K × N; 10. B—B4ch, K—Q5; (on 10. . . . . K × P; 11. N—Q2ch, K—Q5; 12. Q—B4 mate) 11. N—R3, P—QN4; 12. Q—K6, K—B4

White announced mate in three. Can you see it?

1. ________ ________
2. ________ ________
3. ________ **mate**

DIAGRAM 476

ROSSOLIMO — ROMANENKO
Germany, 1948

White Mates in Four Moves

ANALYSIS

In the years before his death in an accidental fall, Nicholas Rossolimo made his New York chess studio a center of instruction for aspiring players. The grandmaster, with the well-earned reputation that came from scores of brilliant mates in grandmaster tournaments, often used his own wins to illustrate how he had become French champion and a leading grandmaster before emigrating to the United States. This fine finish may have been one of his model examples! A hint to aid you—the first move is made by the Bishop! And Black then captured the Bishop in the game!

1. ________ ________
2. ________ ________
3. ________ ________
4. ________ **mate**

DIAGRAM 477

KORCHNOI — POLUGAEVSKI
Leningrad, 1964

White Mates in Four Moves

ANALYSIS

The strongest grandmaster to defect from the Soviet Union or to leave it under normal emigration rules was Victor Korchnoi, whose sudden decision to leave his native country and perhaps head for the United States came in the summer of 1976. His arrival would make the future of American chess more than ever a continuation of a trend evident for two hundred years—the best of other lands seeking personal growth and improvement in the United States. Add his name to the bicentennial memories. Korchnoi, second best player in the world to Karpov in the 1975 world championship matches, has a style that depends less on mate threats than it does on the winning of material—after which his opponents usually resign instead of waiting to be mated. But sometimes a grandmaster too will fight on to the end—and Korchnoi knows how to handle such situations! His mate in three threat becomes a mate in four when Polugaevski gives up a Queen . . . although he resigned after White's second move.

1. ________ ________
2. ________ ________
3. ________ ________
4. ________ **mate**

REMEMBER!

1. This preliminary review of some key mating ideas should have served as a further reminder of key general goals—to remove defenders, to open lines, and to bring your pieces into an enemy King position once you recognize the possibility for a standard mate.
2. Do not forget that most of the mating positions that will occur in your chess career have already occurred in basic form in the past. Recognize the pattern, check your forces, and, by following the suggestions made in this book, more and more of your own games will end in checkmate!

EPILOGUE

It's Harder to Checkmate in Western Asia!

When George Koltanowski submitted the story of his 1974 misadventure, and insisted it had really happened, we accepted it as an act of confidence in a respected chess master, journalist, and the elected head of organized American chess. But when a consultant advised us that the position he described had been printed in the Soviet Union as the composition of someone named Dogorov, we had to check further. We established that George Koltanowski had indeed captained the United States team in the 1974 Olympiad, had disappeared for four days at the end of the competition, and had returned to San Francisco by way of Manila with two thousand dollars in Swiss francs. His insistence that many problems have their origin in actual games could not be denied, and his many examples of problems being composed by different people almost simultaneously convinced us that it would be best to permit our readers to judge the truth of his tale. Our apologies to those who doubt it, and our joy if any believe it, come with this amazing story of an encounter in western Asia.

THE EDITORS

Well, what would you have done in my place? Two thousand dollars in Swiss francs and all expenses paid for a single exhibition of blindfold chess is not easily refused! It was at the Nice Olympiad in 1974 that this bearded gentleman with an Oxford accent approached me and asked if I still played blindfold chess. I did, but no more than ten games simultaneously. That would be fine, and would I be willing to fly to his palace in western Asia (less than five hours away) to play some of his guests at the tenth anniversary of his provincial governorship? He sweetened the invitation with cash in advance and agreed to arrange my flight home via Manila. On the last day of play I sent the United States team home and was soon the single passenger on his private jet—on my way to what proved to be the most difficult chess game I'd ever played.

I had been active for years in efforts to improve chess in the world's less developed countries. But even the much-traveled Dr. Max Euwe, President of FIDE, had not made it to this area! I began to ponder the several columns and articles that would surely develop from this trip. Who knew whether or not I might find some strong player at my exhibition who might be persuaded to organize tournaments in this least known of chess communities?

The jet landed on an isolated airstrip high in the mountains. A waiting car moved me through desolate rocky scenery toward the palace a few miles away, traveling along a winding mountain road that kept the driver to about five miles an hour. Then, at a turn in the road, the car had to stop before a large boulder. The driver got out to examine the obstruction and was immediately seized by three armed men. My door was opened by a bearded heavy-set giant of a man whose pistol gestured me out to the side of the road. My one thought was that I was dreaming, and had become the unfortunate victim of a stagecoach holdup in some Hollywood Western.

My captor spoke in an unknown language and I answered in English, cursed a bit in Flemish, tried Spanish, and finally turned to French. Amazingly, he spoke it! His wife (or one of them) was a French-speaking woman from Lebanon. One of his men opened my bags and when ten chess sets were removed from one of them my captor suddenly grew suspicious.

"Who are you?"

"I am a guest of the governor, and you had better let me go!"

"I eat guests of the governor for breakfast. Why are you here?"

"I am a chess master come to give an exhibition of my skill at the governor's palace."

"What is a chess master?"

To cut the story short, he had me taken to his camp some distance away where he insisted that I set up a chessboard and explain the game to him. I had to, for he had taken my two thousand dollars and had divided it into two piles. His half, he said, was a fee for saving my life from his followers and my half would be my stakes for whatever he decided we would do. It seems that the people of his country love to gamble—for wagers up to and including one's life—and he was beginning to see an interesting kind of bet coming up.

I explained the rules of chess to him, taking my time to make certain each was clear. I showed him how each piece moved and explained that the object is to mate the King. I went into the value of the pieces, the meaning of stalemate, and indicated that a Pawn reaching the eighth rank becomes any piece. It took some time to clarify the fact that White moved first (a strange notion to him, for in the games he knew the first move was always decided by a proof of skill such as the throwing of a knife). Finally, when he understood *en passant,* I told him that he now knew how to play the game. And could I leave now? He could keep the thousand or take the two thousand, so long as I could go on to the governor's palace.

"Let's play a game," he said. "If I win I'll take all the money; if you win you'll take all of it. If we draw I'll shoot you. And in payment for playing me I'll escort you to the governor without charge—living or dead."

What an offer! I decided to teach this bandit a lesson for daring to challenge me after having just learned the game! We tossed knives at a post and, when he won, he chose the Black pieces. I opened with 1. P—K4. He thought for a minute and played 1. . . . . P—KR4. This was going to be so easy! I played 2. B—B4. Then he began to play slowly, toying with a knife or pistol as he made each of his moves. Yes, it unnerved me. A chess master is supposed to have control over his nerves, but whoever played under such conditions?

Two hours later and with darkness approaching, I was four pieces ahead and had an easy win. I could promote a Pawn or mate in two. This was the position after thirty moves—one that I will never forget.

DIAGRAM 478

I played 31. K—B2, and explained to him that he was lost, for my next move would be B—Q4 mate. He looked closely at the board and began to mutter some of the words I hadn't heard since I was a kid in Brussels discovering the beautiful imagery of cursing in French. Then, instead of resigning he played 31. . . . . P—R8 and asked for another King.

"Wait a minute," I shouted. "You cannot have two Kings! A Pawn can be promoted to any piece *but* a King!"

The bandit smiled. "You said that a Pawn that reaches the eighth rank becomes any piece. A King is a piece. I make a King!"

DIAGRAM 479

I looked at him, considered the size of his pistol and the light gleaming from his knife blade, and decided that he was right. I had long ago learned the folly of arguing with people who have very strong convictions. Then I looked at the position and began to tremble. Both Black Kings were stalemated. No matter what I did one of them would remain stalemated and the game would be a draw!

"Sorry, chess master. The game is a stalemate, and that means I will now have to deliver you as promised." And his pistol was in his hand.

"Give me time to make sure of the situation," I pleaded. The next two minutes reminded me of some of the time pressure scrambles that ruin a master's nerves as I searched for a way out. Then it came to me—a flash of chess brilliancy that beat anything I had seen in fifty years at the game! I played 32. P—R8 and told him I was promoting it to a *Black* King.

DIAGRAM 480

"You cannot change a White Pawn into a Black King!" he screamed.

"When did I say that?" I asked in my softest voice. "All I told you was that a Pawn can be promoted to *any* piece. A Black King is a piece, isn't it?"

"Very well, but you still haven't won the game. Let's continue." And he played 32. . . . . K—N1.

The end was in sight at last. I simply played 33. P—R7 and his

DIAGRAM 481

only possible reply was 33. . . . . K—R1. Then, with a sob rather than a sigh of relief, I played 34. P—R8(=Q) and mated all three Kings at once!

That's the story. He kept three of my sets and, money and all else intact, I was taken to the door of the palace. The details of my exhibition are a little fuzzy, for I found myself concentrating on preventing my opponents from advancing Pawns to the eighth rank—which made my play less than brilliant.

A couple of years have passed, and I hear that western Asia is enjoying a chess craze that had its origin in a strange variation of the game played in the mountains. I wonder if the dreamlike quality of my memories of the area could have any connection to this development. Or have I become so involved in the study of checkmates that this story just sprang from a midnight chessboard?

A Quiz Review of "Checkmate!" Ideas

The fifty positions in this quiz were selected from master play to review the basic mating ideas you must know to improve your playing ability. Some are direct applications of mating ideas elaborated on in this book; others are more complex in that they utilize a combination of mating possibilities. All can be understood once you have pictured the final mating positions.

Analyze each position as if it had occurred in one of your own games. Set it up on your chessboard with you as the player whose turn it is to move. Note that you are not told how many moves are needed to achieve the mate or draw. Take no more than ten minutes to find (and write down) the moves that achieve the result called for below the position. If you still haven't found the continuation, turn to page 344, where you will find the *first* move of the best line of play. Play that move and try to find the rest of the continuation. If the next five minutes do not reward you with the solution, turn to the answers (beginning on page 365) and play the winning or drawing line through at least *twice* to clarify the idea illustrated by the position. Then, before continuing with the quiz, review the chapter or chapters indicated in the answer if you did not find the best continuation.

The mating ideas in *Checkmate!* have been scrambled in this quiz. Most of the positions are similar to positions already examined. A few are unique applications of winning ideas that you will probably commit to memory because of their unusual nature. But all should yield to this approach:

1. Seek the mating or drawing idea implicit in the position.
2. Find the barriers to achieving that idea and decide how to remove them.
3. Select your moves and the best replies to them.
4. If you fail to solve the problems set by a position, take the time to review the idea it illustrates before continuing. The same idea may reappear at another point in the quiz.

The range of correct solutions found in informal testing of a number of players of varying ability reveals this pattern of results:

MASTERS get 50 correct answers.

EXPERTS get 40 to 45 correct answers.

CLASS A players get at least 30 correct answers.

INTERMEDIATE PLAYERS get at least 20 correct answers.

BEGINNERS get 10 or fewer correct answers.

You can use these results as a general evaluation of what you have learned, always remembering that there is an unavoidable gap between acquiring knowledge and applying it under the pressures of play. But remember that your goal is a perfect score—not proof of master ability but a reflection of the time you take to review and study the ideas you have examined in this book. It is suggested that you repeat this quiz at least once a month, each time reviewing the chapters containing the ideas you still find unclear. Always follow the procedure of setting up positions rather than trying to solve from diagrams.

A word of caution! Several of the positions involve a mate with Queen and Rook, a type of checkmate included in many of the chapters but not made the subject of a special chapter because the Queen can act as a Rook or Bishop and such situations were examined in the chapters dealing with these pieces. Of course, if the mate is by a supported Queen, study of Chapter 5 will show that the Rook is no more than a supporting piece in a checkmate.

A majority of the positions involve sacrifices to force a final mating or drawing position. Consider such sacrifices at all times—once you have recognized the type of final position implicit in a given situation. Remember! You can do it too, if the ideas of *Checkmate!* have become part of your chess thinking!

1

MARTINS — DUEBALL
West Germany, 1971

White to Move and Force Mate

3

MAJEVSKA — KIRIJENKO
Soviet Union, 1974

White to Move and Force Mate

2

RHEINEIMER — REIDEBACH
West Germany, 1976

Black Resigned in this Position. He Could Have Drawn! Black to Move.

4

JOHANSSON — EKENBERG
Sweden, 1974

Black to Move and Force Mate

5

NOORDYK — LANDAU
Antwerp, 1927

White to Move and Force Mate. Two Mating Continuations Are Possible. Find Both of Them.

7

TARTAKOWER — SCHLECHTER
Vienna, 1908

Black to Move and Force Mate

6

LEVCHENKOV — SHAMKOVICH
Soviet Union, 1972

Black to Move and Force Mate

8

SMYSLOV — CASTRO
Switzerland, 1976

White to Move and Force Mate

9

ROTH — REJNA
Hungary, 1975

White to Move and Force Mate

10

BIELIKI — PARMA
World Junior Championship, 1959

Black to Move and Force Mate

11

SCHULDER — BODEN
London, 1860

Black to Move and Force Mate

12

KAHN — RATSCH
East Germany, 1970

White to Move and Force Mate

13
FOGELOWITSCH — WERLINSKY
Moscow, 1926
White to Move and Force Mate

15
LEVY — FELLER
Spain, 1969
White to Move and Force Mate

14
HANAUER — TREYSMAN
Philadelphia, 1936
Analysis after Black has Resigned. White to Move and Force Mate

16
KLOKIN — GEBREL
Soviet Union, 1969
White to Move and Force Mate

17

LOCASTO — ZACRZEWSKI

Poland, 1974

White to Move and Force Mate

19

BERNSTEIN — SEIDMAN

United States Championship, 1959–60

White to Move and Force Mate

18

LARSSON — ERLANDSSON

Correspondence, 1966–67

Black to Move and Force Mate

20

MICHIGAN — CURRAN

Philadelphia, 1876

Black to Move and Force Mate. There Is a Mate in Three as Well as a Mate in Four in This Position

21

MORPHY — CONWAY
New York, 1859

White to Move and Force Mate

23

BELAVENETZ — SMYSLOV
Moscow, 1936

Black to Move and Force a Draw by Perpetual Check

22

NICHEVSKI — YOFFIE
Yugoslavia, 1969

White to Move and Force Mate

24

KAISZAURI — SZNAPIK
Poland, 1970

White to Move and Force Mate

25

WASJUKOV — GRIGORJAN

Soviet Union, 1975

White to Move and Force Mate

26

UNZICKER — SARAPU

1970 Olympiad

White to Move and Force Mate

27

GEDULT — PATRIKTINO

Paris, 1975

White to Move and Force Mate

28

MORABA — BIELSA

Spain, 1976

White to Move and Force Mate in Two Moves

29

BALACHOV — SABKHOV
Correspondence, 1974

Black to Move and Force Mate

31

ESNAOLA — GALONSKA
Match, Spain—West Germany, 1974

Black to Move and Force Mate

30

STEINKUHLER — BLACKBURNE
England, 1863

Black to Move and Force Mate in Three Moves

32

MEDINA — SANZ
Spain, 1975

White to Move and Force Mate (Give the Moves after Each of Black's Possible Replies to White's First Move)

33

MATULOVICH — KRISTJANSSON
Iceland, 1970

White to Move and Force Mate

34

FLESCH — VADASZ
Hungary, 1971

White to Move and Force Mate

35

TAL — PORTISCH
Switzerland, 1976

White to Play and Force Mate (Give the Replies to Each Possible Black Reply along the Way)

36

POMAR — N. WEINSTEIN
Spain, 1976

White to Play and Force Mate

37

COLJCOV — MOISEIEV
Soviet Union, 1970

White to Move and Force Mate

39

POTEMKIN — ALEKHINE
St. Petersburg, 1912

Black to Move and Force Mate

38

FINE — DAKE
New York, 1933

White to Move and Force Mate

40

SCHWARZ — SZELES
Budapest, 1956

White to Move and Force Mate

41

MARJASIN — KAPENGUT

Soviet Union, 1968

White to Move and Force Mate

42

POMAR — CUADRAS

Spain, 1974

Black to Move and Force the Promotion of a Pawn

43

CORDEN — RUNAU

Hastings, 1971

White to Move and Force Mate

44

SIGURJONSSON — VYZANTEADIS

1972 Olympiad

White to Move and Force Mate

45

TOLOSO — MASCERO
Barcelona, 1896

White to Move and Force Mate

(Position reached after: 1. P–K4, P–K4; 2. N–KB3, P–Q3; 3. P–Q4, P–KB4?; 4. B–QB4, BPXP; 5. N×P, P—Q4; 6. Q—R5ch, K—K2; 7. Q–B7ch, K–Q3; 8. QXPch, K–K2)

47

HERZOG — RANAS
Milan, 1974

White to Move and Force Mate

46

KOVACHEVICH — POPOV
Athens, 1971

Black to Move and Draw by Perpetual Check

48

EUWE — KERES
Holland, 1940

Black to Move and Win White's Queen or Mate (Give Both Continuations)

49

MIRZAJEV — SILJEJEV
Soviet Union, 1974

White to Move and Force Mate

50

SUETIN — POLEAR
Soviet Union, 1965

White to Move and Force Mate

FIRST MOVE IN EACH OF THE QUIZ POSITIONS

1. 1. Q—N5ch
2. 1. . . . . Q—N7ch or
1. . . . . Q—B7ch or
1. . . . . Q—R7ch
3. 1. Q—R7ch
4. 1. . . . . QR—N1ch
5. 1. P—Q3(or Q4) or
1. P—N4ch
6. 1. . . . . Q—K8ch
7. 1. . . . . R—R7ch
8. 1. R—B2ch
9. 1. N—K7ch
10. 1. . . . . Q × Pch
11. 1. . . . . Q × Pch
12. 1. Q—R8ch
13. 1. Q—N6ch
14. 1. R—N7ch
15. 1. R—Q8ch
16. 1. P—R3ch
17. 1. N—N5ch
18. 1. . . . . Q—R6
19. 1. Q × Pch
20. 1. . . . . R × Pch leads to mate in 3; 1. . . . . N—N6ch leads to mate in 4
21. 1. B × Pch
22. 1. R—B8ch
23. 1. . . . . R × Bch
24. 1. Q × RPch
25. 1. Q × RPch
26. 1. Q × Pch
27. 1. Q—N8ch
28. 1. P—B6
29. 1. . . . . Q—K1ch
30. 1. . . . . Q—N8ch
31. 1. . . . . Q—N6ch
32. 1. N—B5ch
33. 1. R—N8ch
34. 1. R—N7ch
35. 1. N—R6
36. 1. R—B7ch
37. 1. R—R6ch
38. 1. Q × Bch
39. 1. . . . . N × P(B4)ch
40. 1. Q × Nch
41. 1. Q × Pch
42. 1. . . . . P—R5
43. 1. R—N3ch
44. 1. Q—R8ch
45. 1. N—N6ch
46. 1. . . . . R × Pch
47. 1. Q—B6ch
48. 1. . . . . B—N5ch
49. 1. B—R6ch
50. 1. N—R6ch

ANSWERS TO QUIZZES

CHAPTER 1

5. 1. P—N7 mate
6. 1. K—K6, P—N8 (=Q); 2. P—B7 mate
7. 1. N—R6ch, K—R1; 2. P—N7 mate
8. 1. Q × Bch, P × Q; 2. P—K6 mate
15. *a.* 1. R × P, B × R; 2. P × B mate
b. 1. R × P, any move other than B × R; 2. R × P mate or R—N8 mate if 1. . . . . N—N3
16. 1. K—B5, P—N5; 2. K—B4, P—N6; P × P mate
17. 1. B—QB5, any; 2. P—R7 mate
18. 1. B—N6ch, N × B; 2. P × N mate
19. 1. Q—B5ch, B × Q; 2. P × B mate
20. 1. . . . . R(K8)—K6ch; 2. K—R4, R—R1ch; 3. K—N5, P—B3 mate
21. 1. R × Bch, P × R; 2. N—Q3ch, P × N; 3. P—B4 mate
22. 1. R—Q5ch, P × R; N—Q3ch, P × N; 3. P—B4 mate

CHAPTER 2

26. 1. R × Pch, R—R2; 2. B—N2 mate
27. 1. R—N5ch, N—N3; 2. R—B8ch, B—B1; 3. P—K7 mate
29. 1. R × Pch, B × R; 2. P—B7 mate (On 1. . . . . K—N1; 2. R(N7)—N7 mate)

30. The solution best illustrating mate by a Bishop is: 1. Q—K8ch, B × Q; 2. R × Bch, Q × R; 3. B—B3ch, Q interposes at K5 or B3; KB × Q mate. There is a shorter mate after 1. Q—K8ch, B × Q; 2. B—B3ch, with mate by the Rook after 2. . . . . B—B3; 3. R—K8 mate or 2. . . . . Q—B3; 3. R × B mate. In both cases, the Bishop on the long diagonal bearing down on a King without escape squares is critical.

33. 1. Q—R8ch, K—B2; 2. R—R7ch, K—K3; 3. B—B5 mate

34. 1. Q × KPch, B—K2; 2. Q × Pch, K—B1; 3. B—R6 mate

37. 1. Q × Q, P × Q; 2. B—R5 mate

38. 1. Q × Pch, P × Q; 2. K—B1 mate. White also mates if Black plays 1. Q × Pch, B—R2; 2. Q × B mate.

39. 1. N × Pch, K—R2; 2. B—Q3ch, B—B4; 3. B × B mate

40. 1. R(K5)—K6ch, N × R; 2. B—K5 mate

41. 1. . . . . Q × Pch; 2. K × Q, B × Pch; 3. B—B3, B × B mate

42. 1. R—N6ch (by the Queen on K5), R × Q; 2. B—B6 mate. Black is also mated after 1. R—N6ch, P—B3; 2. Q × P or B × P mate

CHAPTER 3

48. 1. Q × Pch, Q × Q; 2. N—B7 mate

49. 1. Q × Pch, P × Q; 2. N—R5 mate (for the Knight prevents the Black King from escaping to KB3!)

51. 1. . . . . R—B4 (Black now threatens mate by either 2. . . . . R—N4 or 2. . . . . N—B5. White decides to take the Rook.); 2. P × R, N—B5 mate

52. 1. P × Pch, K—K2; 2. Q—B6ch, B × Q; 3. N—B5 mate illustrates mate by a Knight

54. 1. . . . . Q × QPch; 2. K × Q, B—N2ch; 3. P—K5 (if 3. K—B4, B—K3 mate), B × Pch; 4. K—K4, N—B3 mate

55. 1. Q—R5!, N × Q; 2. N—R7 mate
White threatened mate by 2. Q—B7. If 1. . . . . N—K1 (to protect Black's QB2); 2. R—Q8ch, N × R; 3. N—R7 mate. Black's longest defense follows 1. . . . . Q—Q2; 2. R × Q, N × Q; 3. R—B7ch, K—Q1; 4. N—K5, P × N; 5. N × Pch, K—K1; 6. N × R and White is far ahead in material.

56. 1. N—N4ch, K—R8; 2. K—B1, P—B6; 3. K—B2, P—R7; 4. K—B1, P—B7; 5. N × P mate (as in Diagrams 2 and 3!)

57. 1. . . . . Q × BPch; 2. K—R1, Q—N8ch; 3. R × Q, N—B7 mate

58. 1. R—N8ch!, Q × R; 2. Q—N7ch!, Q × Q; 3. P × Qch, K—N1; 4. N—K7 mate

59. 1. R—R1ch, Q—R5; 2. R (either) × Qch, R—R2; 3. N—N6 dbl ch and mate!

60. 1. N—K2ch (by the Bishop), K—K3; 2. N—B4 mate

61. 1. N—B6 double check, K—N2; 2. Q × P(R7)ch, K × N; 3. N—N4 mate (Check all of the squares adjacent to the Black King. This final position is worth remembering!)

CHAPTER 4

67. 1. B ×Pch, R × B; 2. R × Rch, R—B1; 3. R—R8ch, K × R; 4. R × R mate

68. 1. Q—K8ch, K × Q; 2. R—N8ch, R—B1; 3. R × R mate

69. 1. R—R8ch, K—K2; 2. R—K1ch, K—Q3; 3. R—K6 mate (Also possible is: 1. R—K1, P—B4ch; 2. P × P, K—N1; 3. R—K8 mate)

70. 1. R—R1ch, K—N3; 2. R—R6 mate

71. 1. Q × Pch, N × Q; 2. R—Q8ch, N—B1; 3. R—R8ch, K × R; 4. R × N mate (Black could have delayed the mate by one move if he had interposed his Queen at K1 on his second move.)

73. 1. . . . . Q × Pch; 2. K × Q, R—R2ch; 3. Q—R5, R × Q mate

74. 1. N—R6ch, K—R1; 2. N × Rch, K—N1; 3. R × P mate (Not 1. R × Pch, K—R1!, when mate in three moves is impossible.

75. 1. R—R4, any move; 2. R—R8 mate

76. 1. B—N7ch, K—N1; 2. R × R mate

77. 1. R—K8ch, K—R2; 2. N—N5ch, P × N; 3. R—R3 mate

78. 1. From the position of Diagram 78: 1. . . . . R × N; 2. P × Q, R—Q7; 3. Q × R, B × Bch; 4. Q—N2, R—R6!; 5. Resigns. White cannot prevent Black's next move, ... R × Pch with mate or the win of material to follow. Work it out!

79. 1. . . . . Q × Nch; 2. P × Q, B—R6ch; 3. K—B2, B—R5ch; 4. K—N1, R—K8ch; 5. Q—B1, R × Q mate. If White plays 3. K—N1, R—K8ch; 4. K—B2, B—R5 mate.

80. 1. . . . . Q—R5; 2. Q × B, Q—B7! Black suddenly threatens Q × R mate and Q × KNP mate. There are two variations:

a. 3. R × Q, R—B8ch; 4. Q—K1, R × Qch; 5. R—B1, R × R mate

b. 3. R—KN1, Q × NPch!; 4. R × Q, R—B8ch; 5. Q—K1, R × Q mate

81. 1. . . . . Q—B2ch; 2. K—N3 (or N4), Q—N3ch; 3. K—B4, R—R5 mate (As the analysis indicated, White could have delayed the mate by interposing his Knight at KN5.)

CHAPTER 5

88. 1. Q—K8ch, B—Q1; 2. Q—K6 mate

89. 1. R—Q8ch, R × R; 2. K—R2 dis ch, R—Q5; 3. Q × Rch, Q—N2; 4. Q × Q mate

90. 1. Q—K7ch, K—N1; 2. Q—N7 mate

91. 1. Q—R6ch, K—N1 or B2; 2. Q—N7 mate

92. 1. R—Q8ch, R × R; 2. Q × R mate

94. 1.N × Nch, Q × N (or . . . . P × N or . . . . K—R1); Q × P mate

97. 1. B—B7ch, K—B1; 2. Q—R6 mate

98. 1. B—Q6ch, R—K2 (or any other piece to K2); 2. Q—R8 mate

99. 1. Q—R6, ANY MOVE; 2. Q—N7 mate

101. 1. . . . . N × Pch; 2. K—K2, Q—Q6 mate

102. 1. . . . . R × B; 2. R × P, R × N dis ch; 3. R × B, Q—B3ch; 4. R—B3, Q × Rch; 5. K—N1, Q—N7 mate (In the actual game, White played 4. K—N1 and was mated by 4. . . . . Q—N7) Also possible was 4. Q—Q5, which delays the mate one move 4. . . . . Q × Qch; 5. R—B3, etc.

103. 1. R—B8, R × R; 2. R × R, B × R; 3. Q × Q mate
If 1. R—B8, B × R; 2. Q × Q mate
If 1. R—B8, R × R; 2. R × R, Q × R; 3. Q—K7 mate
If 1. R—B8, K—Q2; 2. Q × BPch, Q—K2; 3. Q × Q mate.

104. 1. . . . . B—R7ch; 2. K × B, Q × Pch; 3. K—N1, Q—R8 mate

105. 1. B—Q6ch, R × B; 2. R—R8ch, K × R; 3. R—R1ch, K—N1; 4. R—R8ch, K × R; 5. Q—R1ch, K—N1; 6. Q—R7 mate

106. 1. R × Rch, Q × R; 2. Q—N2ch, Q—N2; 3. Q × Q mate

CHAPTER 6

112. 1. R × Bch, R × R; 2. Q—N6 mate (If 1. . . . . K—N2; 2. R(B1)—B7 mate)

113. 1. Q—B6ch, K—K2; 2. Q—K6 mate

115. 1. B—N5ch, P—B3; 2. Q × P mate

116. 1. R—B8ch, Q × R; 2. R × Qch, R × R; 3. Q × P mate

122. 1. Q × Pch, K × Q; 2. R—R7ch, K—B1; 3. R—B7 mate

123. 1. R—B3ch, B—B2 (If 1. . . . . B—B4; 2. Q—B6 mate); 2. R × Bch, K × R; 3. Q—B6 mate

124. 1. Q × Bch, K × Q; 2. R—N7ch, K—K1; 3. N—B6 mate

125. 1. N—B7ch, K—B2; 2. Q—Q6 mate

126. 1. R—B8ch, K—N2; 2. R × Nch, K—B3 (if 2. . . . . P × R; 3. Q × P mate, epaulettes!); 3. R—B6ch, B—Q3; 4. R × B mate.
127. 1. . . . . R × Pch; 2. N × R, Q × Nch; 3. K × Q, R—B4 mate

CHAPTER 7

134. 1. B—R6ch, K—R1 or R2; 2. B—B8 mate
135. 1. R × Pch, K—R1; 2. R—N8ch, K × R; 3. R—N1 mate
136. 1. Q × Nch, N × Q; 2. B × Nch, K—N1; 3. R—N1 mate
137. 1. R—B1ch, K—N1; 2. B—B4 mate
138. 1. Q—N8ch, N × Q; 2. R—Q8 mate
139. 1. B × Pch, K—R1; 2. R × Pch, K × R; 3. R—R1 mate
140. 1. B—R6ch, K—N1 (if 1. . . . . K—B3; 2. Q—N5 mate); 2. Q—N5ch!, Q × Q; 3. R—K8ch, B—B1; 4. R × B mate (or 2. R—K8ch and 3. Q—N5ch)
142. 1. Q × Pch, K × Q; 2. R—R4ch, K—N2; 3. B—R6ch, K—R1 or R2; 4. B—B8 mate OR 3. . . . . K—B3; 4. R—B4 mate
143. 1. R—B7ch, K—K4; 2. B—B3 mate
144. 1. R—N1ch, K—R1; 2. B—N7ch, K—N1; 3. B × P mate
145. 1. Q × Pch, P × Q; 2. R—R7 mate
146. 1. R × Pch, K—R1; 2. R × BPch, (if 2. R—N1 dis ch, P—B3 saves Black), K—N1; 3. R—N7ch, K—R1; 4. R—N6 (or N5, N4, N3, N2, N1) dis ch, R—B3; 5. B × R mate
147. 1. . . . . R × Pch; 2. Q × R, Q × Qch; 3. K × Q, R—R1 mate

CHAPTER 8

152. 1. R—Q7, any move; 2. R × P (or R—R7) mate
154. 1. Q × Pch, R × Q; 2. R × R mate
156. 1. . . . . N × Pch; 2. K—R1, R—R6ch; 3. P × R, R—R7 mate
160. 12. Q × Pch, K × Q; 13. R—R5 mate
161. 1. Q × Pch, K × Q; 2. P × B dis ch, K—N1 (or N3); 3. N—K7 mate
162. 1. Q—B8ch, K × Q; 2. R—Q8 mate (and if 1. . . . . K—R2; 2. Q—N7 mate)
163. 1. . . . . R × Pch; 2. K × R, R—B7 mate
164. 1. . . . . R × Nch; 2 B × Rch, R × B mate
165. 1. Q—B5ch, P × Q; 2. R—Q7 mate
166. 1. . . . . N—N6ch; 2. R × N, R × Nch; 3. K × R, R—K8 mate
167. 1. R × Bch, P × R; 2. R—Q3ch, K—K1; 3. N × P mate

CHAPTER 9

172. 1. Either N to Q7ch, Q × N; 2. N × Q mate
173. 1. . . . . N—N4; 2. any move, N × P mate
174. 1. . . . . Q × Bch; 2. K × Q, B—R6ch; 3. K—N1, N—B6 mate
175. 1. . . . . R(N2)—N8ch; 2. Q × R, R—B8ch; 3. Q × R, Q × Rch; 4. K × Q, B—R6ch; 5. K—N1, N—B6 mate
176. 1. K—Q7, P—R6 (or the advance of the KBP with a similar result); 2. K—K7 or K8, P—R7; 3. K × P, P—R8 (=Q); 4. B—N7 mate
177. 1. B—R3, P—K6; 2. B—B8, P—K7; 3. B—R6, P—K8 (=Q); 4. B—N5 mate
178. 1. Q × Pch, N × Q; 2. N—N6ch, K—N1; 3. B—R2 mate
180. 1. Q—R8ch, K × Q; 2. N × NPch (if 2. N × BPch the Knight would be pinned, for the Black Rook prevents 3. N—R6 mate because White's King would then be subject to capture), K—N1; 3. N—K7 mate
181. 1. N—N5 dbl ch, K—R1; 2. N—B7 mate
182. 1. Q × Bch, N × Q; 2. B—B6 mate. If 1. . . . . P—B3; 2. Q or B × P mate
183. 4. N—B7 dbl ch, K—N1; 5. N—R6 mate
184. 1. . . . . Q × N (threatening 2. . . . . Q × P mate); 2. P × Q, B × Pch; 3. K—N1, N—R6 mate
185. 1. Q—R6 (with the threat of 2. Q × NP mate), P × Q; 2. N × P mate

CHAPTER 10

190. 1. N—KN4, any Knight move; 2. N—B6 mate (Thus, if 1. . . . . N—B3ch; 2. N × N mate)
191. 1. . . . . N—Q6; 2. any move, N(Q6)—B7 mate
193. 1. . . . . Q—N7ch; 2. N × Q, N—R6 mate
194. 1. . . . . N—N6ch (forcing Tchigorin's position as in Diagram 193); 2. K—N1, Q—N7ch; 3. R × Q, N—R6 mate
195. 1. N—Q5ch, K—K4; 2. N—B3ch, K × P; 3. N—B3 mate
196. 2. . . . . N—B8 mate
197. 1. R × Nch, P × R (if Black plays R—B6 or B—B6 at once, then 2. N—B2 mate); 2. R × Pch, R—B6 or B—B6; 3. N—B2 mate
198. 1. . . . . Q × Pch; 2. K × Q (if 2. K—B1, mate follows by a Black check at N7 or R8), N—N5ch; 3. K—N1, N—R6ch; 4. K—B1, N—R7 mate

199. 1. Q—K8ch, K × Q; 2. N—B6ch, K—Q1; 3. N—B7 mate

200. 1. Q × Bch, N × Q; 2. N—N3ch, K—R5; 3. N—B3 mate

201. 1. K—B7!, K—R1; 2. N(R5)—B6, P—R4; 3. N—B8 or Q5, P—R5; 4. N—N6 mate. Also 2. N—Q5, K—R2; 3. N—B6ch, K—R1; 4. N—N6 mate.

203. (From the diagram) 1. Q × Pch, R × Q; 2. R × Rch, N × R; 3. N—B6ch, K—R1; 4. N × P mate. White had achieved this mating position by first sacrificing a Rook at his Q7. Black took the Rook with his Bishop, for he would have lost his Queen had he taken it with the Queen instead. Players often permit quick mates rather than resigning or giving up a Queen.

CHAPTER 11

208. 1. Q × Pch, K × Q; 2. B × P mate (If 1. . . . . K—R1; 2. Q—N7 or B—N7 mate)

209. 2. B × P mate

210. 1. Q × Nch, K × Q; 2. B—K5 mate (If 1. . . . . K—B1; 2. Q × R mate. Black could have delayed the mate for a while had he played 1. . . . . K—N1; 2. B—K5, B × Pch; 3. K × B, R—R2; 4. B × Rch, K × B or K—B1; 5. Q—N7 mate. But in the game he played 1. . . . . K × Q, preferring to end the game at once since he is so clearly lost anyway.)

211. 1. . . . . B—R5ch; 2. K—B1, B—B5ch; 3. K—N1, B—B7ch; 4. K—R1, B—K4 mate

213. 1. . . . . Q × Pch; 2. K × Q, B—N2ch; 3. K—N1, B × P mate

214. 1. B × Pch, K—R1; 2. B—N2ch, P—B6; 3. B × Pch, P—Q5; 4. B × Pch, P—K4; 5. B × Pch, P—B3; 6. B × P mate

215. 1. N—R6ch!, K—R1; 2. N(N5) × P mate with two Knights! 1. . . . . P × N; 2. B × P mate with two Bishops!

216. 1. . . . . Q × Pch; 2. P × Q, B—B3ch; 3. K—R2, B—N6 mate

217. (from the diagram) 1. . . . . Q × P; 2. B × Pch, K—B1; 3. N(1)—B3, N × Nch; 4. N × N (if K—N2, Q—R7 mate), B × N; 5. P × Q (to prevent . . . . Q—R7 mate), B—R7 mate

218. 1. . . . . N × Pch! (clearing a path for the Bishop); 2. B × N, R × Pch (opening the short diagonal); 3. P × R, B—R6 mate

219. (from the diagram) 1. . . . . Q × Pch; 2. K × Q, N—N5ch; 3. K—B3, P—K5ch; 4. K × P, N(2)—B3ch; 5. K—B3, N—K4ch; 6. K—B2, N(3)—N5ch; 7. K—N1, B—K6 mate!

220. 1. B—N2ch, K—R2; 2. B—N8 mate

CHAPTER 12

221. 1. Q × Nch, R × Q; 2. R × Rch, R—B1; 3. R(B1 or Q8) × R mate

222. 1. Q × Bch, R × Q; 2. R—K8ch, R—Q1; 3. R(K8 or Q1) × R mate

224. 1. Q × Pch, K ×Q; 2. R—R1 mate

225. 1. . . . . K—N5 dis ch; 2. K—N1, K—R4 dis ch; 3. K—R1 or R2, K—N3 dis ch and mate

226. 1. R(1) × P, any move; 2. R—R8 or R—N8 mate

227. 1. . . . . R × Pch; 2. K—R1, R × Pch; 3. K—N1, R(N7)—N7 mate

228. 1. Q—R7ch, K × Q; 2. R × Pch, K—R1; 3. R—R7ch, K—N1; 4. R(N7)—N7 mate

229. 1. Q × Pch, R × Q; 2. R—N7ch, K—R1; 3. R × R mate

230. 1. . . . . N—N6ch; 2. P × N (if 2. K—N1, R—B8 mate), R—B8ch; 3. K—R2, R—R2 mate

232. 1. N—B6ch, P × N; 2. Q × Pch, K × Q; 3. R—R1ch, K—N3 (if 3. . . . . K—N1; 4. R(KR1)—N1 mate); 4. R(KR1)—N1ch, K—B4; 5. R—R5 mate

233. 1. . . . . R(B4) × Pch; 2. K—K1, R(B7)—QN7!; 3. any move, R—R8 or R—N8 mate (depending on White's third move)

234. 1. Q × Pch, P × Q; 2. R—N7 mate

235. 1. Q × Rch, K × Q; 2. R—Q8 mate

236. 1. . . . . Q × Pch; 2. R × Q (if 2. K—R1, Q × R mate), R—R8ch; 3. R—B1, R(R8 or B2) × R mate

237. 1. . . . . Q × Pch; 2. R × Q, R—N8ch; 3. R—B1, R × Rch; 4. R—N1, R(N3 or B8) × R mate

238. 1. Q—N6ch!, Q × Q (if . . . . R—B2; 2. Q × Q wins. But let's follow the continuation after Black accepts the Queen sacrifice); 2. R(K1) × Nch, K—Q1; 3. R(N7)—Q7 mate

CHAPTER 13

240. 1. Q × Bch, P × Q; 2. B—R6 mate

241. 1. . . . . Q—B6ch; 2. P × Q, B—R6 mate

242. 1. Q × Nch!, R × Q (if 1. . . . . K—Q2; 2. B × P mate anyway); 2. B × P mate

243. 1. Q × Pch, P × Q; 2. B—R6 mate

244. 1. Q × Pch, P × Q; 2. B—R6 mate

245. 1. Q × Pch, P ×Q; 2. B—R6 mate

246. 1. R—B6ch, P × R; 2. Q × Pch, N × Q; 3. B—R6 mate (If 1. . . . . N × R; 2. Q × Nch, P × Q; 3. B—R6 mate)

247. 1. Q × Pch, P × Q; 2. B—N6 mate (if 1. . . . . Q—K2; 2. Q × Q mate)
248. 1. Q × Pch, P × Q; 2. B—R6 mate
249. 1. . . . . Q × Nch; 2. P × Q, B—R6 mate
251. 1. . . . . R × Pch; 2. B × R, R × Bch; 3. P × R, B—R6 mate
252. 1. . . . . R—R3ch; 2. K—N1, B—K6ch; 3. K—B1, Q × Pch; 4. P × Q, B—R6 mate

CHAPTER 14

256. 1. . . . . N × Nch; 2. any move, Q × P mate
257. 1. Q—R8ch, B × Q; 2. R × B mate
259. 1. . . . . P—B6; 2. P—N3, Q—R6; 3. any move, Q—N7 mate
260. 1. . . . . R—KR2; 2. Q—Q1, R—QN1; 3. Q × P, P × Q; 4. any move, R(N1)—KR1; 5. any move, R—R8 mate
261. 1. Q × N!, B × Q; 2. R × P! P × R; 3. R × P, B—R3; 4. R × B, Q—N6ch; 5. K × Q, any move; 6. R—R8 mate
262. 1. B × RPch!, N × B; 2. R × N, K × R; 3. R—R4ch, K—N1; 4. Q—R8 mate or R—R8 mate
263. 1. Q—R8ch, B × Q; 2. R × B mate
264. 1. Q—R6, with Q—N7 mate to follow
265. 1. Q × P!, P × Q; 2. R—R8ch, B × R; 3. R × B mate
266. 1. . . . . Q × Pch!; 2. RP × Q (if 2. K—R1, B—B6 mate), B—B6; 3. any move, R—R8 mate
267. 1. . . . . Q—K8ch; 2. K—R2, B—N8ch; 3. K—R1, B—B7 dis ch; 4. K—R2, Q—N8 mate
268. 1. . . . . N × Nch; 2. N × N (if 2. P × N, Q—N3 mate), Q × N!; 3. P × Q (otherwise Black mates at KN7), B × P; 4. any move, R—R8 mate
269. 1. N—K7ch!, Q × N; 2. Q × RPch, K × Q; 3. R—R5ch, K—N1 (3. . . . . P × R is impossible because the White Bishop at Q3 pins the Pawn); 4. R—R8 mate
270. 1. . . . . Q × RPch!; 2. K × Q, P × P dbl ch; 3. K—N1, R—R8 mate

CHAPTER 15

272. 2. R × Nch, K × R; 3. Q—R5 mate
274. 1. . . . . B—N5ch; (a) 2. Q × B, R—Q8 mate (b) 2. Q—B3, R—Q8 mate (c) 2. B—Q2, B × B mate

275. 1. R × Pch, K × R; 2. Q—R5 mate

276. 2. N—N6ch, P × N; 3. Q—R3 mate

277. 1. . . . . N—N6ch; 2. P × N, Q—R3 mate

278. 1. . . . . N—K7ch; 2. K—R1, Q × Pch!; 3. K × Q. B × P mate

280. *White to Play:* 1. B—N6 dis ch, K—N1 or N2; 2. Q—R7ch, K—B1; 3. Q × P mate
Black to Play: 2. . . . . R × Pch!; 3. Q × R, Q × Qch; 4. K—N1, Q × P mate

282. 1. Q × Pch, K × Q; 2. R—R1ch, B—R6; 3. R × B mate

283. 1. B—B4ch, K—R1 (on K—B1 White plays Q—B7 mate); 2. Q × Pch!, K × Q; 3. R—R3 mate

284. 5. RP(or BP) × P, P × P; 6. P × P mate

285. 1. . . . . B—N8 dis ch; 2. K—N3, Q—B7ch; 3. K—R3, Q—R7 mate

286. 1. . . . . Q × Pch!; 2. Q × Q, N—N6ch; 3. P × N, R—R1 mate

287. 5. R—R5ch, K—N2 (or N1); 6. R—N5ch, K—R2; 7. B—B5 mate

288. 5. Q—B7ch and (a) 5. . . . . K—R3; 6. Q × RP mate or (b) 5. . . . . K—N5; 6. P—B3 mate. Also possible is 5. Q—R6ch. On 5. . . . . K × Q; 6. R × P mate. On 5. . . . . K—N5; 6. P—B3 or R—N7 mate.

CHAPTER 16

294. *a.* 2. B—Q7 mate
b. 2. B—Q7ch, K—B1 or Q1; B × N mate (on 2. . . . . K—Q1; 3. P × N is also mate)

295. 2. B—N5 dbl ch, K—K1; 3. R—Q8 mate

296. 2. . . . . B—Q6 dbl ch; 3. K—K1, R—B8 mate

297. 1. Q—Q8ch, K × Q; 2. B—R5 dbl ch, K—K1 or B1; 3. R—Q8 mate

298. 2. N—B6 mate

299. 1. N—B6 mate

302. 1. Q—N8ch, R × Q; 2. N—B7 mate

303. 1. N—R6ch, K—R1; 2. Q—K7 (threatening Q × R mate), R—N1 (2. . . . . Q—N5 would have prevented the mate but would have meant the loss of Black's Queen); 3. N × P mate (or 2. . . . . N—B3; 3. Q × Rch, N—N1; 4. Q × N or N × P mate)

304. 1. R × Pch, Q × R; 2. N—B7 mate

305. 1. Q × Pch!, P × Q; 2. N—N5 dbl ch, K—R1; 3. R—R7 mate

306. 1. N—K5 dbl ch, K—K2 or K3 (on 1. . . . . K—N1 or N2; 2. Q—B7 mate); 2. Q—B7ch, K—Q3; 3. N—B4 mate (or 2. . . . . K—B4; 3. P—N4 mate)

307. 1. Q—Q8ch, K × Q; 2. N—B6 dbl ch, K—K1; 3. R—Q8 mate

308. 1. . . . . N—Q6 dis ch; 2. K—R1 (2. K—B1, Q—B7 mate), N—B7ch; 3. K—N1, N—R6 dbl ch; 4. K—R1, Q—N8ch; 5. R × Q, N—B7 mate

309. 1. R—K8ch, R × R; 2. N—R6 dbl ch, K—R1 (again K—B1 would permit an immediate mate); 3. Q—N8ch, R × Q; 4. N—B7 mate

310. 1. Q—Q8ch, K × Q; 2. B—R5 dbl ch, K—K1; 3. R—Q8 mate

CHAPTER 17

313. *a.* 2. . . . . P × P dis ch; 3. K—N1, R—R8 mate
b. 2. . . . . Q—R8 mate

314. 2. R—N3ch, K—R3; 3. B—B1ch, K—R4; 4. B—K2ch, K × P; 5. R—R3 or B—KN5 mate

315. *a.* 3. . . . . N(N6 or Q5)—K7ch; 4. Q × N, N × Q mate
b. With the threat of mate at the square KR7 (If 4. P × Q, N—K7 dbl ch is mate!)
c. 5. . . . . N—B6ch; 6. K—R1, Q—R7 mate

316. *a.* 2. Q—B8ch, R × Q; 3. R × R mate
b. 3. P—Q8(=Q), with a winning advantage

317. *a.* 1. Q × Nch, Q × Q; 2. R—Q8 mate (the Black Queen is pinned)
b. 1. Q × Nch, K—N1; 2. Q—K8 or Q—B8 mate

318. *a.* 3. . . . . B—B4ch; 4. K—Q3, N × N mate
b. 3. Q—N2 prevents the mate

319. *a.* 2. N × Pch, P × N; 3. R—R3 mate
b. 2. Q × RPch, K × Q; 3. R—R3 mate

320. On 3. . . . . R × N; 4. R—Q8ch, Q—K1; 5. R × Qch, R—B1; 6. R × R mate

322. 6. B—K2ch, K—N7; 7. R—R2ch, K—N8; 8. K—Q2(or O—O—O) dis ch and mate

323. 1. Q × Pch, B × Q; 2. R × Bch, K—N2; 3. N—B5 mate

324. *a.* 2. B × Pch, K—K2; 3. N—Q5 mate
b. 2. . . . . N—KB3

325. 2. Q × RPch, P × Q; 3. R × R mate

326. 3. R—N8ch!, K × R; 4. P—R7ch, K—B1; 5. P—R8(=Q or R) mate

327. *a.* 3. R—B1, B × Pch; 4. Q—Q3 (for if 4. K—R1, R × R mate), B × Qch; 5. K—R1, R × R mate

b. 3. Q—Q3, B × Qch; 4. K—Q1 or Q2, B × P dis ch; 5. K moves, B × B (or: 3. . . . . P × Q dbl ch; 4. K—Q2, R × R; 5. K × R, P—Q7ch; 6. K—Q1, B—B6ch; 7. K—B2, P—Q8(=Q) mate

328. *a.* R × P mate

b. 3. B × Pch, K—N1 or R1; 4. R—B8 mate

CHAPTER 18

330. 1. . . . . N × BP dbl ch; 2. K—N1, N—R6 mate—or 1. . . . . N × NP dbl ch; 2. K—N1, N—K7 mate. The former was played in the game.

331. 2. R—R8ch, K × R; 3. Q × Rch, K—N1; 4. Q—N7 mate

332. 1. . . . . R × Pch; 2. K × R, Q—R4 mate

333. *a.* 3. . . . . Q × P mate

b. 3. . . . . Q—R6ch; 4. K—N1, R—N1ch; 5. K—R1, Q—B6 or

334. N7 mate

c. 3. . . . . Q—K5 mate

d. 5. . . . . Q × BPch; 6. R—N2, Q × R mate

e. 5. . . . . Q × R; 6. Q—KB1 or KN1, Q × Q mate (or on any other move by White, 6. . . . . Q—N7 mate)

335. *a.* 2. . . . . Q × BP mate

b. 2. . . . . R—N1ch; 3. K—R1, Q—B6ch; 4. K—R2, Q—N7 mate

c. 2. . . . . Q × KNP mate

336. 1. R × Pch, P × R; 2. Q—N6ch, R—B2; 3. Q × R mate

337. 1. R—K8ch, B × R; 2. Q × P mate

338. 4. B × Pch, R—N2; 5. Q × R mate

339. 3. . . . . P—R3ch; 4. K—B4, P—N4ch; 5. K—K5, Q—K3 mate

340. 2. Q—B7ch, K—R1; 3. Q × R mate or 2. . . . . R—N2; 3. Q × R mate

341. 1. R—B8 dbl ch, K × R; 2. N—N6ch, P × N; 3. Q—R8 mate

342. *a.* 4. . . . . B × Pch; 5. R × B, Q—N8 mate

b. 3. . . . . R—N1ch; 4. B—N5, R × Bch; 5. K × R, Q—R3 mate
c. 5. . . . . R—N1ch; 6. B—N5, R × B mate

343. *a.* 2. . . . . Q × P mate
b. 3. . . . . Q—N6ch; 4. K—R1, Q mates on N7 or R7 (or R mates on R7)
c. 4. . . . . Q × B mate
d. 10. . . . . Q—B6; 11. . . . . P—K7; 12. . . . . P—K8(=Q); 13. . . . . Q(K8)—B7 or R8 mate

343. *a.* 2. . . . . Q × P mate
b. 3. . . . . Q —N6ch; 4. K—R1, Q mates on N7 or R7 (or R mate on R7)
c. 4. . . . . Q × B mate *d.* 10. . . . . Q—B6; 11. . . . . P—K7; 12. . . . . P—K8 (=Q); 13. . . . . Q(K8)—B7 or R8 mate

344. *a.* 3. K × R, Q—R5 mate and 3. K—B1, R—R8 mate
b. 7. . . . . P—KR4, for White cannot prevent the advance of this Pawn
c. 3. R—N2, Q—R5 mate

345. *a.* 2. R(R7) × Pch, K—B1; 3. R(B7)—B7 mate (on 2. . . . . K—R1; 3. Q—R5 mate)
b. 2. Q—R5ch, K—N1; 3. Q—B7ch, K moves; 4. Q × P mate

346. 1. . . . . R × Pch; 2. R × R or K × R, Q × RP mate

347. *a.* 2. Q × Nch, Q × Q; 3. R—Q8 mate (or 2. . . . . K—N1; 3. Q × Q mate)
b 4. Q × Nch, K—N1; 5. Q—B8 mate (c) 6. Q × Nch, K—N1; 7. Q—K8ch, Q—B1; Q × Q mate

CHAPTER 19

349. 3. Q—B8ch, Q × Q; 4. R × Q mate

350. *a.* 1. B—B6ch, Q × B (or R × B); 2. Q—B8 mate
b. 1. B—B6, K—N1; 2. B × Q

351. 3. R—R3ch, K—N1; 4. Q—R5, P—B3; 5. P—N6, any move; 6. Q—R8 mate

352. *a.* 5. P—N6, any move; 6. Q—R8 mate
b. 3. P—R5ch, K—B4; 4. P—N4 mate *or* 3. . . . . K—R3; 4. N × KP dis ch, winning the Queen
c. 6. Q—Q3 mate
d. 4. Q—R5, P—B3; 5. P—N6, Q—R5; 6. Q × Q and 7. Q—R8 mate

353. *a.* 3. B × P dis ch, K moves; 4. Q—R7 mate
b. 3. B moves to any square but N8 (dis ch), K—N1; 4. Q—R7ch, K—B1; 5. Q—R8 mate
c. 3. Q—R5, with the threat of 4. Q—R7 mate on any move but 3. . . . . R—K1 or Q1, in which case 4. Q—R7ch, K—B1; Q—R8 mate
d. 4. Q × Pch, K—R4; 5. N—B4ch, K—R5; 6. Q—N3 mate or P—N3 mate (or 5. Q—R7ch, K—N5; 6. P—R3 or P—B3 mate)

354. *a.* 3. N × BP dis ch, K moves; 4. N × Q
b. 3. P—R5ch, K—B3; 4. Q—B3ch, Q—B5; 5. Q × Q mate (or 3. P—R5ch, K—R3; 4. N × BPch, K—R2; 5. N × Q . . . or 3. P—R5ch, K—B3; 4. N—R7ch, K—K3; 5. N × R ch, K—B3; 6. Q—B3ch, Q—B5; 7. Q × Q mate. Take your choice!)
c. 5. Q—R7ch, K—B1; 6. Q—R8 mate

355. *a.* 4. N—Q4, followed by R—K3 and the entry of the Rook will win.
b. 7. Q—R4ch, K—B1; 8. Q—R8ch, K—K2; 9. Q × P mate

356. *a.* 2. . . . . Q × Pch; 3. K—K1, Q—K7 mate
b. 2. . . . . Q—K4ch; 3. B—K3, Q × Bch; 4. Q—K2, Q × Q mate *or* 3. Q—K4, Q × Qch; 4. B—K3, Q × B mate

357. *a.* 2. . . . . N—N6 mate or 2. . . . . N—B7 mate
b. 3. K—B1, Q—B7 mate and 3. K—R1, N—N6 mate; and therefore: 3. B—Q3, Q × Bch; 4. K—B1 or R1 and mate follows (Q—B7 or N—N6).

358. 3. R—N1, N—N6ch; 4. P × N, Q—R6 mate

359. *a.* 2. Q—N5, P—KN3; 3. Q—R6, with the threat of 4. Q—N7 mate. Black can delay the mate one move by playing . . . . Q × Pch.
b. 2. . . . . Q × Pch; 3. B × Q and 4. Q × NP mate
c. 2. . . . . P—KB4; 3. Q × P(B5) and 4. Q × RP mate

360. *a.* 2. Q—R3
b. 4. Q—R7 mate
c. 5. N(B3)—K4ch, P × N; N × P mate (either Knight could have played to K4 on move 5)

361. *a.* 4. N × KP dis ch, winning the Queen
b. 4. P—N4ch, K—B5; 5. B—B1 mate or 4. . . . . K—B3; 5. N—R7 mate
c. 6. P—R6, any move; 7. Q—N5 mate

362. 2. Q—Q5ch, K—B1; 3. Q—B6 mate

363. *a.* 2. . . . . R × Nch; 3. R × R, Q × P mate
b. 3. . . . . R × N mate

c. 2. . . . . Q—K5ch; 3. K—N1, R × Nch; 4. R × R, Q—N7 mate *or* 3. N—B3, Q × Nch; 4. K—N1, Q—N7 mate

CHAPTER 20

365. *a.* 9. R × B
b. 12. B × R, K × B; 13. Q—K7 mate
c. Q—K7 mate
366. 1. . . . . N—N6ch; 2. P × N, P × N mate
367. 2. N—N6ch, P × N; 3. Q—R3 mate
368. *a.* 4. Q—R4, 5 or 6, with the threat of 5. Q—R8 mate
b. 3. Q × P mate
c. 5. Q × Qch, R × Q; 6. R × R mate
369. 1. . . . . N—N5ch; 2. N × N, Q—K6 mate; or 2. P × N, Q—Q5 mate
370. *a.* 1. N—N5, B × N; 2. R × R mate or 1. N—N5, R × R; 2. Q—R7 mate
b. 4. Q—R7ch, K—B1; 5. Q—R8 mate
371. *a.* 3. B—N6ch, K—B1; 4. Q—B7 mate
b. 3. B—N6, winning the Queen after 3. . . . . Q—K1; 4. B × Q
372. *a.* 2. Q × Bch, Q—N4; 3. Q × Q mate
b. 3. N × P mate, or in the second possibility, 3. N × Pch, Q × N; 4. N × Q mate
373. 3. R × Nch, K × R; 4. Q—Q8 mate
374. *a.* 3. Q × KPch, B—K2; 4. Q × B mate
b. 6. R—Q8 mate
c. 6. R—Q8 mate
d. 8. KR—K1ch, B—K7; 9. R—Q8ch, B × R; 10. R × Bch, K—B1; 11. Q × B mate is one of several possibilities.
375. 1. . . . . N—R7ch; 2. R × N or Q × N or K—K1, R—Q8 mate
376. 1. . . . . N—B6ch; 2. K—Q2, R—K7ch!; 3. K × N, Q—Q5 mate
377. *a.* 2. Q × N, Q—KB1; 3. B × Q (threatening 4. Q—N7 mate), K × B; 4. Q—R8 mate
b. 3. Q × N, any move; 4. Q—N7 mate
c. 2. Q × N mate
378. 3. Q—B4ch, B—Q4; 4. Q × Bch, Q—B2 or R—B2; 5. R—R8 mate
379. *a.* 1. . . . . B—N5ch; 2. P × B, N—K6ch; 3. P × N, R—Q1ch; 4. Q—Q5, R × Qch; 5. B—Q2, Q × B mate
b. 4. P—B3
380. *a.* 2. Q—R7 mate
b. 2. N × Nch, any move; 3. Q—R7 mate

CHAPTER 21

384. *a.* 3. . . . . K—K3 and Black stops the White QBP.

b. 5. P—R8(=Q), P—N7; 6. Q—R2, any move; 7. Q × NP (or Q × Q if Black Queens his Pawn)

386. 1. . . . . R—Q8ch; 2. R × R (if 2. K—K2, R(Q1)—Q7 mate), R × Rch; 3. K—K2, P × P

387. *a.* 2. B—K6

b. 2. Q—K8ch, Q × Q; 3. R × Qch, R × R; 4. P × R(=Q or R) mate

388. *a.* 2. P × P

b. 2. P—B7

c. 5. Q—K7ch, K—B1 or N1; 6. R—Q8 mate

389. 1. P—B8 (=Q or B)ch, R × Q (or B); 2. Q × R mate

390. 1. R × R, N × R; 2. P—K8(=Q)

391. 1. Q × Rch, Q × Q; 2. P—K7

392. *a.* 2. Q × Pch, K—B1 or R1; 3. Q—N8 mate

b. 3. P—N8(=Q)ch, K—R3; 4. Q—N6 mate

c. 3. Q—B7ch, K × Q; 4. P—N8(=Q) mate

393. *a.* 2. P—Q8(=Q)ch, Q—K1; 3. Q × Qch, B—B1; 4. Q × B or R × B mate

b. 3. R—B8 mate

c. 3. B × B

394. *a.* 3. Q—B7 mate

b. 4. Q—B7ch, K—N4; 5. B—Q7 mate

c. 5. Q × Pch, K—Q6; 6. Q—B3 mate or R—Q1 mate

395. 7. . . . . P × R(=N) mate

397. 4. Q × Pch, K—R1; 5. Q—B6ch, K—R2; 6. Q—B7ch. Black cannot attempt to escape the checks, for 6. . . . . K—R3; 7. Q—B4ch, K—R4; 8. Q—R4 mate

398. *a.* 1. . . . . R × Bch; 2. K—B4, Q—B6 mate

b. 3. N—B5ch, K—B2; 4. N × Q dis ch, and on 4. . . . . K × N; 5. B × P wins,

399. *a.* 6. . . . . Q—N1ch; 7. K—Q7, Q—B2 mate

b. 3. P—K8(=N)ch, K—B4; 4. R—N5 mate

400. *a.* 3. R—N8 mate

b. 3. P—B8(=N)ch, K—R1; 4. R—N8 mate

c. 2. Q—R7ch, K—B1; 3. Q—R8 mate

401. *a.* 4. P—B7, B—K4; 5. P—B8(=Q)ch, B—N1; 6. Q × B mate or Q—N7 mate or Q—B6 mate

b. 5. N—B6 and 6. B—N7 mate

402. 5. N—R6ch, K—R1; 6. B—B6 mate

403. *a.* 6. R—R8ch, R—R5; 7. R × R mate
b. 6. K—N3, attacking the Rook and threatening R—B1 mate. Black must play 6. . . . . K—N8 to prevent the mate and White wins with 7. K × R.

CHAPTER 22

404. 1. Q—Q8ch, K—R2; 2. Q—R5ch, K—N1; 3. Q—Q8ch
406. 2. R × Pch, K—R1; 3. R—N8ch, K—R2; 4. R—N7ch, K—R3; 5. R—N6ch, etc.
407. 3. R—K8ch, R—B1; 4. R × R mate
408. 3. . . . . Q—N7ch
411. 18. . . . . B—B5; 19. Any move, P—N4 mate
413. 17. N—Q5ch, K—Q2; 18. B—K6ch, K—K1; 19. B—B7ch
414. *a.* 2. . . . . Q × Pch; 3. K—R1, Q—R6ch; 4. K—N1
b. 2. . . . . R—R6ch; 3. K × R, Q—N5ch; 4. K—R2, Q × Pch
416. 1. . . . . R(5) × Pch; 2. P × R, R—R8ch and Black checks at R7 and R8 while the White King can move only to B2 and back to the first rank.
417. 3. B—R6 mate
418. 2. . . . . Q—K3ch; 3. Q × Q stalemate
419. 1. . . . . R—B8ch; 2. K—R2, R—R8ch; 3. K × R, R—B8ch; 4. K—R2, R—R8ch; 3. K × R stalemate
420. 3. . . . . R × Bch; 4. K—R1, B—N7ch; 5. K—N1, B—R6ch
421. *a.* 4. . . . . Q—B5ch
b. 9. . . . . Q—B5ch

CHAPTER 23

422. 1. K—K4, R × Pch; 2. P × R, any move; 3. R—N6 mate (Also good is 1. R—N6ch, K—B4; 2. R—B7ch, R—B3; 3. R(7) × R mate)
423. 3. Q—B3ch, Q—N7ch; 4. Q × Q mate
424. *a.* 3. Q—B5 mate or R—R5 mate
b. 4. R—B5 mate
425. *a.* 2. N—B6ch, K—R1; 3. R—N8 mate
b. 4. B—R5ch, K—R2 or R3; 5. B × P dis ch, Q—R6; 6. R × Q mate
c. 5. B—R5 mate
427. 4. K—K7

428. *a.* 5. . . . . K—R6; 6. K—N1, Q × R mate
b. 7. . . . . Q—K8ch; 8. R—B1, Q × R mate

429. 9. R—Q8ch, Q—B1ch; 10. R × Qch, K—R2; 11. B—Q3 mate

430. *a.* 3. B—B7ch, N × B or K—R1; 4. R—K8 mate (3. B—B7ch, K—R1; 4. B—N7 is also mate)
b. 3. B—B7ch, K—R1; 4. B—N7 mate
c. 7. K—N6, any move; 8. B—N7 mate (In this line 5. . . . . R—KN1 avoids the mate but loses after 6. B × R, K × B; 7. K × P etc.)

431. *a.* 4. P—R6
b. 4. . . . . B—Q5; 5. P—R8(=Q), B × Pch; 6. K—N1, B × Q

432. *a.* 3. . . . . B—B5ch; 4. K—R1, Q—R6ch; 5. K—N1, B—Q6 mate
b. 6. . . . . B—Q6 dis ch; 7. K—Q1, Q—Q7 mate

433. *a.* 3. . . . . B—N7 mate
b. 6. . . . . B—Q5ch; 7. N—N2, B × N mate

434. *a.* 5. Q—K6ch
b. 5. K—N6
c. 5. K—N6

435. *a.* 6. R—N8 mate
b. 7. B × Qch, K—R1; 8. R—B8 mate or B × P mate

CHAPTER 24

GAME ONE:

a. 17. N × P dis ch, R—N2; 18. R × Rch, B × R; 19. Q × B mate
b. 13. B × Pch, K—R1; 14. B—N6 dis ch, K—N1; 15. Q—R7 mate
c. 16. Q × Qch, K × Q; 17. N—B7 (winning the Rook)
d. 18. Q × QPch, B—K3; 19. Q × KP
e. 22. R × Rch, K—R4; 23. R—R6ch, K × R; 24. Q—N5 mate or 23. N—N3ch, K × P; 24. R—R6 mate

GAME TWO:

a. 8. . . . . B—N5ch; 9. Q—Q2, B × Qch; 10. N × B
b. 11. Q—N3!
c. 13. P × P
d. 13. . . . . Q—B3
e. 14. . . . . N × Pch; King moves, N × Q
f. 18. R—N8 dbl ch, K × R; 19. R—N1ch, Q—N4; 20. R × Q mate
g. 20. Q—B6ch, K—N1; 21. R—N1ch, Q—N5; 22. R × Qch, N × R; 23. Q—N7 (or R8) mate

h. 24. R—K1ch, K—B6; 25. Q—N3 mate
i. 23. R—K1ch, K—B6; 24. Q—N3 mate
j. 22. B × Pch, P—B3; 23. B × Pch, R × B; 24. R—N8 mate

GAME THREE:
a. 19. Q—R6ch, K—N1; 20. Q × Nch, K—B1; 21. Q—R8 mate (Mate also follows 20. R—N1ch, when all Black can do is to delay the mate a bit by interposing twice on the KN file.)
b. 16. Q × Pch, B—N2; 17. Q × B mate
c. 17. Q × P mate
d. 25. Q—K2ch, B—K6ch; 26. Q × B mate
e. 23. Q—Q5ch, K—K1 (on 23. . . . . K—B3; 24. Q—K6 mate); 24. Q × Rch, K—Q2; 25. Q × Nch
f. 28. N × Pch, King moves; 29. N × Q
g. 35. Q—K4 or Q—B5
h. 33. N × Qch, R × N; 34. R × Nch

GAME FOUR:
a. 13. Q—R5
b. 17. Q × Rch, Q—B1; 18. N × B or 17. . . . .B—B1; 18. Q × B(QB8)
c. 23. B—N5ch (with 23. . . . . K × B; 24. Q × Q and 23. . . . . K—B2; 24. Q × Qch, K × Q; 25. B × R)
d. 19. Q—Q5ch and 20. Q × B
e. 25. R—B1ch, B—B5; 26. R × Bch, B—B4; 27. R × Bch, Q—B2; 28. Q × Q mate
f. Q—R8 mate
g. 24. R × B
h. 31. B—N6 (on 31. . . . . B × B; 32. Q × Bch, N—N2; 33. Q × B)

GAME FIVE:
a. 13. . . . . B—K3
b. 15. R × P
c. 17. Q—R6ch, K—N1; 18. R—K8 mate
d. 18. Q—R6ch, K—N1; 19. P—B6
e. 22. N—N6ch, K—B2; 23. N × Rch, K—B1; 24. Q × Qch or N—N6ch
f. 23. Q × P mate or R × P mate (epaulettes!)
g. 23. Q—K5ch, K—R1 (if 23. . . . . R—B2; 24. Q × Rch, K—R1; 25. Q—B8 or Q8 mate); 24. N—B7ch, K—N1 (if . . . . R × N; 25. Q—K8 or R8ch, R—B1; 26. Q × R mate); 25. N—R6 dbl ch, K—R1; 26. Q—N8ch, R × Q; 27. N—B7 mate

CHAPTER 25

461. 1. R × Pch, R × R (on 1. . . . . K—R1 or N1; 2. Q—R7 mate); 2. Q—N6ch, K—R1; 3. N × R mate (or 2. . . . .K—B1; 3. Q × R mate)

462. 1. N—B6ch!, B × N; 2. Q × Pch, B—N2; 3. Q—R7 mate

463. 1. N—R6ch, K—R1 (1. . . . . K—B1; 2. Q—B7 mate); 2. Q—N8ch, R × Q; 3. N—B7 mate

464. 4. . . . . R—Q8ch; 5. K—N2 (5. K—K2, R—K8 mate), R—N8ch; 6. K—R3; B—B4ch; 7. P—N4, B × P mate

465. 2. N × P dbl ch, K—R1; 3. R × P mate

466. 3. Q × Nch, R—B4; 4. Q—N7ch, Q—N3; 5. Q × Q mate (or 3. . . . . K—R3; 4. R × P mate or Q—N7 mate and 4. Q × Rch, K—R3; 5. Q (or R) × P mate)

467. 1. N—B6ch, K—N2; 2. Q—R7ch, K—B1; 3. Q—R8 or N8 ch, K—K2; 4. Q—K8 mate (or 1. . . . . K—B1; 2. Q—B8ch, K—K2; 3. Q—K8 mate and in this line 2. . . . . K—N2; 3. Q—N8 mate)

468. 2. Q—B5ch, K—R5; 3. Q—R5 mate

469. 5. Q × Pch, K—N1; 6. R—R1, Q—Q2; 7. Q—R8ch, K—B2; 8. Q—N7 mate

470. 1. R—R6ch, P × R; 2. Q—B6ch, K—R2; 3. Q—B7ch, K—R1; 4. B—B6 mate

471. 2. Q × Pch, K × Q; 3. R—R2 mate

472. 1. Q × Pch, N × Q; 2. R × N mate

473. 1. R—K7ch, K—R3; 2. Q—B4ch, P—N4; 3. Q—B8ch, K—N3; 4. Q—N7 mate

474. 3. Q × Rch, K—R2; 4. R—B7ch, K—N3; 5. Q—N7 mate

475. 1. B—K3ch, K—N5; 2. Q—N3ch, K—R4; 3. Q × P mate (1. P—N4ch is mate in four after 1. . . . . K × P; 2. Q—N3ch, K—B4; 3. Q × Pch, K—Q5; 4. Q—B4 mate.)

476. 1. B—Q8 dis ch, K × B; 2. N—N5, Q—K8ch (to delay the mate); 3. R × Q and now:

—On any move but 3. . . . . N—R3; 4. N × P mate (except 3. N—K2; 4. Q × N mate) . . . .

—And on 3. . . . . N—R3; 4. Q—K7 mate. Black could have delayed the mate by 1. . . . . K—B1; 2. B × Q, but this would have left him too far behind to continue.

477. 1. Q—B7ch, K—R1; 2. Q—K8ch, K—N2 or R2; 3. R—B7 mate is the threat, which Black can delay for a move by 2. . . . . Q—B1; 3. Q × Qch, K—R2; 4. R—B7 mate

ANSWERS TO QUIZ REVIEW OF "CHECKMATE!" IDEAS

1. 1. Q—N5ch, P × Q; 2. R—R8ch, R—R3; 3. R × Rch. (See Chapter 4 for further clarification of mates with a Rook and Chapter 17 for better understanding of when to sacrifice a Queen.)
2. 1. . . . . Q—B7ch, N7ch or R7ch and, on White's King move, 2. . . . . Q—N6ch; 3. K × Q stalemate. (You should have noticed that Black would have no moves if he did not have his Queen, as was explained in Chapter 22.)
3. 1. Q—R7ch, N × Q; 2. N(R4)—N6ch, K—N1; 3. N × Bch, K—R1; 4. N(K5)—N6 mate. (The mate by two Knights should have been the object of your examination of the position once you noticed that they were bearing on an open King position—as explained in Chapter 10.)
4. 1. . . . . QR—N1ch; 2. B—N3 (otherwise, on 2. K—R1, B × P mate), R × Bch; 3. RP × R, B × P (threatening . . . . R—R8 mate); 4. Q—R7, R × Q; 5. ANY WHITE MOVE, R—R8 mate. (A clear example of the Long Diagonal Mate as explained in Chapter 14. If you failed to see the Rook sacrifice re-examine Chapter 18.)
5. 1. P—Q3 or P—Q4 (threatening 2. P—N4 ch and mate on the next move), P—KN4; 2. Q—B7ch, K—R5; 3. P—N3 mate. The second winning line is 1. P—N4ch, K—R5; 2. Q—N3ch, K—N4; 3. P—Q3, P—Q4, P—R4 or P—B4 mate! (Such mates by a Pawn were studied in Chapter 1.)

6. 1. . . . . Q—K8ch; 2. K—N2, B × Pch; 3. K × B or K—R3, Q—B8 mate. (The basic position was examined in Chapter 5, while examples of such a Bishop sacrifice were in Chapter 19.)

7. 1. . . . . R—R7ch; 2. K × R, N—B6ch; 3. K—R1, R × R mate. (This type of Arab Mate was detailed in Chapter 8, while the use of Rook sacrifices to force a mating position was in Chapter 18.)

8. 1. R—B2ch, K × N; 2. K—K2, ANY BLACK MOVE; 3. N—B3 mate. (This use of the King to assist in the mate by limiting the moves available to the enemy King was clarified in Chapter 23.)

9. 1. N—K7ch, K—R1; 2. R × Pch, K × R; 3. R—R1 mate. (This Anastasia Mate was discussed in Chapter 8, and includes the familiar Rook sacrifice to open a line, as illustrated in Chapter 18. The same mate was possible had the White piece on KR1 been a Queen.)

10. 1. . . . . Q × Pch; 2. K × Q, B × N dbl ch; 3. K—Q2, R—B7 mate (or 3. K—N3, B—B7 mate)—a double check attack! (As in Chapter 16, the battery of pieces on the half-open file permits a sacrifice that is followed by mate . . . by Rook and Bishop, as in Chapter 7, or by two Bishops, as in Chapter 11.)

11. 1. . . . . Q × Pch; 2. P × Q, B—R6 mate. (A simple Boden's Mate, as found in Chapter 13.)

12. 1. Q—R8ch, K × R; 2. B—B6 dbl ch, K—N1; 3. R—R8 mate. (Another example of the double check—Chapter 16—in this situation used to force a Long Diagonal Mate—Chapter 14—through a simple Queen sacrifice—Chapter 17.)

13. 1. Q—N6ch, N × Q; 2. P × Nch, B × R; 3. R × B mate. (The Queen sacrifice—see Chapter 17—was clearly indicated because the position calls for the mate by a Rook as explained in Chapter 4.)

14. 1. R—N7ch, Q × R; 2. R × Qch, K—R1; 3. R—N6, N5 or R × KNP mate is the clearest line. Black can delay the mate by 1. . . . . K—R1; 2. R—N5 dis ch, Q—N2; 3. R(from the N file) × Q, N—Q2; 4. R—N6 dis ch, N—B3 or K4; 5. B × N mate. (Such wins were clarified in Chapter 7, and also relate to the attack by two Rooks on the seventh rank as examined in Chapter 12.)

15. 1. R—Q8ch, K—B2 (on 1. . . . . R—B1; 2. R × R mate); 2. N—N5ch, P × N; 3. Q—K8 mate. (An Epaulettes Mate, as explained in Chapter 6, utilizing a Knight sacrifice to open a line, as in Chapter 20.)

16. 1. P—R3ch, K—R5; 2. R—B5ch, P × R or P—N5; 3. B—B6 mate. (Such mates by a Bishop were reviewed in Chapter 2, while Rook sacrifices to open a line were the subject of Chapter 18.)

17. 1. N—N5ch, P × N; 2. N—N7 mate. (Mate by a Knight, as examined in Chapter 3, this time made possible by the type of Knight sacrifice studied in Chapter 20.)

18. 1. . . . . Q—R6; 2. P × Q (to prevent 2. . . . . Q × NP mate), B—B6; 3. B—K7 (delaying mate by one move) 1 K × B; 4. ANY WHITE MOVE, N × P mate. (Such mates by Knight and Bishop were treated in Chapter 9, while Chapter 17 provided the rationale for this type of Queen sacrifice.)

19. 1. Q × Pch, K × Q; 2. R—R4ch, Q—R4; 3. R × Qch, K—N1; 4. N—K7 mate. (A Queen sacrifice—see Chapter 17—designed to bring about a position which is a cross between an Anastasia Mate—see Chapter 8—and a mate by a Knight—see Chapter 3.)

20. The mate in three moves is: 1. . . . . R × Pch; 2. P × R. B—B6ch; 3. K—R2, B—N8 mate. The mate in four moves is: 1. . . . . N—N6ch; 2. K—R2, N—B8ch; 3. K—R1, R × Pch; 4. P × R, B—B6 mate. (Both wins illustrate the Blackburne Mate seen in Chapter 11, while the use of the Rook sacrifice was in Chapter 18.)

21. 1. B × Pch, K × B; 2. Q × Bch, K—N2; 3. Q—B6ch, K—N1; 4. Q—B7 mate or 1. B × Pch, K—B1; 2. Q × B, N—B3; 3. B—B4 dis ch, K—K2; 4. Q—B6ch, K—K1; 5. Q—B7 mate or in the same line 3. . . . . K—N2; 4. Q—B7ch, K—R3; 5. R—B6ch, K—N4; 6. Q—N7ch, K—R4; 7. R—R6 mate. (A Bishop sacrifice to open a King position, as demonstrated in Chapter 19.)

22. 1. R—B8ch, R × R; 2. Q—R8ch, K × Q; 3. P × R(=Q) mate (This position combines the recognition of the timing for a Queen sacrifice—as in Chapter 17—with understanding of when to promote a Pawn—for which see Chapter 21.)

23. 1. . . . . R × Bch; 2. K × R, N × Pch; 3. K—B1 (on 3. K—R1, Q—R7 mate), N—R7ch; 4. K—N1, N—B6ch and draw by perpetual check follows. (Such a draw was demonstrated in Chapter 22.)

24. 1. Q × RPch, K × Q; 2. R—R3ch, B—R5; 3. R × B mate. (This is a Greco Mate as examined in Chapter 15, which, once recognized in the position, justifies the Queen sacrifice according to the guidelines in Chapter 17.)

25. 1. Q × RPch, R—R3; 2. Q × Rch, P × Q; 3. R—R7 mate. (This Damiano Mate, examined in Chapter 15, is the justification for the Queen sacrifice as explained in Chapter 17.)

26. 1. Q × Pch, K—R1; 2. Q—N8ch, R × Q; 3. N—B7 mate. (A different approach to the kinds of smothered mate discussed in

Chapter 16, the Queen sacrifice again following the guidelines of Chapter 17.)

27. 1. Q—N8ch, R—B1; 2. P—B7 mate. (A King lacking escape squares is mated by a supported Pawn, as in Chapter 1.)

28. 1. P—B6, R × B or any other move; 2. R—R8 mate. White can also win but without a mate in sight by 1. R—R8ch, K—N2; 2. R—N8ch, K—B3; 3. P—B8(=Q)ch, R × Q; 3. R × Rch, K—N4; 4. P—B6 and it will be possible to promote the Pawn or win a piece for it. But the mate in two is so simple, especially if you have studied Chapter 4!

29. 1. . . . . Q—K1ch; 2. B × Q, R × Bch; 3. K—Q1, B—K7ch; 4. K—K1, B—N5 dis ch; 5. K—B1, B—R6ch; 6. K—N1, R—K8 mate. (One of the mates illustrated in Chapter 7, the recognition of which justifies the Queen sacrifice according to Chapter 17.)

30. 1. . . . . Q—N8ch; 2. R × Q, N—B7ch; 3. K—N2, B—R6 mate. (Such a mate should have been clear if you had mastered Chapter 9 and its discussion of mate by Knight and Bishop. The Queen sacrifice to force a standard mate position was clarified in Chapter 17.)

31. 1. . . . . Q—N6ch; 2. K × Q (if 2. K—N1, R—B8 mate), N—B8 mate. (This is a difficult mate despite its two-move sequence, but would have been evident if you fully understood Chapter 3 and then applied the rules in Chapter 17.)

32. 1. N—B5ch, P × N; 2. Q × Nch, K—R4; 3. Q—N5 mate is a standard mate with a Queen as clarified in Chapter 5, while the other variation: 1. N—B5ch, K—R4; 2. Q × RPch, N × Q; 3. P—N4 mate is more difficult, requiring understanding of Chapter 17 as well as the recognition of the type of attack spelled out in Chapter 1.

33. 1. R—N8ch, R—Q1; 2. R × Rch, R—B1; 3. R × Rch, K—R2; 4. P—N6ch, K—R3; 5. R—R8 mate. (This direct mate with two Rooks, as examined in Chapter 12, depended on recognizing the impact of White's P—N6 to prevent Black's escape to his KN3.)

34. 1. R—N7ch, K × B; 2. Q—R1 mate. (This unusual example of a Long Diagonal Mate is also reminiscent of mates by a Bishop, two themes studied in Chapters 14 and 2.)

35. 1. N—R6, and Black resigned. The threat is 2. Q—N8ch, R × N; 3. N—B7 mate (smothered mate as in Chapter 16). If Black plays 1. . . . . P × N; 2. Q × P mate (mate by a supported Queen as in Chapter 5). On 1. . . . . R—K2; 2. Q × R, B × Q; 3. N—B7 (mate by two Knights as in Chapter 10.) Another possibility is 1. . . . .

R—K2; 2. Q × R, Q—N1; 3. R—Q8 and on 3. . . . . P × N; 4. Q × P mate or 4. Q × B mate, while on 3. . . . . B × Q; 4. R × Q mate (an Arab Mate as in Chapter 8). Few chess positions demand so thorough an understanding of mating ideas as this fine victory!

36. 1. R—B7ch, K—K3; 2. P—Q5ch, K—K4; 3. R—B4 mate. (In the end it is mate by a Bishop after careful play with the Rooks. See Chapter 2.)

37. 1. R—R6ch, K × R (if. 1. . . . . P × R; 2. Q—N8 mate); 2. Q—R8ch, K—N3; 3. Q—R5 mate. (A standard mate with the Queen, as seen in Chapter 5, justifying the Rook sacrifice according to Chapter 18.)

38. 1. Q × Bch, P × Q (on 1. . . . . K—R1; 2. Q × P mate or R × P mate); 2. N—B6ch, K—R1; 3. R—R7 mate. (An Arab Mate again, as in Chapter 8, with the Queen sacrifice therefore obvious, as Chapter 17 illustrated.)

39. 1. . . . . N × Pch; 2. K—N4, P—R4ch; 3. K—R3, N—B7 mate or on 3. K—N5, B—R3 mate or B—B3 mate. (Illustrating the mate by two Knights as in Chapter 10 and the mate with Knight and Bishop as in Chapter 9.)

40. 1. Q × Nch, K × Q; 2. R × P, N × B; 3. P × N, K—N1; 4. R(1)—R1, Resigns. Mate can be delayed by some sacrifices but cannot be avoided when White plays R—R8 mate. (A mate that begins with a Long Diagonal Mate threat and turns into a mate by two Rooks, as evident from mastery of Chapters 14 and 12.)

41. 1. Q × Pch, K × Q; 2. B—R5ch, K—R2; 3. B—B7ch, B—R3; 4. R × Bch, K × R; 5. R—R1 mate. (A beautiful example of the use of a Queen sacrifice—see Chapter 17—to force a mate by Rook and Bishops—see Chapter 7.) If Black declines the Queen sacrifice by 1. . . . . K—B1; 2. R—R8, Q—B2; 3. R × Rch, K × R; 4. Q—K8ch, B—B1; 5. R—KR1 (threatening mate by Rook and Bishop by 6. R—R8 mate), Q—N2; 6. B × Q, K × B; 7. B—R5, any move; 8. Q—B7ch, K—R1; 9. B—N6ch, and mate follows.

42. 1. . . . . P—R5, and White cannot prevent a Pawn from reaching the eighth rank, becoming a Queen, and winning the game. Thus: 2. P × RP, P—N6; 3. P × NP, P × KP wins, while so does the line played in the game; 2. K × P, P—B6; 3. P × BP, P—R6. (Pawn Promotion was the subject of Chapter 21.)

43. 1. R—N3ch, K—B3; 2. P × Pch, K—K2; 3. R—N7ch, R—B2; 4. Q × R mate. (Black might have delayed the mate a bit by 1. . . . .

Q—N4; 2. R × Qch. Such mates by Queen and Rook are most similar to those by two Rooks as clarified by Chapter 12 as well as mates by a supported Queen as in Chapter 5.)

44. 1. Q—R8ch, K × Q; 2. R × RP dbl ch, K—N1; 3. R—R8 mate. (A simple Long Diagonal Mate as in Chapter 14, the Queen sacrifice being automatic if you also understand Chapter 17.)

45. 1. N—N6ch, P × N; 2. Q—K5ch, K—Q2; 3. Q—K6 mate. If Black plays 2. . . . . B—K3; 3. Q × B mate is also a victory on the critical K6 square. (The position illustrates a Knight sacrifice to vacate a key square—as in Chapter 20—mate by a supported Queen—as in Chapter 5—and is also an Epaulettes Mate in its first variation—as in Chapter 6.)

46. 1. . . . . R × Pch; 2. K × R (if 2. K—N1, Q—R4 can force mate), Q—R4ch; 3. K—N1, N—R6ch; 4. K—R2, N—N4 dis ch; 5. K—N1, N—R6ch; with draw by perpetual check. (As reviewed in Chapter 22, understanding of which would have led you at once to the Rook sacrifice, as discussed in Chapter 18.)

47. 1. Q—B6ch, K—N1; 2. R—N3ch, K—B1; 3. Q—R6ch, K—K2; 4. Q—Q6 mate. (This is an Epaulettes Mate as discussed in Chapter 6, and depends on realization that the Black King on its K2 is in an epaulettes position.) A simpler mate by a supported Queen (Chapter 5) follows 1. R—N3, Q—B1 or Q—N1; 2. Q—B6ch, Q—N2; 3. Q × Q mate. Another possibility is 1. R—N3, N—K3; 2. Q—B6ch, N—N2; 3. Q × N mate.

48. 1. . . . . B—N5ch and on 2. K—N2 or K—N3, B—B4 dis ch wins the White Queen. The mate follows 1. . . . . B—N5ch; 2. K—K4, R—K1ch and there are two mating continuations: a) K—Q3, B—B4 mate or b) 3. K—Q5, B—B6ch; 4. Q—K4, B × Q mate. (A famous win with two Bishops as should have been evident if you had mastered Chapter 11.)

49. 1. B—R6ch, K × R; 2. B—N7ch, K—N1 (if 2. . . . . K × B; 3. Q—R6ch, K—N1; 4. Q—R7 or R8 mate); 3. R—R8ch, K × B; 4. Q—R6 mate. (This double sacrifice—of Rook and Bishop—required understanding of Chapters 18 and 19 combined with comprehension of the mate by a supported Queen, as in Chapter 5.)

50. 1. N—R6ch, K—R1; 2. N—B7ch, K—N1; 3. Q × Pch, K × Q; 4. R—R7ch, K—N1; 5. N—R6 mate. (A final position that is one of the gems of the century, requiring a Queen sacrifice to force a mate by a Knight and a supported Rook—all easy to find if you truly understand Chapters 17 and 8.)